OUR PARLIAMENT

An Introduction to the Parliament of India

Some Other Works by Dr Kashyap

- History of Parliament of India, 6 vols.
- Parliamentary Procedure, Law, Privileges, Practice and Precedents, 2 vols.
- Blueprint of Political Reforms
- The Speaker's Office
- Institutions of Governance in South Asia
- Citizens and the Constitution
- Our Constitution
- Anti-Defection Law and Parliamentary Privileges
- History of Parliamentary Democracy
- Parliamentary Wit and Humour
- Legislative Management Studies
- The Political System and Institution-building under Jawaharlal Nehru
- The Unknown Nietzsche—His Socio-Political Thought and Legacy
- Tryst with Freedom
- Jawaharlal Nehru, the Constitution and the Parliament
- The Citizen and Judicial Reforms (ed.)
- The Framing of India's Constitution, 5 vols. (with Rao Committee)
- Urgency of Value Education and Primacy of Girl Child (ed.)
- National Resurgence through Electoral Reforms (ed.)
- Eradication of Corruption and Restoration of Values (ed.)
- 100 Best Parliamentary Speeches (ed.)
- Reviewing the Constitution? (ed.)
- Dictionary of Political Science—English-Hindi

- Bharat Ka Samvidhan, Sashan aur Hum
- Bhartiya Sansad—Samasyaen avem Samvidhan
- Bhartiya Rajniti aur Sansad—Vipaksh ki Bhumika
- Samvidhanik Vikas aur Samvidhan
- Sansadiya Loktantra Ka Itihas
- Jawaharlal Nehru aur Bharat ka Samvidhan
- Sansadiya Prakriya
- Hamara Samvidhan
- Hamari Sansad

India—The Land and the People

OUR PARLIAMENT

An Introduction to the Parliament of India

SUBHASH C. KASHYAP

NATIONAL BOOK TRUST, INDIA

ISBN 978-81-237-0147-9

First Edition 1989
Revised Editions 1992, 1995, 1999, 2004
Reprints 1989, 1993, 1999, 2000, 2001, 2004, 2005, 2007, 2008, 2010, 2011 (twice), 2014, 2015 (twice), 2017, 2019, 2020, 2023, 2024, 2025 *(Saka 1947)*

₹ 290.00

Published by the Director, National Book Trust, India
5 Institutional Area, Vasant Kunj, New Delhi - 110070
Website : www.nbtindia.gov.in

Contents

Dr Kashyap in this book has explained the parliamentary procedures which ensure order in our respective Chambers. It is extremely important for the health of democracy that the general public understand what is done in their name.... We have to put parliamentary procedures in words and phrases which the general public whom we serve, fully understand. And, in this admirable book, Dr Kashyap has done just that. He has managed to distil a very complicated procedure and put it into simple language.... So, Dr Kashyap, in launching your book, I pay a tribute to you, Sir, for having distilled very complicated procedures into simple words. I hope this book will be widely read by the population and the eloctrate of this great country....

I am sure that it is going to be a great success, and I pray that it will be widely read and widely appreciated by the people of India, and indeed the people of the world because Dr Kashyap, you know, is probably the most distinguished of the Clerks of the Commonwealth and certainly one of the longest serving. When we go to the conferences... we realise how his reputation stands high not only in the Commonwealth parliamentary assembly, but also in the Inter-Parliamentary Union as well.

So, Dr Kashyap, well-done and congratulations; and I wish this book every success.

RT. HON. BERNARD WEATHERILL

Speaker, House of Commons,
United Kingdom, while launching the
first edition of the book *Our Parliament*
on 25 August, 1989.

Preface

The National Book Trust very wisely decided to bring out an introductory work on the Parliament of India for the general public. The first edition of this book was published in English in 1989. The book was well received and within the same year a reprint became necessary. A Hindi edition came out in 1990 followed by editions in several other Indian languages. The second edition of the English version appeared in 1992 and was quickly followed by a reprint in 1993. The third revised edition came in 1995 and underwent reprints in 1999, 2000 and 2001. In the present fourth edition, substantial fresh material has been added including a new chapter on the working of Parliament during the last half-a-century and more. The entire text has been carefully revised and updated. It is hoped that this edition will be widely welcomed as more useful.

There was no simple and short, and yet comprehensive work on Parliament. This book attempts to fill the void and presents in a handy form and in an easy, non-technical language some basic facts, and authentic and up-to-date information about our Parliament. The emphasis through out has been on objectivity and readability; unnecessary details and controversial issues have been avoided to the extent possible. The book seeks to briefly narrate the story of how our Parliament came to its present from, what it is, what it does, why it is needed, how it is constituted and how it functions. In fact, it could very well be titled 'Know Your Parliament' or 'The

What, the Why and the How of Parliament'.

It is essential that everyone knows the system under which he lives and the institutions that govern his life and safeguard his liberties. As somebody said "no more vital truth was ever uttered than that freedom and free institutions cannot long be maintained by any people who do not understand the nature of their own government." Under the political system adopted by us, Parliament is the supreme institution of the people and as the symbol of their freedom and sovereignty they must know it and know it well. The effort here is to place the study of Parliament in its proper historical perspective by describing in the very first chapter the origin and growth of representative legislative institutions right from the Vedic age. Also, it is often missed that Parliament in modern days and, especially so in India, is much more than a legislative body. It is verily a multifunctional institution. Its various functions include the political and financial control over the government, representation and grievance ventilation, conflict resolution and national integration, besides many others. These multifarious activities of the Parliament are sought to be given adequate coverage in the study.

An aspect of the Parliament which most of the books on the subject tend to pass over swiftly with only a cursory look is the actual working of the Houses—the sittings, the role of the Presiding Officers, the Question Hour and the various other procedural devices, like the different types of motions, the budgetary and legislative processes, etc. Needless to say, a grasp of the actual working of the Houses is a must for a meaningful evaluation of our political system. As such, an effort has been made to explain these vital aspects at some length.

It is acknowledged that the enormous range and complexity of legistative and administrative functions of a modern State make it almost impossible for the Parliament to adequately scrutinise legislative proposals and oversee administrative action. The recourse to a system of Parliamentary Committees has, therefore, been the practice adopted by almost all legislatures around the democratic world. The Indian Parliament too has evolved a well-developed system of Committees to help it in performing its tasks effectively. A detailed analysis of the various Committees, financial and general, standing and *ad hoc,* which are in existence in our Parliament, has been given. The study specially covers a description of the 17 departmentally related Standing Committees as well.

The effectiveness of the Parliament depends to a great extent on the services that are provided to it by the Secretariat. The more the Secretariat is independent of the Executive in its day-to-day functioning, the more likely it is to furnish impartial and accurate information with the help of which the parliamentarians can discharge their onerous duties. The importance of an independent Secretariat was realised right from the twenties and the evolution of the Lok Sabha and Rajya Sabha Secretariats as model agencies helping the members of Parliament has, therefore, been included as part of this study.

Parliamentary etiquettes and parliamentary privileges are very frequently discussed in the Press and elsewhere. In fact these concepts do have a place of importance in the dignified and meaningful functioning of our legislative institutions. The scope of parliamentary privileges is something which is too frequently misinterpreted. A clear idea as to their ambit is an essential pre-requisite for the lawyers, for the journalists and for all the citizens. It has been my endeavour to analyse the scope of this important doctrine in the light of judicial interpretations and decisions by the Houses of Parliament, their Committees and Presiding Officers.

Out Parliament is for all the citizens of India. It is written for the non-academic, non-professional, non-expert layreaders, for adult literates, for boys and girls of all ages in schools and colleges. It is hoped it will be widely read with great interest and benefit and will help to bring the Parliament nearer the People by providing to them a better understanding of the institution.

I am deeply beholden to the then Speaker Dr. Bal Ram Jakhar for all the inspiration and encouragement, and for very kindly conttibuting a very thoughtful foreword to the first edition of the work. I am indebted to Rt. Hon. Bernard Weatherill, Speaker House of Commons, United Kingdom who very kindly launched the book. Subsequent Speakers of Lok Sabha, Shri Shivraj Patil, Shri P.A.Sangma and others have been very helpful in many ways. I am most grateful to them. Thanks are also due to my friends and colleagues—too many to be named — who have over the years assisted me during the preparation of this work. Last but not the least, I am grateful to the National Book Trust and its authorities for publishing this work so well in English, Hindi and other Indian languages.

New Delhi
13 April 2003

SUBHASH C. KASHYAP

Abbreviations

Art./ Arts	: Article/ articles of the Constitution of India
B.P.S.T.	: Bureau of Parliamentary Studies and Training
C.A.D.	: Constituent Assembly Debates
C.E.C.	: Chief Election Commissioner
Chair	: The Presiding Officer
Chairman	: Chairman, Rajya Sabha, unless otherwise specified
chambers	: Halls in which the Houses meet
Cl.	: Clause
Constitution	: Constitution of India
Dir	: Direction by the Speaker, Lok Sabha under the Rules of Procedure of Lok Sabha (Sixth Edition)
E.C.	: Estimates Committee
Gazette	: Gazette of India
Handbook	: Handbook for members of Lok Sabha (Eighth Edition)
House	: Lok Sabha
Houses	: Rajya Sabha and Lok Sabha
I.P.U.	: Inter-parliamentary Union
I.P.G.	: Indian Parliamentary Group
J.P.I.	: Journal of Parliamentary Information
Member	: Member of Lok Sabha / Rajya Sabha
Minister	: Member of the Council of Ministers

P.A.C.	:	Public Accounts Committee
P.,pp.	:	Page; Pages
President	:	President of India
Presiding Officer	:	Speaker of the Lok Sabha / Chairman of the Rajya Sabha or anyone duly presiding over the meetings of the House.
R.P. Act	:	Representation of the People Act
Rules	:	Unless otherwise stated, means the Rules of Procedure and Conduct of Business in Lok Sabha (Sixth Edition)
Sec.	:	Section
Secretariat	:	Lok Sabha Secretariat, unless otherwise specified
Secretary-General (S.G.)	:	Secretary/ Secretary-General of Lok Sabha / Rajya Sabha
Speaker (L.S.)	:	Speaker, Lok Sabha
Table	:	Table of the House
w.e.f.	.	with effect from

HISTORY OF PARLIAMENT

ORIGIN AND GROWTH OF REPRESENTATIVE INSTITUTIONS AND THE PARLIAMENTARY SYSTEM

> We choose this system of parliamentary democracy deliberately; we choose it not only because, to some extent, we had always thought on those lines previously, but because we thought it was in keeping with our own old traditions also; naturally the old traditions, not as they were, but adjusted to the new conditions and new surroundings, we choose it also—let us give credit where credit is due—because we approved of its functioning in other countries, more especially the United Kingdom.
>
> **—Jawaharlal Nehru**

Representative Bodies in Ancient India

On the twentysixth day of January 1950, with the commencement of the new republican Constitution, India became for the first time in her long history, a full-fledged parliamentary democracy with a modern institutional framework. Democracy and representative institutions were, however, by no means entirely new to India. Existence of some deliberative representative bodies and democratic self-governing institutions could be traced back to as early as the Vedic age (Circa 3000-1000 BC). The institutions—*Sabha* and *Samiti*—mentioned in *Rigveda*, may be said to have contained rudiments of a modern Parliament. These two institutions were differentiated from each other in their status and functions. The *Samiti* was the general assembly or house of the people, and the *Sabha*, a smaller and select body of elders, broadly corresponding to the

Upper House in modern legislatures. There are enough indications in Vedic texts to suggest that the two bodies were closely associated with the affairs of the State and exercised considerable authority, influence and prestige. Some of the salient features in the functioning of modern parliamentary democracies—free discussion and decision by the vote of the majority—are known to have existed. The decision by the majority was regarded as "inviolable, not be overridden, because where the many meet in an assembly and speak there with one voice, that voice or vote of majority is not to be violated by others."[1] In fact, the foundational principle of ancient Indian society was that the government should be conducted not by the will of a solitary person, but jointly with the aid of councillors whose advice was to be respected. Vedic political theory recognised *Dharma* as the true sovereign. And Dharma was not religion but corresponded most closely to the modem concept of the Rule of Law. Dharma or the Rule of Law was upheld and enforced by the King. Ideally, the powers of the monarch were limited by the will of the people and the customs, usages and injunctions of *Dharmasastra*. The King was required to take an oath of loyalty to the law and the Constitution of the realm and to hold in trust the State for achieving the welfare of his people, both material and moral. While there can be no denying the fact that ancient Indian polity was predominantly monarchical, there were many instances of elective kingship and in any case, certain democratic institutions and practices were often in-built in the monarchical system.

There is ample historical evidence contained in the *Aitareya Brahaman*, Panini's *Ashtadhyayi*, Kautilya's *Arthashastra*, the *Mahabharata*, inscriptions of Ashoka's pillars, writings of contemporary Greek historians and the Buddhist and Jain scholars, and the *Manusmriti*, of the existence of a number of functioning republics during the post-Vedic period of history. Sovereignty in these republics,

Samgha or *Ganarjya* as they were known, vested in a fairly large assembly which elected not only the members of the Executive but also military leaders. It controlled foreign affairs and decided issues of peace and war. Also, the popular assembly exercised full control over the Executive. The Pali texts provide interesting details of the practice and procedure adopted in the assemblies of the ancient republics which according to some scholars, were marked with the underlying concepts of "legalism and constitutionalism of a most advanced type." Thus, for instance, the assembly had its Speaker called *Vinayadhara* and Whip called *Ganapuraka* who were familiar with procedural devices and terms like resolutions, lack of quorum, vote by majority, and so on. Discussions in the assembly were marked by elements of purity, fairness, frankness and freedom. Voting was by tickets (*Salaka*)—slips of wood of different colours to represent different opinions. Complicated and serious matters were often referred to a Special Committee elected from among the members of the assembly.[2]

Grass-roots democracy found its expression in the existence and functioning of Regional Councils (*Janapadas*), City Councils (*Paura Sabhas*) and Village Assemblies (*Grama Sabhas*). These bodies administered local affairs with almost complete freedom of local initiative and self-governance. *Arthashastra, Mahabharata* and *Manusmriti* contain numerous references to the existence of *Grama Sanghas*. Elective local bodies like the *Grama Sabhas, Grama Sanghas* or *Panchayats*, were common features of Indian polity in those days. While the democratic institutions like *Sabha* and *Samiti* and the republican states later disappeared, at the village level *Grama Sanghas, Grama Sabhas* or *Panchayats* survived and continued to function and flourish as effective institutions right through the rule of many Hindu and Muslim dynasties and till the advent of the British rule or even thereafter in one form or the other.[3]

Beginnings of Modern Parliamentary Institutions

Parliamentary government and legislative institutions in their modem connotation owe their origin and growth to India's British connection for some two centuries. It would, however, be wrong to presume that the British institutions as such were at any stage transplanted in India. The Parliament of India and the parliamentary institutions as we know them today had an organic growth on the Indian soil. They grew through many relentless struggles for freedom from foreign rule and for establishment of free democratic institutions, and the successive doses of constitutional reforms grudgingly and haltingly conceded by the British rulers.

Charter Act, 1833: The first faint beginnings of a Central Legislature for India are to be found in the Charter Act of 1833 which introduced important changes in the system of Indian administration and also in the legislative powers of the Indian Government. It established one Legislative Council for all the British territories in. India. For the first time the Governor-General's Government was known as the 'Government of India' and his Council as the 'India Council'. It also introduced an element of institutional specialisation in the government by differentiating the law-making meetings of the Governor-General's Council from its executive meetings. The demarcation made by the Act between the executive and legislative functions of the Governor-General's Council led to the addition of a 'fourth' or legislative member and the appointment of the distinguished jurist Lord Macaulay to occupy this position.

Thus, one may find the seeds of a Legislative Council (as distinct from the Executive Council) in the 1833 Act although it was not to be so described till much later.[4]

Charter Act, 1853: The last of the Charter Acts, the Charter Act of 1853 made important changes in the Governor-General's Council. The 'fourth' or legislative member of the Council, was placed on the same footing as the other members by being given a right to sit and vote at executive meetings. At the same time, the Council was enlarged for legislative purposes by the addition of six special members who were styled as "Legislative Councillors". Thus, along with the Governor-General and the Commander-in-Chief, the Council, as constituted under the Act of 1853, consisted of 12 members. Discussion in the Council, when acting in its legislative capacity, became oral instead of in writing; bills were referred to Select Committees and not to single members, legislative business was conducted in public instead of in secret and reports of the proceedings were officially published. Thus a big step was taken towards differentiating the Legislature from the Executive. The new Council conceived its duties not to be confined only to legislation but, as observed in the Montagu-Chelmsford Report (1918), "contrary to the intentions of Parliament, it began to assume the character of a miniature representative assembly, assembled for the purpose of enquiry into and redress of grievances".

Indian Councils Act, 1861: The Indian Councils Act of 1861 sought "to make better provision for the constitution of the Council of the Governor-General" and "for the local Government of the several Presidencies and Provinces." The Act was said to be the "prime charter of the Indian Legislature" inaugurating the "system of legislative devolution in India." The Act introduced important changes in the machinery for legislation, both at the central and provincial levels. It reconstituted the Council of the Governor-General. Hereafter, it was to consist of five (instead of the erstwhile four) ordinary members. For purposes of legislation, the Governor-General was authorised to nominate to his Council "not less than six nor more than twelve" additional members, at least one half of whom were to be non-officials. Though there was no statutory stipulation to appoint Indians as non-official members of the expanded Council, an assurance was given in the House of Commons that Indians would be so appointed. Notwithstanding this assurance and the fact that the Council was expressly forbidden to transact any business "other than the consideration and enactment of legislative measures introduced," or to entertain any motion other than a motion for leave to introduce such a measure, it could hardly be regarded as being, anywhere near a responsible or representative legislative body.[5] It was merely a legislative committee of the government, by means of which the Executive obtained advice and help in legislation. Not being a deliberative body with respect to any subject but that of immediate legislation and lacking power to inquire into grievances, call for information or examine the conduct of the Executive, the Council did not, in many measure, constitute the germ of responsible institutions. Nevertheless, from the point of view of constitutional development, the 1861 Act did mark an advance over the previous position in that, for the first time since the advent of the British rule in India, it accepted the important principle of representation of non-officials in legislative bodies. Also, hereafter the laws were made after due deliberation and were regular pieces of legislation which could be changed only by the same deliberative and public process by which they were made. Thus the days of legislation by the Executive were practically over, and the making of laws was no longer considered to be the exclusive business of the Executive.

Formation of Indian National Congress: The Indian National Congress was founded in 1885. It initiated the process of gradual relaxation of imperial control and the evolution of responsible government in India. From its very inception, the Congress made gradual introduction of representative institutions in the country as the main plank of its platform. The Congress considered the reform of the Councils "as the root of all other reforms." Speaking on the subject at the fifth session of the Congress (Bombay, 1889), Surendranath Banerjee said: "If you get that, you get everything else. On it depends the entire future of the country and the future of our administrative system.'"

Indian Councils Act, 1892: The Indian Councils Act, 1892 was, in part at least, a step in the direction of responding to the growing Indian demand for representative institutions. The adoption by the British Parliament of the Indian Councils Act, 1892 with a view to "give the people of India a real living representation in the Legislative Council", was regarded as a triumph for the Congress insofar as the British Government for the first time "recognised the representative element in the enlarged Councils." The Congress had the satisfaction of being "responsible for unifying Indians for the common purposes of their political enfranchisement."[6]

The 1892 Act amended the Indian Councils Act, 1861, to reconstitute the Councils of India. The Legislative Council of the Governor-General was further enlarged to consist of "not less than ten nor more than sixteen" (instead of the erstwhile minimum of six and maximum of twelve) additional members. Similarly, the number of additional members in the Provincial Legislative Councils was also increased. The regulations under which the additional members of the Councils were to be nominated on the recommendations of certain recognised bodies or associations representing particular interests. In the case of the Governor-General's Legislative Council, or the Indian Legislative Council as it came to be known, five more 'additional' members were thus brought in, one being nominated by the non-official members of each of the four Provincial Councils and one by the Calcutta Chamber of Commerce. Though the term 'election' was scrupulously avoided, the fact that the non-official members of the Provincial Councils recommended and returned their nominees to the Central Council, indicated implicit acceptance of the principle of indirect election.

Members of the Legislative Council were also granted

the privilege of asking questions, that if of interrogating the government members with a view to eliciting information on important matters. This right, which is one of the fundamental rights of any legislature, was very sparingly used at the time, but its grant marked a definite step forward in the progress of the parliamentary institution. It is interesting that in the initial stages the right was availed of even by official members, and it is amusing to read of one government member questioning another and eliciting information.

The Act of 1892 was certainly an improvement on the 1861 Act, insofar as it brought in a representative element in the Legislative Councils and relaxed to some extent the restrictions on the working of the Councils. The entry of the 'elected' members marked the beginning of new era in the life of the Council. Greater expression began to be given to popular opinion, and the deliberative, as also the critical aspect of the discussions underwent a change.

Indian Councils Act, 1909: The relentless campaign launched by the Congress for greater and more effective representation in running the affairs of the country culminated in the Morley-Minto reform proposals of 1908. The scheme of Morley-Minto constitutional reforms was given effect to through the Indian Councils Act, 1909.[7] The Act as supplemented by regulations framed under it, made important changes in the Constitution and functions of the Indian legislatures. The maximum number of members of the Indian Legislative Council was raised from 16 to 60 (excluding the executive councilors who were ex-officio members) and the size of the Legislative Councils in the Presidencies/ Provinces was also more than doubled. The Act required that the members of the Legislative Councils should include elected as well as nominated members.

The 1909 Act enlarged the functions of the Legislative Councils. It gave to the members the power to move resolutions on the Budget and on any matter of general public interest and to divide the Council upon them. The resolutions were to take the form of recommendations to the executive government, but the government was not bound to accept them. The power to put questions was extended by permitting supplementary questions subject to disallowance by the President.

The biggest defect of 1909 Reforms was the creation of separate or communal system of election providing for representation and reservation of seats in Councils for special interests like Muslims, chambers of commerce, zamindars, etc. The communal system of representation initiated by the Act poisoned the future public life of India and increased separatist tendencies. It was the biggest shock to secular Indian nationalism after the suppression of the 1857 revolt and was indeed the greatest victory for the British policy of 'divide and rule'. In the words of Sardar Pannikar, this was "the first expression of the pernicious two-nation theory" which ultimately resulted in the partition of the country.[8]

Government of India Act, 1919: The Reforms Act of 1919 as supplemented by Rules made under it, introduced many important changes in the Indian constitutional system. At the Centre, the Indian Legislative Council was replaced by a bicameral Legislature consisting of a Council of State (Upper House) and a Legislative Assembly (Lowe House), each with an elected majority.

The Council of State was to consist of not more than 60 members, nominated or elected in accordance with statutory rules, and of these not more than 20 were to be officials. The first Council of State had a total of 60 members, of whom 34 were elected, 20 were nominated officials and 6 nominated non-officials. The strength of the Legislative Assembly was provisionally fixed by the Act of 140 (100 elected, 26 nominated officials and rest nominated non-officials). But there was power, by statutory rule, to increase the total number, and to vary the proportion between the classes of members, so that at least five-sevenths of the total number had to be elected members and at least one-third of the rest non-officials. The first Legislative Assembly, constituted under the 1919 Act, came into being in 1921. It had 145 members, 104 of whom were elected (52 by General, 30 by Muslim, 9 by European, 7 by Landowners, 4 by Commercial and 2 by Sikh constituencies), 26 officials and 15 nominated non-officials.[9]

The elected members of both the Houses were chosen by direct election, but on a very much restricted franchise based on qualifications of property, and tax or education. In the case of the Council of State, property qualifications for voters were pitched extremely high making the House, more or less, an exclusive preserve of wealthy landowners and merchants. The property qualification for voting for election to the Assembly was put at a lower level than that for the Council of State, but it was still considerably higher than that required for the provincial franchise. The total electorate for the Council in 1920 was only 17,644 and for the Assembly 904,746. The normal term of the Council was five years, and that of the Assembly three. The Governor-General could dissolve either House before the expiration of its full term. He could also extend their normal life in special circumstances. The two Houses had coordinate powers, except that only the Assembly could grant or withhold supply.

The 1919 Act while establishing partially responsible governments in the Provinces under a system of what came to be known popularly as 'dyarchy', did not introduce any element of responsibility at the Centre and the Governor-General-in-Council continued to remain responsible only to the Secretary of State for India and through him to the British Parliament. The Central Legislature, though more representative than the previous Legislative Councils and endowed, for the first time, with power to vote supplies, had no power to replace the government and even its powers in the field of legislation and financial control were limited and subject to the overriding powers of the Governor-General. Thus, even as the Central Legislature's power to make laws for the whole of British India, for British subjects and servants of the Crown in India, and for all British Indian subjects within as well as without British India was reiterated, it continued to be subject to many important limitations which were designed either to keep the sovereignty of the British Parliament intact or to maintain the supremacy of the Governor-General and his Council. Broadly speaking, the Indian Legislature had no power to amend or repeal any parliamentary statute relating to British India or to do anything affecting the authority of the British Parliament. The Act also required that measures affecting certain important matters could be introduced in either House of the Indian Legislature only with the previous sanction of the Governor-General. Besides his existing power to veto any Bill passed by the Legislature or to reserve the same for the signification of His Majesty's pleasure, the Governor-General was given the power to secure the enactment of laws which he considered essential for the safety, tranquility or interests of British India, or any part of British India. The Governor-General also continued to have the power to promulgate ordinances for the peace and good government of British India in case of emergency.

Similarly, in the financial field, while power was given to the Legislative Assembly to assent or to refuse its assent to any demand for grant or to reduce the amount referred to in any demand, if the Assembly declined to vote a demand put before it, the Governor-General in Council could restore it by simply declaring that it was essential to the discharge of his responsibilities.

The Indian Legislature under the Act of 1919 was thus only a non-sovereign law-making body and was powerless before the Executive in all spheres of governmental activity—administrative as well as legislative and financial.

Nevertheless, with the constitution of a Legislature, the making of laws ceased to be the business of the Governor-General's Council. That body had now to function in terms of cabinet and submit the financial and legislative proposals of the government to the Legislature, presided over by non-official presidents. A tremendous increase in the scope of legislative activity was witnessed ad several measures of permanent benefit to the country were enacted. The Budget, except for certain reserved heads of expenditure, was subject to vote and the government had to weather many a storm when supplies and services were refused, or the entire Budget thrown out by the House. With freedom of speech in the Houses being assured and with their right to ask questions, move resolutions and motions of adjournment, the members had opportunities to criticise and expose the government. Some of the members were afforded additional opportunity, through Standing Committees, of influencing the government and familiarising themselves with the working of the executive departments.

The emergence of the Central Legislature was a matter of historic importance. For the first time it gave the representatives of the people a voice in making laws and influencing governmental policies. It also played a great role in the shaping of the political destinies of the country. While the country was fighting to overthrow foreign domination, the representatives of the people assembled in the Legislature carried the battle into the House. The world saw an alien government bow to the wishes of the people to accept defeat. Defeat, of course, did not make any difference to the government because the government, consisting as it did of nominated Executive Councillors, had no obligation to vacate. Nevertheless, the existence of a highly critical Legislature encouraged the exercise of care and discretion on the part of the Executive and instilled in it a consciousness of its obligation to the people.

Lokmanya Tilak termed the 1919 Reforms as "dissatisfying, disappointing and a sun without morning", but he declared that he would accept what had been given, agitate and work harder, and use it for obtaining more as soon as possible. His policy of responsive cooperation included both cooperation, and constitutional assertion, and if need be, constitutional obstruction.[10] Annie Besant declared the scheme to be "unworthy to be offered by Britain and received by India." A sort of schism was thus created in the Congress over the 1919 Reforms. In 1918, some moderates leaving the Congress, had formed a separate organisation called the National Liberation Federation under the leadership of Surendranath Banerjee. These moderates hailed the Reforms but the Congress at its 1919 Amritsar session called them "inadequate, unsatisfactory, and disappointing."

The Legislature Under the 1919 Reforms: The constitutional reforms of the 1919 Act came into force in 1921. The largest and the most influential political party in the country, the Indian National Congress, boycotted the 1920-21 elections and was thus not represented in the legislatures that came into being in 1921. Only the National Liberal Federation formed by the moderates who had left the Congress in 1918 took active part in the elections and a number of eminent members of the Party were elected to seats in the legislatures. As was expected of them, and as the terms of their pledge to their constituents demanded, they discharged their function as legislators and ministers. Their programme in the Councils was described by them as "a policy of uniform, continuous and consistent obstruction."[11]

In 1923, Deshbandhu C.R. Das and Pandit Motilal Nehru formed the Swaraj Party which advocated fighting elections and entering the Councils with a view to either changing or wrecking the system from within "the enemy's camp". The special Delhi Session of the Congress held in September 1923 under the presidentship of Maulana Azad adopted the Swarajist plan of Council entry and thereafter the Swaraj Party became the legislative wing of the Congress. Swaraj Party leaders justified entry into the legislature saying that under the contemporary situation, it was the best course to make the administrative system hollow and ineffective.

The Swaraj Party achieved remarkable success at the polls in 1923. By winning 45 seats out of a total of 145, the Swaraj Party became the largest party in the Central Legislature. According to Maulana Azad, the biggest victory of the party lay in the fact that it secured even those seats which were reserved for the Muslims. And, with the support of some independents and of the members of the Nationalist Party led by Pandit Madan Mohan Malviya, it got an absolute majority. The Swarajists under the leadership of Motilal Nehru defeated the government on several motions of national importance and repeatedly prevented the passage of the budget and many legislative measures. They staged several walk-outs. As a result of the Swarajist efforts, resolutions on 'National Demand' were passed with overwhelming majorities in 1924 and 1925.

The Swaraj Party had a poor showing at the 1926 elections. On 7 March 1926 the All India Congress Committee called upon the Swarajists, owing to the absence of any sign of cooperation from the government, to walk out of the legislatures as a protest. Thus the Swarajist experiment came to an end.

One important development during the period was the evolution of the office of the Speaker. While the first President (Speaker) of the Central Legislative Assembly, Sir Frederick Whyte was nominated in August, 1925, Shri Vithalbhai Patel was elected and became the first non-official President (Speaker) of the Assembly. He along with several other members of the House realised that the independence of the elected Speaker was prejudicially affected because the Secretary of the Assembly was the Secretary of the Legislative Department under the Government of India. On 22 September 1928, Pandit Motilal Nehru moved a resolution in the House that a separate Assembly Department be constituted. It was adopted unanimously. The Secretary of State for India accorded his approval with certain modifications and a separate self-contained department known as Legislative Assembly Department was created with effect from 10 January 1929. The Speaker was made the *de facto* head of the new department and the staff was appointed with the approval of the Speaker.

The limited reforms brought about under the Government of India Act, 1919 proved totally inadequate to satisfy the popular demand for a representative responsible government. The national opinion gathered momentum against a legislature with limited powers, and with every passing year the demand for a fully sovereign Parliament and responsible government became more insistent.

Appointment of Simon Commission: The years 1920 to 1935 were fateful years. During this period considerable political consciousness developed in the country. The Indian National Congress, under the leadership of Mahatma Gandhi, developed into a mass organisation. The Act of 1919 had provided for the appointment for a Royal Commission at the expiration of ten years "for enquiring into the working of the system of government...and the development of representative institutions in British India..." and of reporting "as to whether and to what extent it is desirable to establish the principle of responsible government, or to extend, modify, or restrict the degree of responsible government...existing therein, including the question whether the establishment of second chambers of the local legislatures is or is not desirable." In November 1927, two years before it was due, the appointment of a Commission was announced. But, the Commission's Chairman, Sir John Simon, and all its members were chosen from the British Parliament. The all-white Simon Commission was boycotted by most of the Indian parties. The report of the

Commission published in May 1930 was rejected by all political parties. The Indian National Congress presided over by Jawaharlal Nehru at its Lahore session in 1929 had already declared complete independence or *Purna Swaraj* as its aim.

The Government of India Act, 1935: The Act of 1935 aimed at providing a federal structure. The Governor-General was to have a Council of Ministers, not exceeding ten in number, "to aid and advise" him "in the exercise of his functions" except where he was required to exercise his functions in "his discretion" or in "his individual judgement". There was no reference in the Act to either collective or individual responsibility of the ministers to the Federal Legislature, although every minister was required to be a member of either House of that Legislature. Also, there was no reference to a Prime Minister. The functions of the Governor-General with respect to the appointment and dismissal of the ministers were to be exercised in his "discretion". He was empowered in his "discretion" to preside at meetings of the Council of Ministers.

The Federal Legislature was to consist of His Majesty, represented by the Governor-General, and two Chambers to be known respectively as the Council of State (the Upper Chamber) and the House of Assembly (the Lower Chamber). The Council of State was to consist of 156 representatives of British India and not more than 104 representatives of the Indian States while the Assembly was to consist of 250 representatives of British India and not more than 125 representatives of the Indian States. The Council of State was to be a permanent body not subject to dissolution, but one-third of its members were to retire every third year. Every Federal Assembly, unless sooner dissolved by the Governor-General in his "discretion", was to continue for five years. In a rather strange and involved provision, the Act provided for the representatives of British India to be elected to the Upper Chamber by provincial constituencies through direct election, and, representatives to the Lower Chamber to be elected by electoral colleges constituted by members of Provincial Assemblies, through indirect elections.

Each house was to elect its Chairman and Deputy Chairman and would have power to regulate, subject to the provisions of the Act, its own procedure and business. The Governor-General was empowered to summon and prorogue the Legislature, and to dissolve the Lower House at his "discretion". No Bill would become law unless agreed to by both Houses and assented to by the Governor-General or, in the case of Bill reserved for the significance of His Majesty's pleasure, by His Majesty. Even an Act assented to by the Governor General could be disallowed by His Majesty. The Governor-General could remit a Bill to the Houses for reconsideration. In the case of disagreement between the Houses, the Governor-General could summon a joint sitting in which a decision would be reached by a majority vote.

The two Houses were given nearly equal powers; the difference lay in the sphere of finance. Money Bills could be introduced only in the Lower House, but the Upper House had the power to amend or reject them in the same way as the Lower House, and the Governor-General was empowered to resolve the differences by summoning a joint sitting.

The 49th and the 50th Sessions of the Congress held in Lucknow (April, 1936) and Faizpur (1937) respectively, rejected in its entirety, the new Constitution embodied in this Act as it "in no way represents the will of the nation". The Congress felt that the Act had been imposed on India against the declared will of its people. The Indian people, the Congress declared, could only recognise a constitutional structure which had been framed by them.

The Federal part of the 1935 Act, however, never came into operation as the Princely States could not be persuaded to accede to the Federation. As a result, the Constitution of the Central Government in India remained the same as it was under the Act of 1919 with such modifications as were necessitated by the introduction of autonomy in the Provinces. Thus, no Council of Ministers, responsible to the Legislature, was appointed at the Centre and the powers and functions of the Central Legislature, as provided in the 1919 Act, remained unchanged until the Indian Independence Act, 1947. The Legislative Assembly as constituted in 1934 had 44 members of the Congress Party and 11 nationalists who ordinarily voted with them, under their leaders, Bhulabhai Desai and Aney. The independents, who held the balance between the national parties and the government bloc, were led by M.A. Jinnah. The main purpose of the Nationalists was to prove the irresponsible character of the Government of India and to demonstrate that the Indian people had no confidence in the government and were not prepared to support it. Two important occasions to oppose the government were when voting took place on the Railways and secondly, in the General Budget. The demands for grants on many items were rejected in pursuit of the object. The cut motions were moved in order to ventilate Indian grievances and censuring the government for its negligence in action and antipathy to the interests of the people. The government restored most of the cuts in compliance with the special powers of certification vested in the Governor-General. This attracted the stigma that India was being ruled by the autocratic fiat of the Governor-General and not with the consent of the elected representatives of the people.

Fresh elections to the Central Legislative Assembly which were overdue were held in the last quarter of 1945. The Congress contested the elections on the issue of its 'Quit India' resolution of 1942 while for the Muslim League the issue was 'Pakistan'. The result showed that the Congress secured a majority of the elected seats (56 out of 102). Sarat

Chandra Bose was the leader of the Congress Legislature Party. The Indian Independence Act 1947 introduced some changes. The provisions of the Act of 1935 which required the Governor-General or a Governor to act in his discretion or in exercise of his individual judgement ceased to have effect. The Dominion Legislature was vested with "full power to make laws..., including laws having extra-territorial operation".

The First Sovereign Legislature

In pursuance of the Indian Independence Act, the Government of India Act, 1935 was modified and adapted by the Governor-General to make it the provisional Constitution of the Dominion, until some other provision was made by the Constituent Assembly. There was a Council of Ministers "to aid and advise the Governor-General in the exercise of his functions". The legislative powers of the Governor-General were removed and power was conferred on him to promulgate ordinances only in case of emergency for the peace and good government of the Dominion. The Governor-General ceased to be a part of the Dominion Legislature and his power of dissolution ended. Thus, the Governor-General became a mere constitutional head of the country and the sovereignty of the Dominion Legislature was complete.[12] The Indian Independence Act, 1947, declared the Constituent Assembly of India to be a fully sovereign body and on the midnight of 14-15 August 1947, the Assembly assumed full powers of the governance of the country. Section 8 of the Act conferred on the Constituent Assembly full legislative power. It has, however, soon felt that it would be desirable to maintain distinction between the Constitution-making function of the Constituent Assembly and its ordinary function as a legislature. The House having agreed, a Committee under the Chairmanship of G.V. Mavalankar was appointed on 20 August 1947 to consider the matter.

On 29 August 1947, after considering the Mavalankar

Committee Report, the Constituent Assembly resolved that the business of the Assembly as a Constitution-making body should be clearly distinguished from its function as the Dominion Legislature and that a provision should be made for the election of a Speaker to preside over the Assembly while functioning in the latter capacity.[13]

In accordance with the aforesaid Resolution, the Legislative Assembly Rules in force immediately before the establishment of the Dominion of India were modified and adapted by the President of the Constituent Assembly.

The Constituent Assembly (Legislative) as a distinct body met for its first sitting in the Assembly Chamber on 17 November 1947, with the President of the Constituent Assembly (Dr. Rajendra Prasad) in the Chair.

Only one nomination, that of G.V. Mavalankar, was received for the office of the Speaker and he was declared as duly elected. Later Dr. Rajendra Prasad vacated the Chair which was then occupied by Speaker Mavalankar. Meanwhile, the Constituent Assembly was engaged in the task of framing a Constitution for independent India.

The Constituent Assembly accepted the principle of the parliamentary executive collectively responsible to the popular House of the Parliament, as recommended by the Union Constitution Committee and as subsequently incorporated into the Draft Constitution prepared by the Drafting Committee. While introducing the Draft Constitution and recommending the parliamentary system in the Constituent Assembly on 4 November 1948, B.R. Ambedkar, Chairman of the Drafting Committee said that "The Draft Constitution in recommending the parliamentary system of executive has preferred more responsibility to more stability." While some dissentient voices were heard against the concept of the parliamentary type of government, the overwhelming opinion was in favour of the Drafting Committee's proposal[14] and finally with the coming into force of the republican Constitution of independent India on 26 January 1950, a full-fledged parliamentary system of government with a modern institutional framework and all its other ramifications was established. The Constituent Assembly became the Provisional Parliament of India and functioned as such until after the first General Elections based on adult franchise. The Parliament was constituted under the provisions of the new Constitution.

The first general elections under the new Constitution were held during the year 1951-52, the first elected Parliament with the two houses—the Rajya Sabha and the Lok Sabha—came into being in May 1952, the Second Lok Sabha came in May 1957, the Third in April 1962, the Fourth in March 1967, the Fifth in March 1971, the Sixth in March 1977, the Seventh in January 1980, the Eighth in December 1984, the Ninth in December 1989, the Tenth in June 1991, and the Eleventh, Twelfth and Thirteenth in May 1996, March 1998 and October 1999 respectively.[15]

The Rajya Sabha first constituted in 1952 is a continuing, permanent House, not subject to dissolution. One-third of its members retire every two years.

REFERENCES

1. Radha Kumud Mookerjee, *Glimpses of Ancient India*, Bombay, 1970, pp. 5-6, 41; Balashastri Hardas, Glimpses of the Vedic Nation, Madras, 1967, p. 514.
2. A.S. Altekar, *State and Government in Ancient India*, Delhi, 1949, pp. 83-86; Mookerjee, *op.cit.*, pp. 45-46.
3. For further discussion of the theme, see P.L. Bhargava, *India in the Vedic Age*, Lucknow, 1971; Mookerjee, *op.cit.*, Balashastri Hardas, *op.cit.*, Altekar *op.cit.*, S.N. Mishra, *Ancient Indian Republic*, Lucknow, 1976; J.P. Sharma, *Republics in Ancient India*, Leiden, 1968; S.K. Roy, *Democracy in India*, Calcutta, 1960; K.P. Jayaswal, *Hindu Polity*, Bangalore, 1955; and R.K. Mookerjee, *Local Government in Ancient India*, Oxford, 1920.
4. C. Ilbert, *The Government of India*, Oxford, 1922, pp. 83-87.
5. *Montagu-Chelmsford Report*, paras 63 to 65 and *Report of the Indian Statutory Commission* (Simon Commission), Vol. 1, 1930, para 133

and John Cumming (ed.), Political India (1832-1932), Oxford, 1932, p. 161.

6. B.P. Sitaramayya, *History of the Indian National Congress*, Vol. 1, 1935, p. 37; A.M. & G. Zaidi, *The Encyclopaedia of the Indian National Congress*, New Delhi, 1976, Vol. V, pp. 229 and 615.
7. Zaidi, *op.cit.*, 227.
8. K.M. Pannikar, *Asia and Western Domination*, 1953, p. 155; Zaidi, *op.cit.*, Vol. V, pp. 545-46.
9. Data regarding the composition of the two Houses is based on R. Coupland, *The Indian Problem 1833-1935*, Madras, 1943, p. 64.
10. R.G. Pradhan, *India's Struggle for Swaraj*, 1930, p. 136.
11. Bisheshwar Prasad, *Bondage and Freedom*, 1979, p. 364.
12. P.N. Murty and K.V. Padmanabhan, *The Constitution of the Dominion of India 1947*, Introduction.
13. *Constituent Assembly Debates*, Vol. V, 29-8-1947, pp. 359-60.
14. *Constituent Assembly Debates*, Vol. VII, pp. 32-33.
15. For further study, see Subhash C. Kashyap, *History of Parliamentary Democracy*, Delhi, 1991; *History of Parliament of India*, Delhi, 6 Vols., 1994-2000.

2

THE POLITICAL SYSTEM

STRUCTURE OF PARLIAMENT AND ITS POSITION IN INDIAN POLITY

Representative Parliamentary Democracy

We have adopted a system of representative parliamentary democracy. The three words—representative, parliamentary and democracy—are the cardinal features of our political system.

Democracy implies the right of the people to self-determination and faith in the rationality and ingenuity of the human mind. The basic premise of true democracy is that every individual irrespective of his caste, creed, colour or sex and irrespective of the level of the educational, economic or professional backgrounds, is capable of governing himself and of managing his affairs, the way he deems fit. In a democracy the people are their own masters.

The Constitution of India, in the words of its Preamble, speaks of "we the people of India having solemnly resolved...to give to ourselves this Constitution", thereby clarifying beyond all shadow of doubt that sovereignty under the Indian political system vests in the people. But, except in a primordial or revolution situation, sovereignty of the people is merely an abstraction. Also, it may imply a state of anarchy. Sovereignty in the hands of the people may be likened to power in the waters of a wild mountainous river. In order to be useful, it has to be tamed and harnessed. The people need an institution, an instrumentality for expressing and exercising their sovereign powers. Under the scheme of our Constitution and its provision of universal adult franchise, the people exercise their sovereign power while casting their votes to elect representatives to the Union Parliament. And, the Parliament becomes the people's institution *par excellence* through which the sovereign will of the people finds expression.

Initially, in the ancient Greek City-States and also during the Vedic period in India, the people themselves assembled together to decide the issues of governance. People, thus, exercised their power directly in deciding matters of the State and this kind of polity could be called direct popular democracy. But the with gradual increase in the size and population of the political units and ultimately with the advent of modern Nation-States, it became impossible to arrange for the people to assemble at a place to discuss matters of the State and arrive at decisions smoothly. All forms of direct democracy, therefore, soon became practically extinct all over the world except in a few Swiss Cantons where issues could still be decided by the people-at-large through vote. Modern democracy has of necessity, to be a representative democracy where people exercise their sovereign power through their elected representatives.

The term 'parliamentary' refers specifically to a kind of democratic polity wherein the supreme power vests in the body of people's representatives called Parliament. The parliamentary system is one in which the Parliament enjoys primacy of place in the governance of the State. Under the Constitution of India the Union Legislature is called 'Parliament'. It is the pivot on which the political system of the country revolves.

Composition of Parliament

The Parliament of India consists of the President and the two Houses—the Rajya Sabha (Council of States) and the Lok Sabha (House of the People).[1]

The President: The President of the Republic is directly elected by an electoral college consisting of the elected member of both Houses of Parliament and the elected members of the Legislative Assemblies (popular Houses) of the States.[2] Though the President of India is a constituent part of Parliament, he does not sit or participate in the discussions in either of the two Houses. There are certain constitutional functions which he has to perform with respect to the Parliament. The President summons the two Houses of Parliament to meet from time to time. He can prorogue the two Houses of Parliament and dissolve the Lok Sabha. His assent is essential for a Bill passed by both Houses to become a law. Not only that, when both the Houses of Parliament are not in session and he is satisfied that circumstances exist which render it necessary for him to take immediate action, the President can promulgate Ordinances having the same force and effect as a law passed by the Parliament.[3]

At the commencement of the first session after each general election to Lok Sabha and at the commencement of the first session of each year, the President addresses both Houses of Parliament assembled together and informs the Parliament of the causes of its summons. Besides, he may address either House of Parliament or both Houses assembled together and for that purpose require the attendance of members. He is also empowered to send messages to either House whether with respect to a Bill then pending in Parliament or otherwise, and a House to which any message is so sent has to, with all convenient dispatch, consider any matter required to be considered by the message.[4] Bills belonging to certain categories can be introduced and proceeded with only after the recommendation of the President is obtained.[5]

There are certain other functions which the President is required to perform under the Constitution in relation to the Parliament. He appoints the Speaker *pro-tem* of Lok

Shabha and an acting Chairman of Rajya Sabha, as and when the need arises.[6] He summons the joint sitting of both Houses in case of disagreement between them on a Bill.[7] The President causes to be laid, every year, before the Parliament, the Budget of the government, referred to in the Constitution as the "Annual Financial Statement"[8], and certain other reports of constitutional functionaries like the Comptroller and Auditor-General of India, Finance Commission, Union Public Service Commission, Special Officer for Scheduled Castes and Scheduled Tribes and Backward Classes Commission.[9] He may nominate not more than two members of the Anglo-Indian community to the Lok Sabha, if he is of the opinion that the community is not adequately represented[10] in the House. The President also nominates 12 members to the Rajya Sabha from amongst persons having special knowledge or practical experience in respect of such matters as literature, science, art and social service.[11] Besides, he is empowered to decide, after obtaining the opinion of the Election Commission, whether any member duly elected, attracts the disqualifications laid down in Article 108 of the Constitution. His decision, in this matter is final.[12]

Rajya Sabha: The Rajya Sabha is, as its name indicates, the Council of States. It represents the people in an indirect way inasmuch as they are grouped into several components of the Union—the States and the Union Territories—and members of Rajya Sabha are elected by the elected members of the State Legislative Assemblies in accordance with the system of proportional representation by means of single transferable vote.[13] The different States of the Union have not been given equal representation in the Rajya Sabha. The number of representatives from each State in India depends largely on its population. Thus, while Uttar Pradesh has 31 members in the Rajya Sabha, smaller states like Manipur, Mizoram, Sikkim, Tripura, etc. have only one member each. The populations in some of the Union Territories such

Andaman and Nicobar Islands, Chandigarh, Dadra and Nagar Haveli, Daman and Diu, and Lakshadweep are too small to have any representative in the Rajya Sabha. Under the Constitution, the Rajya Sabha consists of not more than 250 members. It includes 12 members nominated by the President and 238 members elected by the States and the Union Territories.[14] The Rajya Sabha at present consists of 245 members (See Annexure 2.1 and Diagram 4).

Unlike the Lok Sabha, which has a fixed term but can be dissolved by the President at any time, the Rajya Sabha is a permanent body and is not subject to dissolution. While the term of an individual member of the Rajya Sabha is six years, as nearly as possible, one-third of its members retire at the expiration of every second year in accordance with the provision made in that behalf by Parliament by law.[15] The term of office of the members begins from the date on which names of the members are notified by the Government of India in the Gazettee.[16] The Vice-President, who is elected by the members of both Houses of Parliament, is the ex-officio Chairman of the Rajya Sabha, whereas the Deputy Chairman is elected by the members of the Rajya Sabha from amongst themselves.[17]

Lok Sabha: The other House—the Lok Sabha—is the House of the People. It is directly elected by the people. Every citizen of India who is not less than 18 years of age is entitled to vote in the elections to the Lok Sabha unless he is otherwise disqualified under law (Art. 326). The Constitution provides that the Lok Sabha shall consist of not more than 530 members chosen by direct election from territorial constituencies in the States, and not more than 20 members to represent the Union Territories, chosen in such manner as Parliament by law provides.[18] In addition, the President may nominate not more than two members to represent the Anglo-Indian community. The maximum strength of the House envisaged in the Constitution is thus 552. The total elective membership is distributed among the States in such a manner that the ratio between the number of seats allotted to each State and the population of the State is, as far as possible, the same for all States.[19] Population for this purpose means the population as ascertained at the 1971 census. There shall be no change in the number of seats in the Lok Sabha until the year 2026 [Art. 81(3)]. Seats in the Lok Sabha are reserved for the Scheduled Castes and Scheduled Tribes Statewise on the basis of population ratios. Originally it was only for ten years but is being extended every time for the next ten years. Under the latest amendment it is now for 60 years i.e. until the year 2010 (Art. 330 and 334). At present, the Lok Sabha consists of 545 members (See Annexure 2.2 and Diagram 5).

Lok Sabha has been provided with a fixed term as in the case of the popularly elected House of Representatives in the United States of America and the House of Commons in the United Kingdom. The *raison d'etre* of representative democracy is that the government should obtain the mandate of the people periodically in order to continue in office legitimately. The term of the House in India is five years from the date appointed for its first meeting. The expiration of the period of five years operates as its dissolution. The House may be dissolved before the expiration of its full term under certain circumstances.[20] When a proclamation of Emergency is in force, the term of the Lok Sabha can be extended by the Parliament for a period not exceeding one year at a time and not exceeding in any case a period of six months after the proclamation has ceased to operate.[21]

Relative Roles of the Two Houses

The two Houses of Parliament enjoy co-equal power and status in all spheres except in financial matters and in regard to the responsibility of the Council of Ministers, which are exclusively the domain of the Lok Sabha. Accordingly, the following limitations have been placed on the powers of the Rajya Sabha:

(i) A Money Bill cannot be introduced in the Rajya Sabha.

(ii) Rajya Sabha has no power either to reject or amend a Money Bill. It can only make recommendations on the Money Bill. If such a Bill is not returned to the Lok Sabha within a period of 14 days, the Bill shall be deemed to have been passed by both the Houses at the expiration of the said period in the form in which it was passed by the Lok Sabha.[22]

(iii) Whether a particular Bill is a Money Bill or not is to be decided by the Speaker of the Lok Sabha.[23]

(iv) Rajya Sabha may discuss the Annual Financial Statement.[24] It has no power to vote on the Demands for Grants.

(v) Rajya Sabha has no powers to pass a vote of no-confidence in the Council of Ministers.[25]

It should not, however, be taken to mean that the Rajya Sabha is less important or has been given a secondary position in relation to the Lok Sabha. The powers of the Rajya Sabha are on par with those of the Lok Sabha in case of other Bills. Every non-financial measures must be passed by both the Houses individually before it can become an Act. Rajya Sabha has equal powers with the Lok Sabha in important matters like the impeachment of the President, removal of the Vice-President, constitutional amendments, and removal of the judges of the Supreme Court and the High Courts.[26] President's Ordinances, proclamation of Emergency and the proclamation of the failure of constitutional machinery in a State must be placed before both Houses of Parliament.[27] Disagreement between the two Houses on a Bill, other than a Money Bill and a Constitutional Amendment Bill is resolved by both the Houses in a joint-sitting where matters are decided by majority vote. Such a joint-sitting of the two Houses is presided over by the Speaker of the Lok Sabha.[28]

Further, the Constitution has assigned some special powers to the Rajya Sabha. It alone has the power to declare that it would be in national interest for the Parliament to legislate in respect of a matter in the State List. If by a two-thirds majority, Rajya Sabha passes a resolution to this effect, the Union Parliament can make laws for the whole or any part of the country even with respect to a matter enumerated in the State List.[29] Also, under the Constitution, Parliament is empowered to make laws providing for the creation of one or more All-India Services common to the Union and the States, if the Rajya Sabha declares by a resolution supported by not less than two-thirds of the members present and voting, that it is necessary or expedient in the national interest to do so.[30]

Parliament and the Executive

The term 'Executive' is often used rather loosely to connote several different things. Under the Constitution of India, the head of the Executive is the President. All executive power is vested in him and is to be exercised by him either directly or through officers subordinate to him. All executive action, therefore, is taken in the name of the President.[31] He is, however, required to act only on the aid and advice of the Council of Ministers with the Prime Minister at its head. As such, the President is only the formal constitutional or nominal executive. The real or the political executive is the Council of Ministers.[32] The Ministers constitute the Government of India and the head of the government is the Prime Minister. Then, there is the permanent administration comprising the civil services—the huge staff of administrators, experts, technocrats and others forming the administrative apparatus which really helps the ministers in the formulation and implementation of policies. For the sake of conceptual clarification, therefore, the term 'Executive' may be used to indicate the political executive, i.e. the Council of Ministers, while the terms 'administration' or 'administrative' may refer to the permanent services or the administrative machinery.

After a new Lok Sabha is duly elected and constituted, the President invites the leader of the party or parties commanding the support of more than half of the members of the Lok Sabha, to form the Government. Thus, the Prime Minister is appointed by the President. The other ministers are appointed by the President on the advice of the Prime Minister.[33] It may be pointed out here that the President has little opportunity of exercising a personal choice in appointing the Prime Minister. Only, if a situation arises where none of the parties gets a clear majority in the Lok Sabha, President may have to use his judgement to pick up the leader who, in his opinion, is likely to command the support of the majority in the House.

While the Prime Minister usually is a member of the Lok Sabha, ministers are drawn from both Houses of Parliament. A person other than a member of Parliament may also be appointed as a minister, but he has to vacate the office after six months unless, in the meanwhile, he manages to get himself elected to either of the tow Houses. Ministers hold office during the pleasure of the President and Council of Ministers is collectively responsible to the Lok Sabha.[34] So, the ministers are under a constitutional obligation to resign collectively as soon as they loose the confidence of the Lok Sabha. At the same time, every minister holds office during the pleasure of the President and shall be liable to dismissal by him. But since the President does so only on the advice of the Prime Minister, this power actually rests with the latter.

The Indian political system represents a real fusion of the highest executive and legislative authorities. The relationship between the Executive and the Legislature is one that is most intimate and ideally does not admit any antagonism or dichotomy. The two are not visualised as competing centre of powers but as inseparable partners or co-partners in the business of government. Parliament is a large body. It does not and cannot govern by itself. The

Council of Ministers may in a sense be described as the grand executive committee of the Parliament, charged with the responsibility of governance on behalf of the parent body. In other words, the Executive is not a separate or outside body. It is in Parliament, inasmuch as the Council of Ministers is drawn from the remains part of the Parliament and responsible to the Lok Sabha, the relationship may be said to be that of a part to the whole and one of interdependence. There is, however, a clear distinction between the functions of the Executive and the functions of the Parliament.[35] Parliament is to legislate, advise, criticise and ventilate public grievances. The Executive is to govern, *albeit* on behalf of the Parliament (See Diagram 1). In the words of the first Secretary of the Indian Parliament:

> Parliament should not any time share in the executive responsibilities of the Government of the day because once it begins to do that, the parliamentary and the executive responsibilities get blurred. Parliament tends to weaken and does not exercise the full power of criticism.[36]

While the Executive has almost unlimited right to initiate and formulate legislative and financial proposals before Parliament and to give effect to approved policies unfettered and unhindered by Parliament, the latter has the unlimited power to call for information, to discuss, to scrutinise and to put the seal of popular approval on proposals made by the Executive. The Executive remains responsible and the administration accountable to Parliament. The function of Parliament is to exercise political and financial control over the Executive and to ensure parliamentary surveillance of administration.

Parliament and Judiciary

The Judiciary in India is an authority co-ordinate with the Legislature and the Executive. The Supreme Court of India and the High Courts in States form a single integrated judi-

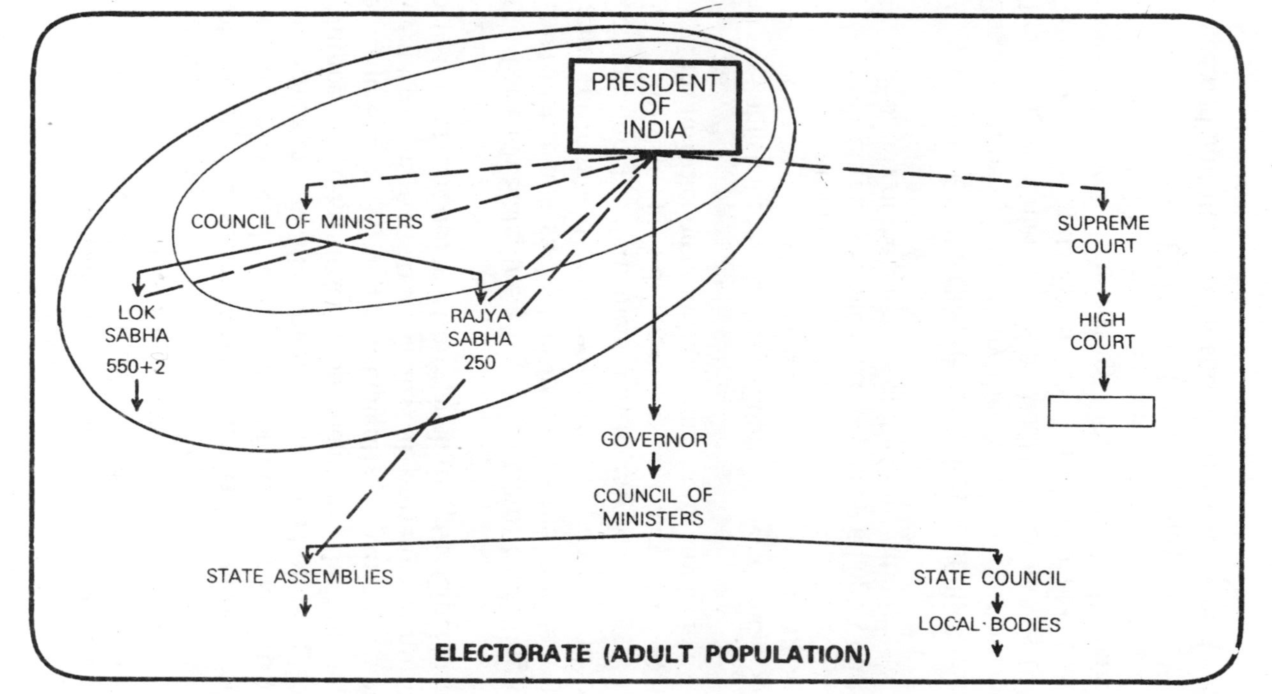
PRESIDENT OF INDIA
COUNCIL OF MINISTERS
SUPREME COURT
LOK SABHA 550+2
RAJYA SABHA 250
HIGH COURT
GOVERNOR
COUNCIL OF MINISTERS
STATE ASSEMBLIES
STATE COUNCIL
LOCAL·BODIES
ELECTORATE (ADULT POPULATION)

ciary. The Supreme Court stands at the apex of the judicial system; it is the highest tribunal of the country.

Parliament has the power to make laws regulating the constitution, organisation, jurisdiction and powers of the Courts. Supreme Court of India consists of the Chief Justice and other judges. It was laid down in the Constitution that the number of judges other than the Chief Justice, would not be more than seven. Parliament was, however, empowered to prescribe a larger number of judges by law.[37] Under this provision, the Parliament passed the Supreme Court (Number of Judges) Act, 1956, increasing the number of other judges to 10, and subsequently by various amendments to this Act, to 25. Thus, at present the number of judges of the Supreme Court, including the Chief Justice, is 26.

For each State, there is a High Court consisting of a Chief Justice and such other judges as the President may from time to time deem it necessary to appoint.[38] Under the Constitution, the Parliament may by law:

(i) extend the jurisdiction of a High Court to, or exclude the jurisdiction of a High Court from, any Union Territory;[39]
(ii) establish a common High Court for two or more States or for two or more States and a Union Territory;[40] and
(iii) constitute a High Court for a Union Territory or declare any Court in any such territory to be a High Court for all or any of the purposes of the Constitution.[41]

According to the Constitution, Judges of the Supreme Court shall be appointed by the President after consultation with the Chief Justice and such other judges of the Supreme Court and of the High Courts in the States as the President may deem necessary. Judges of a High Court are to be appointed by the President after consultation with the Chief Justice of India, the Governor of the State concerned and the Chief Justice of that High Court.[42] But, by its decisions in the Judges' cases, the Supreme Court has practically taken over the power of selecting the judges for appointment in its own hands.

A judge of the Supreme Court or a High Court may by writing under his hand, addressed to the President, resign his office but he cannot be removed from his office except through a process prescribed in the Constitution. Contrary to common belief, there is no provision in the Constitution for the impeachment of a judge. The impeachment procedure is only for the President of India. A judge can be removed from his office by the President on grounds of misbehaviour or incapacity, after an address passed by both Houses of Parliament with a special majority, (i.e. by a majority of the total membership of the House and by a majority of not less than two-thirds of the members of each House present and voting) is presented to him[43] in the same session.

The Parliament is not empowered to discuss the conduct of any judge of the Supreme Court, or a High Court in the discharge of his duties except in the case of a motion for presenting address to the President praying for the removal of a judge.[44] This has apparently been done to secure the independence of the judges both from the Executive as also from the Legislature. The protection of the Judge in this regard is, however, restricted to his judicial duties and does not apply to his private conduct.

The Parliament may by law provide for the establishment of an administrative tribunal for each State or for two or more States. The law made under this provision may specify the jurisdiction and powers of the tribunals. Such a law may exclude the jurisdiction of all Courts, except the jurisdiction of the Supreme Court under Art. 136, with respect to certain specified matters.[45] Further, the Constitution empowers the Parliament to create an All-India Judicial Service which shall not include any post inferior to that of a district judge.[46]

The validity of any proceedings in either House of Parliament cannot be questioned before a court of law on the ground of any alleged irregularity of procedure.[47] The Presiding Officer of each House or any other officer or member of Parliament who is for the time being vested with the powers to regulate procedure, or to enforce or carry out the decision of either House of Parliament, is not subject to the jurisdiction of the courts in exercise of those powers.[48] The courts have no jurisdiction to issue a writ, direction or order relating to a matter which affects the internal affairs of the House.

In the framework of a Constitution which guarantees individual fundamental rights, divides powers between the Union and the States and clearly defines and delimits the powers and functions of every organ of the State including the Parliament, Judiciary plays a very important role under its powers of judicial review. The Courts may declare a law made by Parliament *ultra vires* the Constitution and as such, null and void and unenforceable. Article 13 of the Constitution clearly prohibits the making of any law Parliament or the State Legislature or by any other authority, which may be inconsistent with, or in derogation of, any of the fundamental rights contained in Part III of the Constitution. Articles 32 and 226 confer power on the Supreme Court and the High Courts, respectively, for the enforcement of these rights. Thus, the constitutional validity of a law can be challenged in India on the ground that the subject matter of the legislation:

(i) is not within the competence of the Legislature which has passed it,
(ii) is repugnant to the provisions of the Constitution, or
(iii) it infringes one of the fundamental rights.

It is sometimes assumed and often said that just as it is for the Legislature to make laws and for the Executive to execute them, it is for the Courts to interpret the

Constitution and the laws. This is very misleading and patently wrong. The Judiciary in our polity is not the sole interpreter. There are many authorities who very legitimately interpret the Constitution almost daily during the discharge of their functions. For example, the Presiding Officers in the Houses of Parliament have to interpret the provisions of the Constitution while giving their rulings, which are final in their respective chambers. The basic function of the Courts is to adjudicate disputes between individuals, between individuals and the State, between the States and between the Union and the States and while so adjudicating, the Courts may be required to interpret the provisions of the Constitution and the laws. And, the interpretation given by the Supreme Court becomes the law honoured by all Courts of the land. There is no appeal against the judgement of the Supreme Court. It remains the law of the land unless its interpretation is reviewed or reversed by the Supreme Court itself or the law or the Constitution is suitably amended by Parliament. If an Act of the Parliament is set aside by the Judiciary, the Parliament can re-enact it after the removing the defects for which it was set aside. Also, the Parliament may, within the limits of its constituent powers, amend the Constitution in such a manner that the law no longer remains unconstitutional.

Thus, the Parliament in India is not as supreme as the British Parliament where no judicial review of legislation is permitted. At the same time Judiciary in India is not as supreme as in the United States of America which recognises virtually no limit on the scope of judicial review.

Parliament and the State Legislatures

The Constitution of India has established a federal structure of government in the country inasmuch as there is a distribution of legislative, executive and financial powers between the Union and the States. But it is extremely doubtful if Indian polity can be described as federal. The word 'federation' is nowhere used in the text of the Constitution. In fact, the proposal to describe India as a 'federation' was specifically turned down in the Constituent Assembly. Article 1 of the Constitution described India as a 'Union of States'. There are many features of the Constitution and a large number of its provisions which very clearly and strongly militate against it being a federal Constitution. Unlike in the United States of America, the citizenship in India is one; the flag is one; the Constitution is one. The Judiciary also is one integrated whole and not divided between the Union and the States. The brief point here, however, is that there can be difference of opinion in regard to whether Indian polity is federal, unitary or quasi-federal or it is a polity which is unitary in spirit but federal in structure.

The Union of India as of today is composed of 28 States and 7 Union Territories as specified in the First Schedule of the Constitution. The territory of the Union is divided amongst the States and the Union Territories. A law made by a State Legislature can be applicable only in the territory of that State. The Union Parliament can make laws for the whole or any part of the territory of India. Parliament also enjoys the power of extra-territorial legislation[49], i.e. a law made by it will be applicable not only to the people and property within the territory of India but also to Indian citizens living abroad. No such power of legislation is available to the States.

The Constitution provides for a three-fold distribution of legislative powers between the Union and the States. List I or the Union List contains 97 subjects over which the Parliament has exclusive power to make laws. List II or the State List includes 66 entries over which State Legislatures have got exclusive power of legislation. List III or the Concurrent List contains 47 items on which both the Parliament and the State Legislatures can make laws. While in their own respective spheres as allotted by the Constitution the

Parliament as well as the State Legislatures enjoy complete autonomy, the scheme of distribution of powers emphasises the general predominance of the Parliament in the legislative field.

The Union List, the longest of the three lists, contains important subjects like Defence, Foreign Affairs, Railways, Communication, Banking and Currency, etc. The residuary powers, i.e. power to legislate on a matter not enumerated in any one of the three lists belongs to the Parliament. Further, in the concurrent sphere, in the event of any repugnancy between a Union and a State law relating to the same subject, the former prevails. In other words, the Union law has got "right of way" in this respect. An exception to this rule is made in favour of a State law with respect to a matter in the concurrent field which, in case of a conflict with an earlier law of the Parliament, prevails, if it has been reserved for consideration, and received the assent, of the President. But this provision does not prevent the Parliament from subsequently amending, varying or even repealing the law made by the State Legislature.[50] The executive power of every State is required to be so exercised as to ensure compliance with the laws made by the Parliament.[51]

Even in the spheres exclusively reserved for the States, the Parliament is authorised to legislate under certain circumstances. It may thus legislate on any specified matter in the State List, whenever the Rajya Sabha by a resolution[52], supported by a special majority, declares it necessary or expedient in the national interest to do so.[53] Further, when a proclamation of Emergency is in operation, the legislative competence of the Parliament widens so as to extend to any matter in the State List. Although any power exercised by the Parliament in the national interest or during an Emergency does not restrict the normal legislative power of a State Legislature, in case of any conflict the law made by the Parliament prevails and so long as it remain in force, the State Law, to the extent of its repugnancy, remains inoperative.[54]

The Parliament also enjoys the power to legislate for implementing any treaty, agreement or convention with any country or any decision made at an international conference, association or other body on any subject, even if it falls in the State List.[55]

The Parliament may enter the State List by invitation also. If two or more State Legislatures consider it desirable that any of the matters within their exclusive legislative competence should be regulated by parliamentary legislation and pass resolutions to that effect, the Parliament can undertake necessary legislation. However, the legislation so passed has effect only in the States which had requested and those others which may adopt it afterwards by resolutions passed in that behalf.[56] Some of the entries in the Union List themselves empower Parliament to take over to itself, by making the requisite declaration by law, certain spheres and subjects from the State field.[57]

Our Constitution envisages that if the President receives a report from the Governor of a State, or if the President himself is satisfied that a situation has arisen in which the government of the State cannot be carried on in accordance with the provisions of the Constitution, the President may, in such a case, assume to himself by proclamation, all or any of the executive functions of the State and declare that the powers of the Legislature of the State shall be exercisable by, or under the authority of Parliament.[58]

Predominance of the Parliament is again indicated in the matters of establishment and formation of new States. The Parliament has been empowered—

(i) to form a new State by separation of territory from any State or by uniting two or more States;
(ii) increase or diminish the area of any State;
(iii) alter the boundaries of any State; and
(iv) alter the name of any State.[59]

These alterations are not to be treated as amendments to the Constitution and can be effected if the Parliament passes a Bill by a simple majority on the recommendation of the President. Such a Bill is required to be referred to the legislatures of the States concerned for expressing their views thereon within the time allowed for the purpose. However, this reference in practice, does not fetter the hands of the Parliament in making the change as it thinks fit. Also, the Parliament has been empowered to abolish or create a Legislative Council in a State by a simple procedure not involving an amendment of the Constitution. It can be done by an Act of Parliament, if the Legislative Assembly of the State passes a resolution to that effect by a special majority.[60]

Last but not the least, the Parliament exercises its control over the States through the office of the Governor. The President, as we know, is a constituent of the Parliament and at the same time the Executive head of the Union. Governors of the States are appointed by him and they hold their office during the pleasure of the President.[61] Further, the President may make such provisions as he thinks fit for the discharge of the function of the Governor of a State in any contingency not provided for in the Constitution.[62]

All this, however, does not imply that the States in India have been intended to be made merely administrative agents of the Union. Within the limits laid down in the Constitution, the Union and the States are independent of each other. One is not subordinate to the other in its own field. In the words of Dr. Ambedkar, "the States are as sovereign in the field which is left to them by the Constitution as the Centre is in the field which is assigned to it." The authority of one is to coordinate with the other. In fact, the relationship between the Union and the States in India represents a compromise between the following two conflicting considerations:

(i) normal division of powers under which States enjoy autonomy within their own spheres;
(ii) need for national integrity and a strong Union under exceptional circumstances.

Thus, in practice there exist, as Granville Austin prefers to call, a 'coopreative federation'[63] in India which produces a predominance of the Parliament without necessarily resulting in weak States.

Conclusion

To sum up, in our scheme of things, the adult population, i.e., those who have attained the age of 18, constitute the electorate; they elect the members of the Lok Sabha and the Legislative Assemblies of their States. The State Assemblies, in turn, elect the members of the Rajya Sabha. The President is elected by an electoral college consisting of the elected members of the Rajya Sabha, the Lok Sabha and the Legislative Assemblies of the States (See Diagram 2). He is the nominal or the constitutional executive, the real or the political executive being the Council of Ministers. The ministers must be members of Parliament and are collectively responsible to the Lok Sabha. According to the Constitution, the judges of the Supreme Court and of the High Courts are to be appointed by the President but the Supreme Court has held that the decisive authority in the matter would vest in the Judicial Wing.

Ideally, in our political system, the question of conflict between the Parliament and other organs must never arise because the relationship here is that of the part to the whole, of the agent or the servant to the principal. As between the Executive and the Legislature, there is no adversary situation. The two are partners in the service of the people.

The Parliament of India, representing as it does all constitutionally organised shades of public opinion at the national level, occupies a pre-eminent and central position

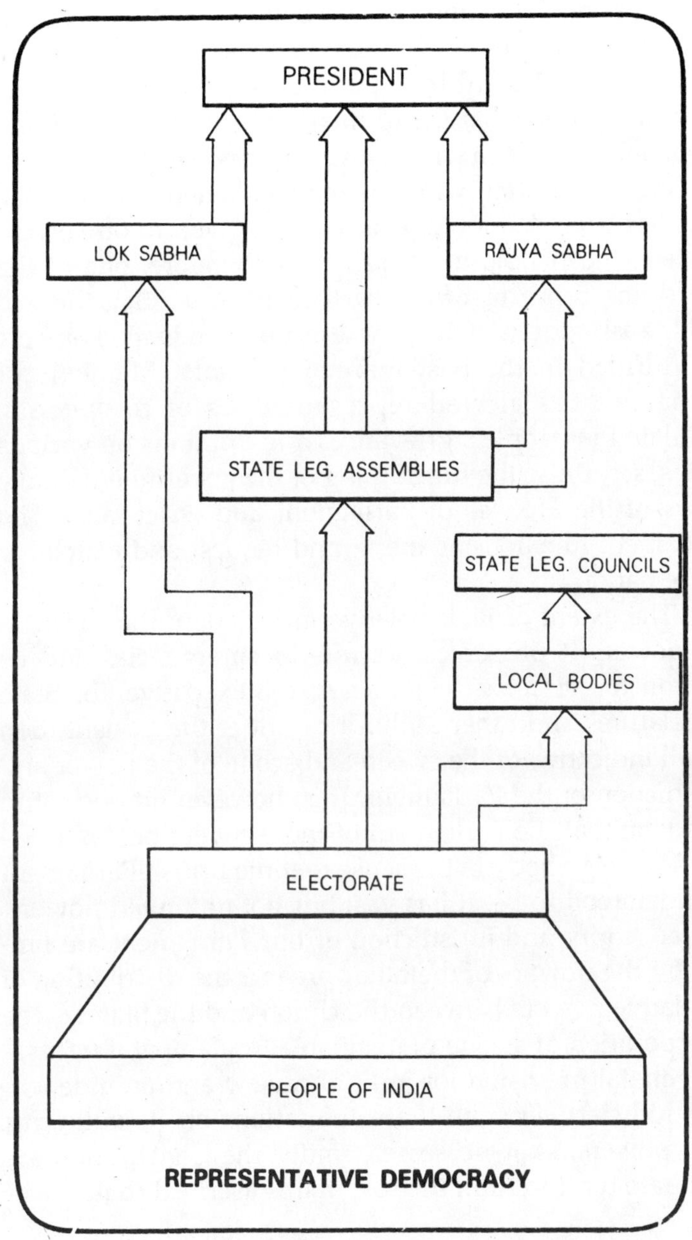
PRESIDENT
LOK SABHA
RAJYA SABHA
STATE LEG. ASSEMBLIES
STATE LEG. COUNCILS
LOCAL BODIES
ELECTORATE
PEOPLE OF INDIA
REPRESENTATIVE DEMOCRACY

Diagram 2.

in Indian polity. It embodies and epitomises the 'sovereign will' of the people; it is the mirror and the voice of the nation. The Preamble to the Constitution makes it abundantly clear that the ultimate source of all power are the people of India in whom sovereignty vests (see Diagram 3). The Constitution which is the fundamental law of the land has been "adopted, enacted and given to ourselves" by "we, the people of India". It is, therefore, one of the overriding concerns of the Parliament to see that the will and the aspirations of the people as reflected in its chambers are fulfilled in the best manner possible. Members of Parliament, as elected representatives of the people, ventilate the people's grievances and opinions on various issues, scrutinise the functioning of the government on the floors of the Houses of Parliament and enact laws. The Parliament functions as the 'grand inquest and watchdog of the nation'.

The extent of its legislative jurisdiction, the constituent powers it possesses, its role in emergencies and its relationship *vis-à-vis* the judiciary, the Executive, the State Legislatures and other authorities under the Constitution are all indicative of the sweep and scope of the power and jurisdiction of the Parliament. It is, however, important to note here that the Parliament of India cannot be described as a sovereign body in the sense that the British Parliament is understood to be. It has vast but not unlimited powers. The authority and jurisdiction of our Parliament are limited by the powers of the other organs, the distribution of legislative powers between the Union and the States,[64] the incorporation of a code of justifiable fundamental rights,[65] the general provision for judicial review and an independent judiciary. Despite these limitations on its authority, such powers, as it possesses, under the Constitution are adequate for it to fulfil the role that is ascribed to it.

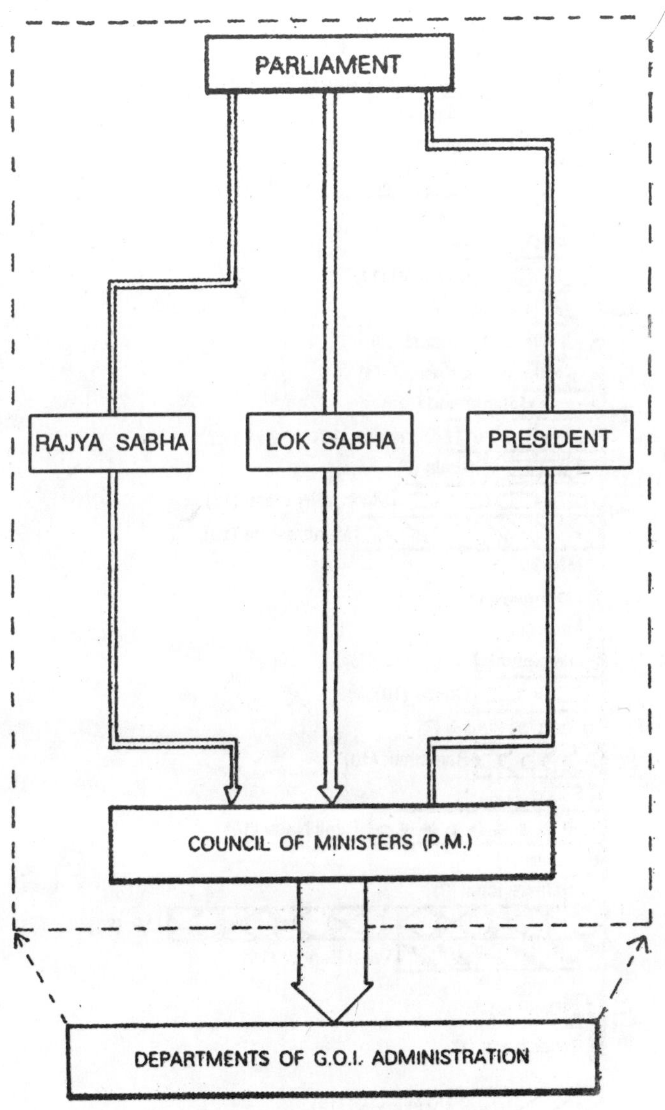
PARLIAMENT
RAJYA SABHA
LOK SABHA
PRESIDENT
COUNCIL OF MINISTERS (P.M.)
DEPARTMENTS OF G.O.I. ADMINISTRATION
SUPREMACY OF PARLIAMENT

Diagram 3.

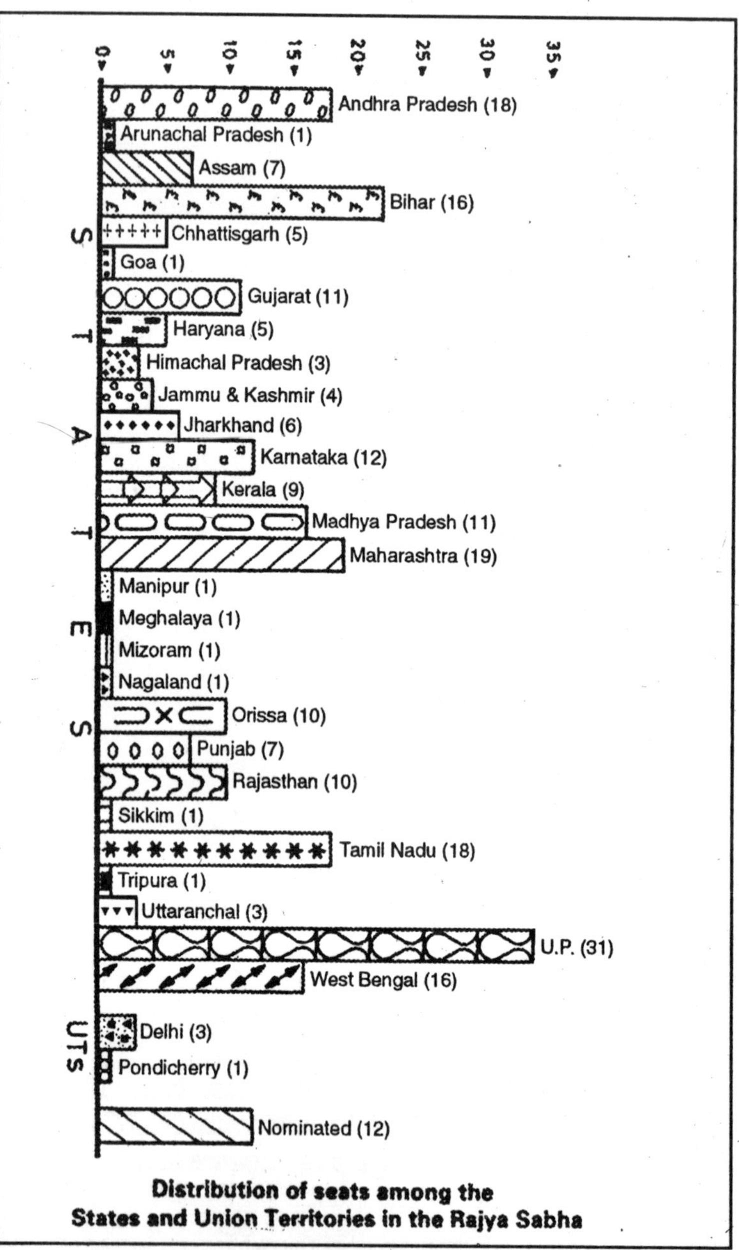

Distribution of seats among the States and Union Territories in the Rajya Sabha

Diagram 4.

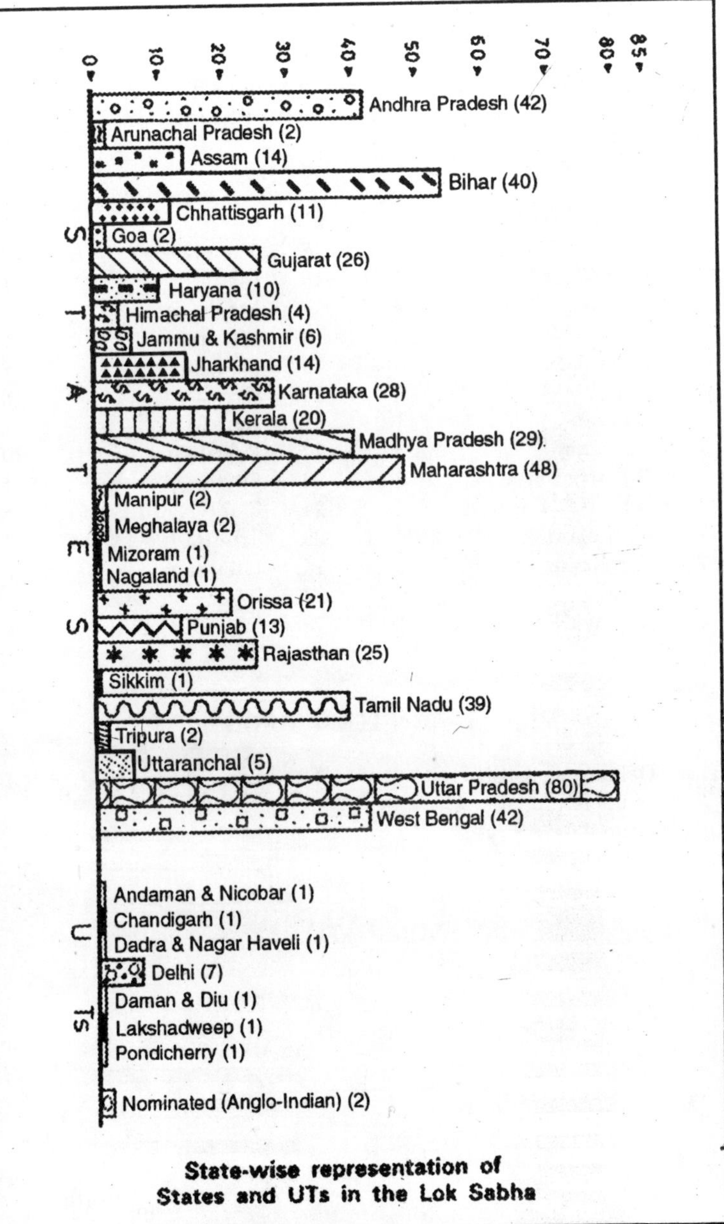

State-wise representation of States and UTs in the Lok Sabha

Diagram 5.

Annexure 2.1

Number of Seats Allotted to Various States and Union Territories in Rajya Sabha

STATES

1.	Andhra Pradesh	18	15.	Maharashtra	19
2.	Arunachal Pradesh	1	16.	Manipur	1
3.	Assam	7	17.	Meghalaya	1
4.	Bihar	16	18.	Mizoram	1
5.	Chhattisgarh	5	19.	Nagaland	1
6.	Goa	1	20.	Orissa	10
7.	Gujarat	11	21.	Punjab	7
8.	Haryana	5	22.	Rajasthan	10
9.	Himachal Pradesh	3	23.	Sikkim	1
10.	Jammu & Kashmir	4	24.	Tamil Nadu	18
11.	Jharkhand	6	25.	Tripura	1
12.	Karnataka	12	26.	Uttaranchal	3
13.	Kerala	9	27.	Uttar Pradesh	31
14.	Madhya Pradesh	11	28.	West Bengal	16

UNION TERRITORIES

1.	Delhi (now termed as the National Capital Territory)[66]	3	2.	Pondicherry	1

NOMINATED 12

Annexure 2.2

Present Strength of Lok Sabha and Number of Seats Allotted to the States and Union Territories

STATES

1.	Andhra Pradesh	42	15.	Maharashtra	48
2.	Arunachal Pradesh	2	16.	Manipur	2
3.	Assam	14	17.	Meghalaya	2
4.	Bihar	40	18.	Mizoram	1
5.	Chhattisgarh	11	19.	Nagaland	1
6.	Goa	2	20.	Orissa	21
7.	Gujarat	26	21.	Punjab	13
8.	Haryana	10	22.	Rajasthan	25
9.	Himachal Pradesh	4	23.	Sikkim	1
10.	Jammu & Kashmir	6	24.	Tamil Nadu	39
11.	Jharkhand	14	25.	Tripura	2
12.	Karnataka	28	26.	Uttaranchal	5
13.	Kerala	20	27.	Uttar Pradesh	80
14.	Madhya Pradesh	29	28.	West Bengal	42

UNION TERRITORIES

1.	Andaman & Nicobar Islands	1	5.	Delhi (now termed as the National Capital Territory)	7
2.	Chandigarh	1	6.	Lakshadweep	1
3.	Dadra & Nagar Haveli	1	7.	Pondicherry	1
4.	Daman & Diu	1			

NOMINATED

(Anglo-Indian) 2

REFERENCES

1. Art. 79
2. Art. 54
3. Arts. 85, 111 & 123
4. Arts 86 & 87
5. Arts 117 & 274 (1)
6. See Arts 95 (1) & 91 (1)
7. Art/ 108 (10)
8. Art. 112
9. Arts. 151 (1), 281, 323 (1), 338 (2), 340 (3) & 350 B(2)
10. Art. 31
11. Art. 80 (1) (a) & (3)
12. Art. 103
13. Art. 80 (4)
14. Art. 80 (1)
15. Art. 83 (1); Representation of the People Act, 1951 Sec. 154 (1)
16. Representation of the People Act. 1951, Sec. 155
17. Arts. 64, 66 & 89
18. Art. 81 (1)
19. Art. 81(2) (a)
20. In fact, right from the First Lok Sabha, every House has been dissolved before completing its full term. Once when during the Emergency its life was extended by one year, the House was dissolved before the completion of the extended term. For further study see Subhash C. Kashyap, 'Dissolution of Lok Sabha', *The Parliamentarian*, LVII, Jan. 1977. Also see *History of Parliament*, op.cit.
21. Art. 83
22. Art. 109
23. Art. 110 (3)
24. Art. 113
25. Art. 75 (3)
26. Arts 56, 61, 67, 124 (4) & 217 (1) (b)
27. Arts 123, 352 (4) & 356 (4)
28. Arts 108 & 118 (4)
29. Art. 249
30. Art 312
31. Arts 52-53 & 77
32. Arts 74 and 78. Also see *Rai Sahib Ram Jawaya Kapur* v. *The State of Punjab*, A.I.R. 1955 S.C. 549.
33. Art. 75 (1)
34. Art. 75

35. Art. 75; *Rai Sahib Ram Jawaya Kapur Case*, op.cit.
36. M.N. Kaul, *Parliamentary Institutions and Procedures*, New Delhi, 1978, p. 18.
37. Art. 124
38. Arts 214 and 216
39. Art. 230
40. Art. 231
41. Art. 241
42. Arts 124 (2) and 217 (1)
43. Arts 124 (4) and 218
44. Art. 121
45. Arts 313 A and 323 B
46. Arts 312 (4) & (3)
47. Arts 122 (1) & 212 (1); *M.S.M. Sharma v. Shree Krishna Sinha*, A.I.R. 1960 S.C. 1186.
48. Art. 122 (2) & 105 (3)
49. Art. 245
50. Art. 254
51. Art. 256
52. Such a resolution initially remains in force for a period not exceeding one year and has to be renewed for a period of one year every time.
53. Art. 249
54. Arts 250 (1) & 251
55. Art. 253
56. Art. 252
57. Seventh Schedule, List I, Entries 7, 23, 24, 27, 52, 54, 56, 62, 63, 64 & 67.
58. Arts 356 & 357
59. Art. 3
60. Art. 169
61. Arts 155 and 156
62. Art. 160
63. Granville Austin, *The Indian Constitution*, Oxford, 1966, p. 187.
64. Arts 245-46 and the Seventh Schedule
65. Arts 12-35 and 226
66. The erstwhile Union Territory of Delhi which had a Metropolitan Council and Executive Councillors has now emerged as the National Capital Territory with a Legislature and a Council of Minsiters (Arts 239 AA and 239 AB inserted by the 69th Amendment in 1991).

3

FUNCTIONS OF PARLIAMENT

ROLE AS A MULTIFUNCTIONAL INSTITUTION

Parliament today is not a law-making body only. It has become more and more a multifunctional institution performing a variety of roles—many of these interrelated and often meshing into one another. This, however, is often not appreciated and disproportionate emphasis is laid only on one or two aspects of the working of the Parliament. Any attempt at a comprehensive identification of roles and analysis of functions of the present-day Parliament in the language of modern parliamentary Political Science may be quite misleading and may even amount to pettifogging—it may befog more and enlighten less. Nevertheless, with a view to clarifying the concepts, some of the cardinal roles and functions of the Parliament may be described:

Functions of Parliament

- Political and financial control (or Executive Responsibility)
- Surveillance of administration (or Administrative Accountability)
- Informational (Right to Information)
- Representational, grievance ventilation, educational and advisory
- Conflict-resolution and national integrational
- Law-making, developmental, social engineering and legitimatisational

- Constituent (Amending the Constitution)
- Leadership (Recruitment and Training)

Political and Financial Control (or Executive Responsibility): Executive or ministerial responsibility to Parliament or what is often termed parliamentary control over the Executive or the Government is based on:

(i) The constitutional provision of collective responsibility of the Council of Ministers to the popular House of Parliament,

(ii) the Parliament's control over the Budget.[1]

In both the matters, parliamentary control over the Executive is political in nature. The answerability of the Executive is direct, continuous, concurrent and day-to-day. When the Parliament is sitting, the continuance of the government in office depends from moment to moment on its retaining the confidence of the House of the People. The House may at any time decide to throw out the government by a majority vote, i.e. if the ruling party loses the support of the majority of the members of the House, its Government goes. No grounds, arguments, proofs or justification are necessary.[2] When the House clearly and conclusively pronounces that the government of the day does not command its support, it must resign. Want of parliamentary confidence in the government may be expressed by the House of the People by:

a. Passing a substantive motion of no-confidence in the Council of Ministers;[3]

b. defeating the Government on a major issue of policy;

c. passing an adjournment motion;[4] and

d. refusing to vote supplies or defeating the government on a financial measure.

The Executive enjoys the right to formulate the Budget. The Constitution provides for an annual statement of the estimated receipts and expenditure to be placed before the Parliament. The Executive is completely free to suggest what the level of its expenditure should be and specify the purposes for which various amounts may be required. It also has full freedom to suggest how revenue should be raised to meet the expenditure. Thus, the entire initiative in financial matters is with the government. Nevertheless, parliamentary control over public finance—the power to levy or modify taxes and the voting of supplies and grants—is one of the most important checks against the Executive assuming arbitrary powers. No taxes can be legally levied and no expenditure incurred from the public exchequer without specific parliamentary authorisation by law.[5]

In fact, except in the theoretical sense of budgetary control or the ultimate sanction of a vote of no-confidence, parliamentary control over the government is a myth. The 19th century British concept of parliamentary control over the Executive is no more valid even in the 'Mother of Parliaments'. Parliament does not control the government. In actual practice, it is the government which control the Parliament through its majority in the House of the People and through its power to have the House dissolved and fresh election ordered by the President. As has been said elsewhere:

> The operative reality of politics today is that the real power resides in the Prime Minister and his or her Cabinet and not in Parliament. The Prime Minister is the leader of the majority in Lok Sabha and also the head of the Government. The Council of Ministers, with the Prime Minister at its head, controls both government and Legislature, not the least because it has extensive patronage and the power to take and implement decisions.[6]

And, this is as it should be:

> There should not be repudiation of the authority of the Prime Minister because then the Cabinet Government does not function. After all the Prime Minister is the pivot. He may consult two or three colleagues and go ahead. That is why you have the system of Cabinet Committees. It is ultimately the Prime Minister who is responsible to the Parliament and the Nation for the policies which the government pursues.[7]

Surveillance of Administration (or Administrative Accountability): Administrative accountability means the accountability of the administration to the Parliament. Administration is run by the permanent civil services. The Parliament does not interfere with day-to-day administration nor does it control administration. Accountability to it is technical and indirect, i.e. through the ministers, and it is ex post facto, i.e. after something is done, after the action has ended. Also, it has to be based on specific grounds. Under our system, after a policy is laid down, a law is passed or moneys are sanctioned, it is the administration which is required to execute and implement. The Parliament itself cannot administer and nor can the ministers. It is, therefore, the officers—and not ministers—who have to explain if things go wrong in the process of implementation.

In a parliamentary polity, since Parliament embodies the will of the people, it must, therefore, be able to oversee the way in which public policy is carried out so as to ensure that it keeps in step with the objectives of socio-economic progress, efficient administration and the aspirations of the people as a whole. This, in a nutshell, is the raison d'etre of parliamentary surveillance of administration. The Parliament has to keep a watch over the behaviour of the administration. It can enquire and examine ex post facto whether the administration has acted in conformity with its obligations under the approved policies and utilised the powers conferred on it for purposes for which they were intended, and whether the moneys spent were in accordance with parliamentary sanction. This ensures that the officers function in the healthy awareness that they would be ultimately subject to parliamentary scrutiny and be answerable for what they do or fail to do. But in order to be able to conduct meaningful scrutiny and call the administration to account, the Parliament must have the technical resources and information wherewithal.[8]

The various procedural devices like the system of Parliamentary Committees, Questions, Calling Attention Notices, Half-an-Hour discussions, etc. through which the Parliament gets informed, also constitute very potent instruments for effecting parliamentary surveillance over administrative action. Significant occasions for the review of administration are provided by the discussions on the Motion of Thanks on the President's Address, the Budget demands, and particular aspects of governmental policy or situations. These apart, specific matters may be discussed through motions on matters of urgent public importance, private members' resolutions and other substantive motions.

Informational (Right to Information) Role: Information is vital to Parliament. It is the first essential requisite for effective discharge of any of its functions. The Parliament gets informed in many ways—through a wide variety of sources—but in as much as the Government is the greatest single monopolist of information, the Parliament and its members have to rely very heavily on the government departments for their information requirements.[9] To call for information is perhaps the greatest power of the Parliament. Parliament's right to be informed is unlimited except that if divulging of certain information is likely to prejudice vital national interest or the security of the State it may not be insisted upon. So far as the activities of the Government are concerned, it is the duty of the Government itself to feed the Parliament with information which is full, truthful, precise and supplied in time. This is done by the ministers making statements on the floor of the House, laying reports and papers on the Table of the House or placing documents in the Parliament Library. All these constitute a wealth of information which becomes immediately public and can be used to raise discussions in the House.

The most well-known and effective mechanism through which members on their own elicit information is that of asking questions in the Houses of Parliament. It has been rightly said that during the Question Hour in Parliament, "a piercing searchlight is thrown in every nook and corner of the vast length and breadth of the administration and nothing falls outside the scrutiny of the Parliament". The minister may be put to a gruelling test by means of searching supplementaries which may be so framed as to expose the weakness of the administration. Through the members' questions sometimes, the ministers concerned themselves get better informed about the departments under their charge and the weak spots therein requiring priority attention. As follow up of what may be an incomplete answer to a question, a member may demand a half-an-hour discussion. Members may ask on matters of urgent public importance Short Notice Questions for oral answers. Still another procedural device is that of the Calling Attention Notices. A member may, with the previous permission of the Speaker, call the attention of a minister to any matter of urgent public importance and request the Minister to make a statement on the subject. Members can also write to the concerned ministers and ask for the information they may need and the information is usually supplied.[10]

On an institutional plane, another method for the Parliament to inform itself and receive necessary feedback is through the reports of various parliamentary committees. In the process of their scrutiny, the committees ask searching questions and collect extensive and valuable information from the government ministries and departments, public undertakings, etc. under examination. This procedural device has also become an important tool for eliciting information on matters of urgent public importance and has been very popular with members from both sides of the House.

Some political parties have their own research and reference staff who feed their members with the necessary information particularly from the party position angle. Visits to constituencies and other places, correspondence with constituents and others, membership of governmental consultative or other official Committees, Boards, etc., official and unofficial publications, periodical literature and mass media—the Radio, T.V., the newspapers—also help members keep themselves abreast of developments and well-informed about matters of administration and public policy.

The Press plays a particularly important informational role in parliamentary life. But, this also casts a tremendous responsibility on the Press to follow its own code of conduct, to resist the temptation to yield to sensationalism, to remember the overriding duty not to sacrifice national interest for petty journalistic gains, to ensure factual accuracy and reliability of the news stories and above all, to be honest and objective and devoted to serving the people at large. Often, the Press struggles hard to unearth the administrative lapses, scandals and shortcomings, gives expression to public grievances and difficulties and reports on how policies are being carried out. Most of the raw material for parliamentary questions, motions and debates comes from the daily Press and this is an important instrument on which a member relies. Simultaneously, the Press keeps the people informed of what is happening in Parliament. This two-way traffic enables the Press to maintain an important and strong link between the public and the Parliament. Considering the space that is devoted to these matters and the volume of information that is given, the Press in our country fulfils a great need felt alike by the members of Parliament and the public.

Even though so much information from such a variety of sources is available to Parliament, it is not enough. The information supplied by the official government sources is efficiently collected and processed but it may sometimes, consciously or unconsciously, get slated or biased and may not always be strictly complete, factual and objective. Information from other sources like the mass media, political parties, interest groups or lobbyists would be even less so. Hence the need for the Parliament developing its own institutionalised sources of information, an independent information reservoir and specialised dissemination procedures. This is sought to be achieved through what is called the Parliament Library and its Research, Reference, Documentation and Information Services. These remain at the disposal of members and supply non-partisan, objective and strictly relevant information on demand, promptly and often at short notice, as also in anticipation of the members' needs in discharge of their parliamentary duties. Since legislators are busy men with multifarious pressure on their time, the information has to be precise, to the point and in easily digestible and readily usable form.[11]

Representational, Grievance Ventilation, Educational and Advisory Role: The primary function of the Parliament in a modern democracy is to represent the people. In recent decades, emphasis has shifted more and more to the representational and grievance ventilation role of the Parliament. It is the people's institution par excellence. It is the supreme forum through which the people seek to realise their aspirations, urges and expectations, ventilate their grievances and difficulties and even articulate their passions, anxieties and frustrations. The Parliament represents the changing moods and needs of the people. It is not only a microcosm and mirror of the people, but also a barometer of their mood and pulse rate.

It may be interesting to study the self-perceptions of their roles by the members of Parliament, i.e. to examine what and how the members themselves perceive their legitimate roles to be and also whether the changing complexion of the Houses of Parliament is in any way reflected in on the members' own role perceptions and the actual functioning of the Houses. On the basis of the analysis of empirical data, while the pre-Independence central legislature was an elitist body, the Lok Sabha, with each successive election has been becoming a more representative body. As analysed in an earlier study:

> ...the Parliament of India more and more truly mirrors the mosaic of Indian society. Parliament is becoming more representative of the people of India, of the level of their political awareness, of their lack of sophistication, and of their problems, hopes and aspirations. Elitist politics is gradually giving way to a healthy ruralised politics. The polished urban lawyer who knew the law and the niceties of parliamentary procedure is being replaced by the village farmer or the political/social worker with his innate common sense and acute awareness of what the people need. The foreign educated, public or convent school-trained, upper middle class urban elite are being elbowed out by the rural, educated, indigenous counter-elite.[12]

Also, an average member of Parliament himself views his primary duty to be that of representing his people and giving expression to their difficulties, problems and grievances and seeking their removal and redressal. For, if the Executive is responsible to the Parliament, the Parliament and its members are also answerable to the people. The member is the chief communication channel and link between the people he represents and the Parliament and the government. Also, the member has an educational role. He has to understand and be involved in what goes on in the Parliament, in order to be able to educate the people about the Parliament and generally feed them with information. For, if he has to represent the people in Parliament he has also to present its proper image, its working and its problems to the people. He must know his constituents and their problems and needs and do his best to contribute to their welfare. This the member can try to achieve by making full use of the various procedural devices available and snatching every possible opportunity in the House and through the Petitions Committee and other Parliamentary Committees.

During debate and discussion on legislative proposals or Finance Bills, motion to consider and approve government policies, Motion of Thanks on the President's Address, Budget, etc. members are free to express themselves and to say what is good for the country and what modifications in the existing policy are required. The government is sensitive to parliamentary opinion; in most cases they anticipate it; in some cases they bow to it and in some others they may feel that they cannot make any change consistent with their commitments and obligations and political philosophy. Nevertheless during discussions members have full liberty to criticise the administration for their past performance and suggest how they should behave in the future or how a particular measure should be carried out or implemented. The discussions are important for they indicate parliamentary mood and bring the impact of public thinking on the administrative apparatus which may otherwise remain immune to public sentiments and feelings. It is as well that the parliamentary debates should serve to remind the administration of their duties and obligations. Parliamentary debates effect the administrative thinking and action in a variety of ways and the subtle influence which cannot be measured in terms of any visible units pervades through all the ranks of administration—high and low. While the administrators have complete freedom to implement the policies approved by the Parliament in the best manner possible, they are nevertheless haunted and guided by the various viewpoints expressed on the floor of the House. And, this may be called the Advisory Role of the Parliament.

Conflict Resolution and National Integrational Role: Conflict is natural to man—conflict of ideas and interest and struggle for power by various contending forces. The emergence of Parliament as a potent conflict resolution mechanism and a leading mediating force in national politics is now an accepted fact of the Indian political life.

Parliamentary democracy is considered to be a better and more civilised system of government inasmuch as under it debate and discussion on the legislative floor take the place of physical strife on the streets or on the battle fields. Debates and discussions bring out into the open the underlying tensions and resentments in society. The Parliament becomes the legitimate arena for power struggle, for crystallisation of political activity or for acting out the conflicting roles and interests with parliamentary rules and procedures, facilitating eventual reconciliation. Instead of fighting to annihilate each other, the parties tend to agree to disagree and to accommodate or tolerate each other. It is on the legislative floor that some very delicate problems get resolved. The contending forces struggle to have their way and finally get reconciled. In performing this conflict resolution role, the parliamentary institution acts as a great national integrator and mediator in change. This conflict resolution and integrational role of Parliament is specially significant in the context of our highly pluralistic society.

Besides the role played by the formal parliamentary forums and parliamentary procedures, attention may be drawn to the Central Hall of the Parliament House which is almost an institution in itself. It is a big club and a great purgatory. Here members of Parliament from all parts of the country irrespective of caste, creed, region or religion meet informally and discuss in groups or with individuals, problems which affect the country as a whole. In creates feelings of national integrity of a high order which no other forum can. Even those who before entering its portals, may have some separatist, regional or parochial views, get cleansed and all feel one—people of one country—after they have passed through the purgatory of the Central Hall. Fissiparous tendencies, if any, lose their sharp edges. What may seem alright and quite acceptable—even laudable—in some state capitals may become a subject matter of laughter inside the Central Hall. The atmosphere itself compels a larger national perspective.

Law-making—Developmental, Social Engineering and Legitimatisational Role: Law-making is the traditional function of a legislature. Under the Constitution of India, Parliament is the supreme legislative body at the national level. It can make laws on a wide range of subjects allotted to it under the Union and the Concurrent Lists in the Seventh Schedule of the Constitution.[13] Since residuary power vests in the Parliament, it can also make laws in areas not specifically assigned to States. Even in the specifically assigned areas a subject in the State List, i.e. falling within the sphere exclusively reserved for the States ceases to be so reserved in certain circumstances under which the Union Parliament may legislate in that subject are also.

The most important aspect of legislation lies in its vital social or sociological ramifications. Laws are necessary not only for maintaining peace and law and order, for securing the country from external dangers and internal disturbances, for ensuring sound and efficient administration but also for bringing about public welfare by facilitating economic and social change. In a society particularly in a state of flux like ours, the Parliament alone can provide the basis and the catalytic agency for social change and economic development. Concretisation of socio-economic transformation may involve a restructuring of existing institutions and bringing about a new balance between different societal forces and conflicting group interests. This can be done only through legislation by Parliament. In fact, the Parliament has been in the forefront of social reforms. A large number of social reform measures have been passed by the Parliament since the commencement of the Constitution, e.g. laws providing special consideration, guarantees and benefits to backward, down-trodden or traditionally ill-treated sections of the society in the form of reservations, social security, removal of disabilities, minimum wages, old-age pensions, housing and the like.[14]

While Parliament's role in law-making—the opportunity to review, examine and discuss the proposed legislation and possibly to influence the final shape—is of immense value, there is another side to the picture. Parliament does not make laws. It has neither the time nor the necessary know-how for the purpose. Initiative in legislation as insomuch else has passed almost completely to the Executive and the departments of the administration.

> The formulation of the legislative proposal implies a preparation at the technical level and harmonisation of several competing claims and considerations that cannot, in the very nature of things, be accomplished in the legislature because the resources vital to legislation—technical data and statistics, accumulated administrative experience and expertise—are available only to the Executive.[15]

Parliament only discusses, scrutinises and, by putting its seal of approval, legitimatises legislative proposals—bills, rules and regulations, etc.—formulated by the Executive. Its role is thus more a legitimatisational role that a law-making role.

On the one hand, Parliament does so much else which is not law-making—only about 1/5th of its time is devoted to legislation—on the other, Parliament is not the sole actor in the drama of law-making. It is only one of the many. The modern concept of law is not that of a body of rules of action of general application, established by authority, etc. Law is a process—a long and complicated process—beginning in the pre-natal social urges, the first felt need and demand for action, conception of the policy-makers and the play of political forces and various interest groups, involving role of the concerned and the law departments in drafting the Bill, the ruling party, the concerned minister and the Cabinet, the Houses of Parliament and their Committees and the President; and proceedings to making rules and regulations and then actual implementation by the administration and, in case of dispute, interpretation and judicial review by Courts. At every stage law is being actually made and in effect modified. Thus, the act of law-making cannot be attributed to any one body of persons or any constituent organ of the State; all the three organs of State—the Executive, the Legislature and the Judiciary—have a participating role in legislation.[16] Annexure 3.1 at the end of this chapter shows the time spent (percentages) on different kinds of functions by the Lok Sabha.

Constituent (Amending the Constitution) Role: Under Art. 368 of the Constitution, which is the specific provision dealing with the amendment of the Constitution, Parliament is the repository of the constituent power of the Union. The procedure for constitutional amendment, as spelled out in that article, has certain distinctive features which clearly mark out the Parliament's constituent capacity from its ordinary role as a legislature. First, an amendment of the Constitution can be initiated 'only' by the introduction of a Bill either House of Parliament so that the initiative in the matter of constitutional amendment has been exclusively reserved for Parliament. Second, for the most part, the provisions of Constitution can be amended by the Parliament by a special majority, namely, a majority of not less than two-thirds of the members of each House present and voting. It is only in the case of a limited category of constitutional provisions (i.e. those relating to the lists in the Seventh Schedule, representation of States in Parliament, provisions of Art. 368, etc.) that the amendment Bill having been passed by each House of Parliament with the prescribed special majority, needs to be ratified by the legislatures of not less than half of the States. Third, on a Constitution Amendment Bill, as duly passed/ratified, being presented to the President, the President's assent is mandatory and, unlike as in case of ordinary legislative Bills, he has no option to withhold his assent or return the Bill to the House for reconsideration.[17] And, lastly, it is significant that no provision of the Constitution is 'unamendable' inasmuch as Parliament can in any way amend, alter or repeal any provision of the Constitution and such amendments are in order unless they tend to alter or violate what may be considered as the basic features of the Constitution.

During the period 1950-1972, the question of the amendability of fundamental rights came before the Supreme Court in three different cases, namely, *Shankari Prasad v. Union of India,*[18] *Sajjan Singh v. State of Rajasthan*[19] and *Golak Nath v. State of Punjab.*[20] Until the Supreme Court decision in the *Golak Nath* case, the law was as follows:

(i) Constitution Amendment Acts are not ordinary laws and are passed by Parliament in exercise of its constituent powers as contradistinct from ordinary legislative powers. There is no separate constituent body for the purposes of amendment of the Constitution, constituent power also being vested in 'Parliament'.

(ii) There is no limitation placed upon the amending power, that is to say, there is no provision of the Constitution which cannot be amended. The terms of Art. 368 are perfectly general and empower Parliament to amend the Constitution, without any exception whatever.

(iii) Fundamental Rights guaranteed under the Constitution (Part III) are subject to Parliament's power to amend the Constitution.

In the *Golak Nath* case, the Supreme Court by a 6:5 majority reversed its earlier decisions and held that the fundamental rights enshrined in the Constitution were transcendental and immutable, that Art. 368 of the Constitution laid down only the procedure for amendment and did not give to Parliament any substantive power to amend the Constitution or any constituent power distinct or separate from its ordinary legislative power, that a Constitution Amendment Act was also law within the meaning of Art. 13 and as much Parliament could not take away or abridge the fundamental rights even through a Constitution Amendment Act passed under Art. 368.

In 1973, in the *Kesavananda Bharati* v. *State of Kerala*[21] case the Supreme Court reviewed the decision in the *Golak Nath* case. Ten of the 13 judges held that Art. 368 itself contained the power to amend the Constitution and that 'law' in Art. 13(2) did not take in a constitutional amendment under Act. 368. The law declared in the *Golak Nath* case was accordingly overruled. On the question whether the amending power under Art. 368 is absolute and unlimited, seven judges, constituting a majority, held that the amending power under Art. 368 was subject to an implied limitation; a limitation which arose by necessary implication from it being a power to "amend the Constitution". By a majority of 7:6 the Court ruled that "article 368 does not enable Parliament to alter the 'basic structure' or framework of the Constitution". What constituted the basic structure was, however, not clearly made out by the majority and remained an open question.[22] This is, however, not to dispute the opinion of some learned judges who may still regard the judgement in *Kesavanand Bharati* case "as our Republic's greatest contribution to jurisprudence" and its underlying philosophy as of "momentous significance for the survival of democracy in our country".

Following the decision in *Kesavananda's case,* clauses (4) & (5) were inserted in Art. 368 by the Constitution (42nd Amendment) Act, 1976, to dilute the limitation of 'basic feature' to the amending powers of Parliament. The clauses provided that (a) there were no limitations, expressed or implied, upon the amending power of the Parliament under Art. 369 (1), which is a 'constituent power' and that (b) a Constitution Amendment Act would not, therefore, be subject to judicial review, on any ground. But the applicability of the doctrine of basic structure was reaffirmed by the Supreme Court in *Minerva Mills v. Union of India case* by holding clauses (4) & (5) as void, on the ground that this amendment sought to totally exclude judicial review, which was a 'basic feature' of the Constitution.

Present state of the doctrine of basic feature is that so long as the decision in *Kesavananda's case* is not overturned by another Full Bench of the Supreme Court, any amendment to the Constitution is liable to be interfered with by the court on the ground of affecting one or other of the basic features of the Constitution.

In *Kesavananda's case*, Justice Sikri had tried to tabulate the basic features of the Constitution as follows:[23]

(i) Supremacy of the Constitution
(ii) Republican and democratic form of government
(iii) Secular character of the Constitution
(iv) Separation of powers and
(v) Federal character of the Constitution.

In the same case, Justice Hegde and Justice Mukherjee, included the sovereignty and unity of India, the democratic character of our polity and individual freedom to the elements of basic structure of the Constitution. They believed that the Parliament had no power to revoke the mandate to build a welfare State and an egalitarian society.[24] Justice Khanna also said that the Parliament could not change our democratic government into a dictatorship or hereditary monarchy nor would it be permissible to abolish the Lok Sabha and the Rajya Sabha. The secular character of the State could not, likewise, be done away with.[25]

In *Indra Gandhi v. Raj Narain case*, Justice Chandrachud found the following to be the fundamental elements of the basic structure of the Constitution.[26]

(i) India as a sovereign democratic republic;
(ii) equality of status and opportunity;
(iii) secularism and the freedom of conscience;
(iv) rule of law.

The same Judge in *Minerva Mills' case* added the 'amending powers of Parliament', 'judicial review' and 'balance between the Fundamental Rights and the Directive Principles' to the list of elements basic to the Constitution.[27]

In some cases there is a difference of opinion among the judges as regards a particular element forming an element of the basic feature. For example, Chief Justice Ray did not find it possible to hold the concept of free and fair elections as a basic structure, whereas Justice Khanna, in the same case found this principle to be an element of the fundamental features of the Constitution.[28] Justice Chandrachud did not subscribe to the view that the Preamble to the Constitution holds the key to its basic structure.[29] Justice Beg, on the other hand found that the Court can find the test (of constitutional validity) primarily in the Preamble to the Constitution. The Preamble, he believed, furnished the yardstick to be applied even to constitutional amendments.[30]

In the *S.R. Bommai case* regarding the dismissal of three BJP governments in Madhya Pradesh, Rajasthan and Himachal Pradesh, Justice Jeevan Reddy and Justice Ramaswamy reiterated that federalism inter alia was a basic feature of the Constitution. Justice Ramaswamy said:

> The Preamble of the Constitution is an integral part of the Constitution, democratic form of government, federal structure, unity and integrity of the nation, secularism, socialism, social justice and judicial review are basic features of the Constitution.

It is thus evident that so far, there has been no consensus in this regard among the judges and no majority judgement is available laying down all the features of the Constitution that may be considered 'basic'. The Court has not foreclosed the list of the basic features as suggested by different judges in different cases. In *Indira Gandhi's case,* Justice Chandrachud has observed that "the theory of basic structure has to be considered in each individual case, not in the abstract, but in the context of the concrete problem."[31]

Since the commencement of the Constitution in 1950 as many as 86 constitutional amendments have been effected. All this has been done in exercise of the Parliament's constituent powers and often to meet unforeseen difficulties created and situations brought about as a result of the decisions of courts and their interpretations of constitutional provisions. Sometimes, the amendments became necessary to clarify the constitutional intent—the intention of the framers of the Constitution behind particular provisions—and to bring the text of the Constitution closer to accepted national goals and objectives as understood by Parliament.

Leadership (Recruitment and Training) Role: Last but not the least, an important function of the Parliament is to serve as a national reservoir and nursery of political leadership. Parliament is the recruiting and training ground for ministers. The performance of members in the two Houses and their committees helps the Prime Minister to select the best from among those available. While serving on various parliamentary committees, members acquire considerable knowledge and expertise in specific fields and they usually make good ministers.[32]

REFERENCES

1. Arts 75, 114-116 and 265 of the Constitution of India.
2. See Inter-Parliamentary Union (ed.), *Parliaments of the World*, London, 1976, pp. 801-802 and 825-827.
3. *Rules of Procedure and Conduct of Business in Lok Sabha*, (7th edn), 1989, Rule 198.
4. Rule 56
5. Arts 114-116 and 265
6. Subhash C. Kashyap, 'Committees in the Indian Lok Sabha in John D. Lees and Malcolm Shaw, *Committees in Legislatures*, Durham, 1979, p. 291.
7. M.N. Kaul, *Parliamentary Institutions and Procedures*, New Delhi, 1978, p. 14.
8. Also see S.L. Shakdher, *Glimpses of the Working of Parliament*, New Delhi, 1977, pp. 180-184.
9. Subhash C. Kashyap, 'Information Management for Parliamentarians', *Monthly Public Opinion Surveys*, XVIII, 6, 1973; and his report

on 'Means of Information at the Disposal of the M.P.' in *The Member of Parliament: His Requirements for Information in the Modern World*, Vols. I and II, Inter-Parliamentary Union, Geneva, 1973 (Papers and Proceedings of the International Symposium).

10. Shakdher, *Glimpses*, op.cit., pp. 186-187.
11. Kashyap, 'Information Management', *op.cit.*
12. Kashyap, *Committees, op.cit.* p. 296.
13. Arts 245-246 and the Seventh Schedule
14. Subhash C. Kashyap, *Human Rights and Parliament*, New Delhi, 1978, Chapter 9, 'Parliament and Socio-economic Legislation', pp. 124-133.
15. Subhash C. Kashyap in Inter-Parliamentary Union, (ed.), *Who Legislates in the Modern World*, Geneva, 1976, p. 68.
16. *Ibid.*, pp. 65-69
17. Kashyap, *Human Rights, op.cit.*, Chapter 10, 'Constituent Power of Parliament and Judicial Review', pp. 134-143.
18. A.I.R. 1951, S.C. 458
19. A.I.R. 1965, S.C. 845
20. A.I.R. 1967, S.C. 1643
21. A.R.R. 1973, S.C. 1461
22. Subhash C. Kashyap, 'Parliament and Recent Constitutional Developments in India', *The Table*, (London), Vol. XXIV, 1976, pp. 15-18.
23. *Kesavananda Bharati v. State of Kerala*, A.I.R. 1973, S.C., 1461, para 302.
24. *Ibid*, para 682
25. *Ibid.*, para 1437
26. *Indira Nehru Gandhi v. Raj Narain*, A.I.R. 1975, S.C. 2299, para 665.
27. *Minverva Mills Ltd. v. Union of India*, A.I.R. 1980, S.C. 1789.
28. *Indira Gandhi case*, op.cit., paras 55 and 213.
29. *Ibid.*, para 665
30. *Ibid.*, para 623
31. *Ibid.*, para 2465
32. Also see, Subhash C. Kashyap, *Parliamentary Procedure, Law, Privileges, Practice and Precedents*, Universal, New Delhi, 2000, Vol. I, Chapter 3.

Annexure 3.1

Time Spent (Percentage of Total) on Different Procedural Divices in Lok Sabha

Lok Sabha	I	II	III	IV	V	VI	VII	VIII	IX	X	XI	XII
Total Duration (Hours)	3784	3651	3733	3029	4071	1753	3224	3324	754	2528	813	575
Percentage of Total												
1. Legislative Business	48.80	28.20	23.00	22.08	27.55	23.51	23.99	25.00	16.23	22.16	15.66	16.60
2. Budget	18.50	20.90	25.00	19.30	21.64	23.26	30.84	21.74	16.00	17.38	17.60	14.68
3. Questions	14.60	15.10	15.10	15.94	12.61	13.70	12.20	12.80	10.14	11380	9.58	8.96
4. Resolutions	6.30	5.50	5.90	6.45	5.17	3.72	3.96	5.47	5.77	6.23	4.59	4.45
5. Motions	7.00	13.70	13.20	9.22	6.55	10.71	6.35	3.35	4.34	6.33	17.33	10.45
6. Other Discussions under Rule 193 (Short Duration Discussion) and Rules 55 (Half-an-Hour Discussions), etc.	4.80	16.60	17.80	27.01	26.48	25.10	32.66	31.33	47.52	36.10	35.24	44.86

4

THE ELECTORAL SYSTEM

ELECTIONS TO PARLIAMENT

Representative parliamentary democracy calls for a system of choosing representatives of the people and for a suitable machinery for the purpose. The Constitution provides for universal adult franchise. Every citizen who is 18 years or above has full voting rights irrespective of religion, race, caste, sex or place of birth. It is most important that the elections are free and fair and are seen to be so. These are, therefore, to be conducted under the superintendence and direction of an independent authority called the Election Commission. In a country of India's vast size (nearly 3.3 million sq.km.) and its large population (over 1 billion) and with a massive electorate (nearly 620 million), the conduct of nation-wise elections becomes a gigantic undertaking.[1] In addition to the elections to the two Houses of Parliament and the State Legislatures, the Election Commission is required to conduct elections to the high offices of the President and Vice-President of India.

The Election Commission

The Election Commission consists of the Chief Election Commissioner and such other Election Commissioners as may be appointed by the President. In October 1992 two Election Commissioners were appointed and by an ordinance given the same position and status as the Chief Election Commissioner. Also, the Commission was required to act as a body taking decisions unanimously or by majority. The ordinance (which was later replaced by an Act) was challenged by the Chief Election Commissioner but the Supreme Court held the Act to be valid.

Taking into consideration the importance of the duties that the Chief Election Commissioner has to perform, persons of eminence with rich administrative experience, legal knowledge and high social standing are appointed to this post. The conditions of service and tenure of office of the members of the Commission cannot be changed to their disadvantage after the appointment. The Chief Election Commissioner cannot be removed from his office except through the same process as in the case of a judge of the Supreme Court. Other Election Commissioners cannot be removed from office without the recommendation of the Chief Election Commissioner. The Union and State governments are enjoined to make available to the Commission such officers and staff as may be necessary for the proper discharge of its duties and responsibilities and while performing any functions in connection with the elections all such officers and staff are fully answerable to the Election Commission.[2]

For every State, there is a Chief Electoral Officer nominated by the Election Commission to supervise the preparation, revision and correction of electoral rolls and to conduct all elections in the State. Likewise, for each district there is a District Election Officer who coordinates and supervises all work in his district relating to elections under the direction of the Chief Electoral Officer.[3] Usually the District Collectors or Deputy Commissioners are designated as the District Election Officers. They appoint presiding and polling officers for the polling stations. The presiding officer plays an important role on the day of the election. His general duty at a polling station is to keep order there and to see that the poll is fair and free.[4] It is the duty of the polling officers at a polling station to assist the presiding officer in the performance of his functions.[5]

The Election Commission, in consultation with the State Government, appoints a Returning Officer for every parliamentary and assembly constituency and for every election to fill a seat or seats in the Rajya Sabha. The Returning Officer is authorised to do all such acts and things as may be necessary for conducting the elections according to election laws.[6]

Election of Members

A general election to the Lok Sabha is held either on the expiration of its term or on its dissolution.[7]

The Constitution empowers the Parliament to make laws concerning elections to either House of Parliament or to either House of the Legislature of a State, including the preparation of electoral rolls, the delimitation of constituencies and all other necessary matters for securing the due constitution of such House or Houses.[8] The Representation of the People Act, 1950 and the Representation of the People Act, 1951 are two of the most important statutes enacted in pursuance of this provision. Supplementing the provisions of these statutes are the Registration of Electoral Rules, 1960 and the Conduct of Election Rules, 1961. The Acts and Rules are amended and updated from time to time to meet the exigencies of developing situations.

Qualifications and Disqualifications for Membership

To be qualified to become a member of Parliament a person must be:

(a) a citizen of India;

(b) not less than 30 years of age in the case of the Rajya Sabha and not less than 25 years in the case of the Lok Sabha; and

(c) and elector for any parliamentary constituency in India, but in the case of the Rajya Sabha a candidate mu t be registered as an elector in the State or Union Territory from where he is to be chosen.

Additional qualifications may be prescribed by Parliament by law.[9]

There are also certain disqualifications for becoming a member. A person, for example, shall be disqualified for being a member of either House of Parliament if:

(a) he holds any office of profit under the government other than an office declared by Parliament by law not to disqualify its holder;
(b) he is of unsound mind;
(c) he is an undischarged insolvent;
(d) he has ceased to be a citizen of India;
(e) he is so disqualified by any law made by Parliament; and
(f) he is so disqualified on the ground of defection.[10]

The office of a minister is not deemed to be an office of profit.[11] Besides the above constitutional requirements, the election laws lay down some more disqualifications. Under the Representation of the People Act, 1951, if a person has been convicted, among other things, for promoting enmity between different groups or convicted for the offence of bribery or has been punished for preaching and practising social crimes such as untouchability, dowry and sati, then he is disqualified from being chosen as a member. Again, a person convicted for any offence and sentenced to imprisonment for not less than two years stands disqualified for a period of five years after his release. A government servant dismissed for corruption or for disloyalty to the State is disqualified for a period of five years from the date of his dismissal.

Mode of Election

Rajya Sabha: Members of the Rajya Sabha are the representatives of the people of the States and of Union Territories. They are elected in the case of a State by the elected members of the Legislative Assembly of the State and in case of a Union Territory by an electoral college. They are elected through a system of indirect election and in accordance with the system of proportional representation by means of single transferable vote. This is intended to provide some representation to minority community and parties.[12]

For the purpose of filling seats in the Rajya Sabha, the President, by issuing notification on a date as may be recommended by the Election Commission, calls upon the electors to elect the members of the Rajya Sabha. No such notification is issued more than three months prior to the date on which the term of office of the retiring members is due to expire.[13] The Returning Officer, with the approval of the Election Commission, fixes and notifies the place at which the polling is to be held.

Lok Sabha: For the purpose of electing a new Lok Sabha, the President, by notification published in the Gazette, on such date as suggested by the Election Commission, calls upon all parliamentary constituencies to elect members to the Lok Sabha. After the notification has been issued, the Election Commission fixes the dates for filing of nominations, scrutiny, withdrawal and polling.[14] Every candidate for election has to deposit a security amount to validate his nomination. The amount is forfeited if the candidate fails to secure a minimum percentage of votes polled in that constituency.[15] A candidate for election has to make and subscribe an oath or affirmation bearing true faith and allegiance to the Constitution according to the form set out for the purpose in the Third Schedule of the Constitution. Under the latest judgement of the Supreme Court and directions issued by the Election Commission thereunder, every candidate has also to declare on affidavit his criminal background, if any, educational qualifications, assets and liabilities, etc. The Returning Officer, after examining the validity of nomination papers, publishes a list of validly nominated candidates.

The election to the Lok Sabha, being direct, requires

the territory of India to be divided into suitable territorial constituencies. Thus, each State is divided into several parliamentary constituencies in such a manner that the ratio between the population of each constituency and number of seats allotted to it is, so far as practicable, the same throughout the State. Every parliamentary constituency is a single member constituency.[16]

After the polling has been completed, counting of votes takes place on the date and time fixed by the Returning Officer. He declares the result and reports it to the Election Commission and to the Secretary-General of the concerned House.

If any question arises as to whether a member of either House of Parliament has become subject to any of the disqualifications specified in the Constitution, the President's decision shall be final. However, before giving his decision, he is required to obtain the opinion of the Election Commission in this matter.[17]

Vacation of Seats

If a member of one House is also elected to the other House, his seat in the first House becomes vacant with effect from the date on which he is elected to the other House.[18] Similarly, if he is chosen also as a member of a State Legislature, he ceases to remain a member of Parliament, unless he resigns his seat in the State Legislature within a period of 14 days from the publication of declaration in the State Gazette. A member may vacate his seat by submitting his resignation to the Chairman, Rajya Sabha or Speaker, Lok Sabha, as the case may be. If a member does not attend any of the meetings of the House for a period of 60 days, without the permission of the House, it may declare his seat vacant.[19] Further, a member has to vacate his seat in the House if (i) he holds any office of profit; (ii) is declared to be of unsound mind or an undischarged insolvent; (iii) voluntarily acquires citizenship of a foreign State; (iv) his election is declared void by the Court; (v) he is expelled upon the adoption of a motion of expulsion by the House; or (vi) he is elected President, Vice-President or appointed Governor of a State.[20]

A member may also cease to be a member on being disqualified on grounds of defection under the provisions of the Tenth Schedule of the Constitution (see chapter 15).

Election Disputes

Elections give rise to disputes also. It has been provided that no election to either House of Parliament or of a State Legislature shall be called in question except by an election petition presented to a High Court.[22] The petition can be presented by any candidate at such election, or by any voter. The petition can be presented on the ground of disqualifications to fill the seat or adopting during the election, any corrupt practices forbidden by law. The High Court is empowered to declare the election of a returned candidate void on any of the grounds mentioned above, if proved.[23]

If in a petition, a claim has been made by the petitioner that he received the majority of valid votes and that the returned candidate may not have won but for the corrupt practices adopted by him, the Court, if satisfied, can declare the election of the returned candidate void and declare the petitioner duly elected.[24]

A right to appeal to the Supreme Court from the order of the High Court, is available to the aggrieved party.

Electoral Reforms

During recent years, widespread concern has been felt in the matter of the influence of what is called 'money, muscle and mafia power' in the electoral process. The tenth general elections of 1991 were reported to be particularly brutal, violent and associated with all sorts of crime, riots, murders and mayhem. The then Prime Minister himself had gone on record to deprecate the prevalent "criminalisation of politics and politicisation of criminals". Video and other media coverage of elections and stories of booth capturing, rigging, bogus voting, impersonation, misuse of religious and caste identities and various other corrupt practices made the need for electoral reforms imperative. From time to time various suggestions were made by academics, the Election Commission, Law Commission, other commissions and committees including the Goswami Committee and Indrajit Gupta Committee. The Election Commission has of late been trying to enforce a code of conduct, various rules, etc. with a view to cleanse and streamline the electoral process. The latest have been the two Supreme Court judgements of May 2002 and March 2003 on Public Interest Petitions. The first judgement and related Election Commission direction were debated in an All-Party meeting and a consensus legislation was passed by Parliament. The Supreme Court did not find it satisfactory and reiterated its May 2002 judgement. The Election Commission has since issued fresh directives making it necessary for all candidates for membership of legislatures to give on affidavit information about the educational qualifications, assets and liabilities of self and close family, and criminal record, if any. The government was also toying with the idea of bringing a comprehensive legislation for electoral reforms but the entire exercise got embroiled in political controversies and party differences.

The most comprehensive and meaningful recent exercise in the field of electoral reforms was the one undertaken by the National Commission to Review the Working of the Constitution. The Commission submitted its report on 31 March 2002. It noted that nearly 70 per cent of all our representatives were elected by minority of votes cast, i.e. more votes were cast against every winning candidate than for him. The representational legitimacy of our representatives was thus doubtful. There were substantial advantages in following the policy of 50 %+one vote. On the one hand, it would resolve the problem of representation, on the other, it would be in the self-interest of various political parties to widen their appeal to the electorate. It could help push political rhetoric in a direction where the mobilising language might take on comparative "universal' tones as opposed to "sectoral" tones of the present day. With the need to be more broad based in their appeal, issues that had to do with good governance rather than with cleavages and narrow identities might start to surface in the political vocabulary. This one proposal had the greatest potential of service to the cause of national integration and ridding Indian politics of the scourge of casteism and communalism. The Commission recommended that the Government and the Election Commission should examine this issue of prescribing a minimum of 50% plus one vote for election in all its aspects, consult various political parties, and other interests that might consider themselves affected by this change and evaluate the acceptability and benefits of this system.

The Commission found that most of the independent candidates are dummies and only vitiate the sanctity of the electoral process. Only a few—6 out of 1900 in 1998 and 9 out of over 10,000 in 1996—got elected. Such independent candidates should be discouraged and only those who have a track record of having won any local election or who are nominated by at least twenty elected members of Panchayats, Municipalities or other local bodies spread out in majority of electoral districts in their constituency should be allowed to contest for Assembly or Parliament.

Also, the Commission recommended (i) a foolproof method of preparing electoral rolls and multi-purpose ID Cards, (ii) introduction of Electronic Voting Machines in all the constituencies, (iii) authorising the Election Commission to take a decision in regard to booth capturing, countermanding the election or ordering repoll etc., and (iv) use of tamper-proof video and other electronic surveillance at sensitive polling stations/constituencies. Some of the other significant recommendations of the Commission for legislative action were (i) mandatory imprisonment and disqualification for spreading caste or communal hatred during election campaigns, (ii) disqualfication of those charged with serious offences and derecognition of parties putting up such candidates, (iii) permanent disqualification for life of those convicted of heinous crimes, (iv) speedy trial of election petitions and of cases involving candidates, (v) disqualification on conviction to apply to sitting legislators also, (vi) ceiling of election expenses to be progressively raised with increasing costs but to cover all expenses by party, friends etc. and an audited statement of expenses to be submitted, (vii) declaration by every candidate and every holder of political office of all assets and liabilities and these declarations to be subjected to audit and public scrutiny, (viii) security deposits of candidates securing less than 25% votes be forfeited, (ix) Chief Election Commissioner and Election Commissioners to be appointed on the recommendations of a body consisting of Prime Minister, Leaders of the Opposition in Lok Sabha and Rajya Sabha, Speaker of Lok Sabha and Dy. Chairman of Rajya Sabha, and (x) candidates to clear all government dues and vacate unauthorised government accommodation etc. before being allowed to go to polls.

With a view to reducing costs of elections, the Commission recommended that (i) to the extent possible, State and parliamentary elections should be held simultaneously, (ii) campaign period should be reduced, (iii) no one should be allowed to contest from more than one constituency, (iv) code of conduct should be made into a law and its violation should attract penal action. Lastly, besides intra-State delimitation of constituencies, the Commission categorically recommended rotation of reserved seats.[25]

REFERENCES

1. Arts 324 (1), 325 & 326
2. Art. 324
3. Representation of the People Act, 1950, Secs. 13 A & 13 AA
4. *Ibid.*, Sec. 27
5. *Ibid.*, Sec. 28
6. R.P. Act, 1951, Secs 21 & 24
7. Art. 326; See also R.P. Act, 1951, Sec. 16
8. Art. 327
9. Art. 84, and R.P. Act, 1951, Secs 3 & 4
10. See Tenth Schedule and Arts 102 (2) and 191 (2)
11 Art. 102
12. Art. 80 (4) (5) and R.P. Act, 1951, Secs 27A & 27 H
13. R.P. Act, 1951 Sec. 12
14. *Ibid.*, Sec. 14
15. *Ibid.*, Secs 34 & 158
16. See arts 81 (2) & 3 and 82
17. Art. 103
18. R.P. Act, 1951, Sec. 69
19. Art. 101 (3) & (4)
20. See Arts 59 (1), 66 (1), 102 (1), 158 (1) and R.P. Act, 1951, Sec. 100 (1)
21. The Constitution (52nd) Amendment Act, 1985 and the Lok Sabha (Disqualification on Ground of Defection) Rule, 1985.
22. R.P. Act, 1951, Secs 80 & 80A
23. *Ibid.*, Sec. 100
24. *Ibid.*, Sec. 101
25. For further study see Subhash C. Kashyap (ed), *National Resurgence through Electoral Reforms*, Shipra, New Delh, 2002; *Blueprint of Political Reforms*, Shipra, New Delhi, 2003. Also see *The Report of the National Commission to Review the Working of the Constitution*. Vol. 1, Universal, New Delhi, 2003.

5

PARLIAMENT IN SESSION

SITTINGS OF THE HOUSES

Of the two Houses of Parliament—Rajya Sabha and Lok Sabha—the Rajya Sabha is a continuing House. One-third of its members retire every two years and new members are elected to take their place. The Lok Sabha is constituted by a notification issued by the Election Commission after every general election.[1] First sitting of the Lok Sabha takes place when it meets for the first time for the purpose of the newly elected members taking and subscribing the prescribed oath or affirmation to "bear true faith and allegiance to the Constitution of India" to "uphold the sovereignty and integrity of India" and to "faithfully discharge the duty" of a member of Parliament. Such an oath or affirmation is essential for every member "before taking his seat".[2] And unless he has taken his seat in the House after taking and subscribing an oath or affirmation, a person elected as a member of Parliament does not become entitled to immunities and privileges of such membership nor does he acquire a right to vote and participate in the proceedings.

Summoning of the Houses

The President from time to time summons each House of Parliament to meet. After the conclusion of every session, the President must summon the Houses to meet for the next session within six months.[3] While the power to summon the Houses is vested in the President, in practice, the proposal is initiated by the government. The Department of Parliamentary Affairs intimates the proposed date of commencement and the duration of a session to the Secretaries-General of the Rajya Sabha and the Lok Sabha.

After the proposal is agreed to by the Chairman of the Rajya Sabha and the Speaker of the Lok Sabha, orders of the President to summon the Houses on the date and time specified are obtained by the Secretaries-General of the two Houses. They notify the President's order in the Gazette Extraordinary and issue a Press Communique in the matter. Thereafter, the Secretaries-General issue summons to members individually.[4]

Sessions of Parliament

Normally, there are three sessions of Parliament each year viz. the Budget Session (February-May), the Monsoon Session (July-September) and the Winter Session (November-December). In the case of the Rajya Sabha, however, the Budget Session is split into two sessions with a three to four week recess in between so that it has four sessions in a year.

Speaker *pro tem*

When the Lok Sabha is summoned to meet for the first time after a General Election, the President appoints a member of Lok Sabha as the Speaker pro tem. Normally, the seniormost member is chosen. The Speaker *pro tem* presides over the House for the purpose of enabling the new members to take oath, etc. and elect their Speaker.

President's Address

After the newly-elected members have taken oath/affirmation and the Speaker has been elected, the President addresses both the Houses of Parliament assembled together in the Central Hall of the Parliament House. The President also addresses the Houses together at the commencement of the first session of each year.

The President's Address is a very solemn occasion. It is marked with great splendour befitting the dignity of the Head of the State. The President arrives in the State Coach at the Parliament House where he is received at the gate by the Chairman, Rajya Sabha, the Speaker, Lok Sabha, the Prime Minister, the Minister of Parliamentary Affairs and the Secretaries-General of both the Houses. He is then conducted in a ceremonial procession to the high-domed Central Hall of Parliament along a red-carpeted route. After the National Anthem has been played, the President reads the printed Address. It contains a statement of policies and programmes the government proposes to pursue in the ensuing year and a review of its activities and achievements during the preceding year. Being a statement of policy of the government, the Address is drafted by the government.

Half-an-hour after the President's Address, both the Houses meet in their respective Chambers where the copies of the President's Address are laid on the Table of the House by the Secretary-General concerned. A discussion on the President's Address is held in both the Houses on a Motion of Thanks proposed by a member of the respective House and seconded by another member.[5] The scope of discussion on the Address is very wide and any or all aspects of administration may be brought into focus. Members are free to speak on all sorts of national and international problems. Even matters which are not specifically mentioned in the Address may be covered through amendments to the Motion of Thanks.[6] The only limitations during the discussion are that members cannot refer to matters which are not the direct responsibility of the Government of India and the name of the President cannot be brought in during the debate. The idea behind the latter restriction is that it is the government and not the President who is responsible for the contents of the Address and the policy.

At the end of the discussion, usually the Prime Minister replies to the debate on the President's Address.[7] After the Prime Minister's reply, amendments are disposed of and the Motion of Thanks put to vote in the House. After the Motion is passed, it is conveyed to the President by the Speaker through a letter.[8]

Election of Speaker/Deputy Speaker

The Constitution requires the Lok Sabha to elect two members of the House as Speaker and Deputy Speaker as soon as it may, after the first sitting. The President, after receiving the suggestion of the Prime Minister through the Secretary-General of the Lok Sabha, approves the date for the election of the Speaker. The Secretary-General, thereafter, sends a notice of this date to every member.

At any time, one day before the date fixed for the election of the Speaker, any member may give notice of the motion, that another member, (i.e. a member other than himself) be chosen as the Speaker of the House. The notice has to be accompanied by a statement by the member, whose name is proposed in the notice, that he is willing to serve as Speaker, if elected.[10] Normally, the notice of motion for election of the candidate selected by the ruling party is given by the Prime Minister or the Minister of Parliamentary Affairs.

All the notices of motion which are found in order are entered in the List of Business in the order in which they are received at the point of time.

On the day fixed for the election, the member in whose name a motion stands on the List of Business is called upon to move it. He also has the option to withdraw it. The motions which have been moved and duly seconded are put to vote in the House one by one in the order in which they have been moved, and decided, if necessary, by division. If the motion is carried, the person presiding, without putting the other motions, to vote, declares that the member proposed in the motion, which has been carried has been chosen as the Speaker of the House.[11]

The Speaker shall vacate his office: (a) if he ceases to be a member of Lok Sabha; (b) if he sends his resignation to the Deputy Speaker; and (c) if a resolution removing him has been passed by the Lok Sabha by a majority of all the then members.[12]

The Speaker continues in office even after the dissolution of the House and until "immediately before the first meeting of the House".

Sittings of the Houses

Along with the summons for a session, a Provisional Calendar of Sittings showing the programme of sittings, the nature of business (government or private members') to be transacted and a question chart giving information about days allotted to various ministries for answering questions, and dates fixed for holding ballots are issued to members. This information is also published in the Bulletin along with the other information on various matters connected with the commencement of the session.

Sittings of the House, unless the Speaker otherwise directs, ordinarily commence at 11.00 a.m. and the normal hours of sittings are from 11.00 a.m. to 1.00 p.m. and from 2.00 p.m. to 6.00 p.m. leaving one hour from 1.00 p.m. to 2.00 p.m. for lunch break.[13] There are, however, many occasions when the House decides to dispense with the lunch break and even sits late hours.

The number and duration of Lok Sabha sittings from the first to the twelfth Lok Sabha period is given in Annexure 5.1 at the end of this chapter. Annexure 5.2 gives the yearwise break-up of sittings of the two Houses—Lok Sabha and Rajya Sabha.

Arrangement of Business and List of Business

Parliamentary business can be divided into two broad

headings viz. government business and private members' business.[14] Government business may be further sub-divided into two categories (a) items of business initiated by government and (b) items of business initiated by private members but taken up in government's time.

Daily business is arranged according to priorities fixed in Direction 2 of the Directions by Speaker viz. oath or affirmation. Obituary references, Questions, leave to move Adjournment Motion, questions involving a breach of privilege, papers to be laid on the Table, communication of messages from the President, Calling Attention statements, statements and personal explanations, motions for elections to Committees, Bills to be introduced, matters under Rule 377, etc.

Apart from the private members' business, i.e. Bill and resolutions which are discussed for two-and-a-half hours on every Friday or such other day as the Speaker may fix[1]5, there are certain items of business which though initiated by private members are transacted during the time allotted for the transaction of government business. Besides statements pointing out mistakes or inaccuracies in statements made by a minister or another member and personal explanations by members, the other items of business which fall under this category of business are—Questions, Adjournment Motions, Calling Attention to matters of urgent public importance, questions of privilege, discussion on matters of urgent public importance for short duration, Motion of No-Confidence in the Council of Ministers, Half-an-Hour Discussions on matters arising out of answers to questions, matters under Rule 377, etc. Allocation of time to various kinds of business to be transacted in the House is normally recommended by the Business Advisory Committee, sittings of which are normally held once a week.

Conduct of Business and Procedure

Each house is the matter of its procedure and may make

rules for regulating its procedure and conduct of business subject to the provisions of the Constitution (Art. 118). The validity of any proceeding in Parliament cannot be questioned in a court of law on grounds of any alleged irregularity of procedure and no officer or member of Parliament is subject to jurisdiction of courts in respect of exercise of any powers in the matter of regulating procedure or conduct of business in the Parliament (Art. 122).

Some of the basic rules of procedure and conduct of business have been laid down in the Constitution itself. Thus, Art. 100 provides (1) that except where otherwise provided in the Constitution, (e.g. in the case of constitutional amendments, impeachment of the President, removal of the presiding officers, judges, etc.), all questions at any sitting of either House or joint sitting of the Houses shall be determined by a majority of votes of the members present and voting, other than the Presiding Officer who shall exercise a casting vote only in case of an equality of votes; and (2) all proceedings of either House shall be valid irrespective of any vacancies in membership or any unauthorised participation in debate or voting.

Quorum of the House

The quorum to constitute a sitting of the House is 55 members (on-tenth of the total membership) including the Speaker or the person acting as such. At the beginning of the sitting each day, before the Speaker takes the Chair, the existence of quorum is ascertained. If on some day, it is found that there is no quorum at 11 a.m., the quorum bell is rung and the Speaker takes his seat only after there is a quorum. The same is true of the procedure followed whenever the House reassembles after the lunch break or after any adjournment. During the rest of the sitting of the day, by a sort of unwritten understanding or convention, the question of quorum is usually not raised by any member. More particularly, it is not questioned during extended hours of sittings—either during lunch-time or after 5 p.m. But, even if a single member questions it at any time, proceedings have got to be interrupted, the quorum bell has to be rung and proceedings can be resumed only after there is a quorum.

Voting Procedure: Decision of the House on any question can be taken only by means of a motion moved by a member. In most cases matters are decided by a voice vote. But if the opinion of the Speaker as to the decision on a question is challenged, the Speaker orders that the lobby be cleared. After the lapse of about three and a half minutes, the Speaker puts the question a second time and declares whether in his opinion the 'Ayes' or the 'Noes' have it. If the opinion so declared is again challenged, the Speaker directs that the votes be recorded either by operating the automatic vote recorder or by using 'Aye' and 'No' slips in the House or by members going into the lobbies. However, the practice of going into the lobbies for the purpose of vote recording is not in vogue for many years now.

When a division is ordered by the Speaker, division bells ring normally for three and a half minutes. Immediately after the bells stop ringing, all the outer doors of the inner lobby of the Chamber are closed to prevent any entry until division is concluded.

Under the automatic vote recorder system, each member casts his vote from the seat allotted to him pressing the requisite button provided for the purpose. A push-button set containing a pilot light and three push buttons—a green button for 'AYES', a red button for 'NOES' and a black button for 'ABSTAIN'—together with a push switch suspended by a wire, is provided at the seat of each member. After the result of the voting appears on the indicator board, the result of the division is announced by the Speaker. When the automatic vote recorder is out of order or when seats or division numbers have not been assigned, the method of distribution of slips is used. Members are supplied at their seats with 'Ayes'/'Noes' printed slips for recording their votes. An 'Ayes' slip is printed in green, both in English and Hindi on one side and 'Noes' in red on its reverse. On these slips members are required to record votes of their choice by signing and writing their names, division numbers and dates legibly at the appropriate places. Members who desire to record 'Abstention' may fill in the abstention slip printed separately in yellow both in English and Hindi. In case, a member has not been allotted a seat/division number, he may write his name, constituency, state and date legibly below his signature. The officer at the Table scrutinises the 'Ayes'/'Noes' and 'Abstention' slips and counts the votes recorded thereon and compiles the result. The result so arrived at is announced by the Chair. The Presiding Officer does not have the right to vote in the first count but in case of equality of votes he has a casting vote which may be decisive.

Record of Proceedings: A full verbatim record of the proceedings of the two Houses of Parliament is prepared and published. While the uncorrected mimeographed copies of debates are made available to members the very next day, the printed debates are usually available within a month of the sitting. Certain words or phrases held unparlimentary and expunged by the Presiding Officer or portions 'not recorded' under his orders are not included in the official record of the proceedings.

Proceedings are tape-recorded. Also parliamentary reporters take down the proceedings in shorthand in relays or turns of five or ten minutes each. After transcribing their portions, the reporters check their doubts with the help of the tape-recorded version. Sessionwise printed volumes of debates are available in Hindi and English versions.

Language in Parliament: Hindi and English have been declared by the Constitution to be the languages for conducting business in Parliament. The Presiding Officers may, however, allow any member not proficient in either to address the House in his mother tongue (Art. 120). Facilities of simultaneous interpretation from 12 languages into the floor languages, i.e. Hindi and English, exist in both the Houses.

Parliament and the Media: Freedom of the Press has not been expressly provided for in the Constitution, but it has been settled by judicial decisions that freedom of speech and expression includes the freedom of the Press.

Absolute immunity from proceedings in any court of law has been conferred under the Constitution on all persons connected with the publication of proceedings of either House of Parliament, if such publication is made by or under the authority of the House [Art. 105 (2)]. Statutory protection has been given to the publication in newspapers or broadcast by wireless telegraphy of substantially true reports of any proceedings of either House of Parliament, provided the reports are for the public good and are not actuated by malice (Art. 361A). The protection has been accorded within the overall limitation that the house has the power to control and, if necessary, to prohibit the publication of its debates or proceedings and to punish for violation of its debates or proceedings, and also to punish for the violation of its orders. Normally, no restrictions are imposed on reporting the proceedings of the House.

The Parliament is entitled to take action for any malicious writing, speech, etc. casting reflection or aspersion on its functioning or on the functioning of its members or its committees. No action is, however, taken if the criticism is fair and *bonafide*.

Facilities provided to the Press in Parliament include those of a press gallery, press rooms, supply of parliamentary papers and press releases, access of lobbies and Central Hall, use of library and reference services, etc.

Telecasting/Broadcasting of Proceedings: With a view to taking the Parliament closer to the people, a beginning was made in 1989 by telecasting/broadcasting live, the

President's address to the members of the two Houses. From December 1991, the Question Hour in the two Houses, was being telecast after necessary editing, on the following day. The broadcasting of the Question Hour started in 1992. Also, from 1992 important occasions like the presentation of the Railway Budget and the General Budget were being telecast live. Important speeches were also telecast from time to time and telefilms were being made of the entire proceedings for archival purposes and future use. From December 1994 the proceedings of the Houses of Parliament are being telecast/broadcast live. But, while the Question Hours in the Lok Sabha and Rajya Sabha are telecast on the primary channel on alternate weeks—one week Lok Sabha and the other Rajya Sabha—other proceedings of the two Houses are telecast daily on two separate low power transmission channels with a reach of 15 km. only.

Adjournment *sine-die* and Dissolution

The President may from time to time prorogue the Houses or either House and dissolve the Lok Sabha.

The Speaker has the power to adjourn the House *sine-die*. Once the House is adjourned *sine die*, he is empowered to call it again.[16] But, on prorogation, it is only the President who can summon the Houses.

Normally, after the House is adjourned *sine die*, it is prorogued within the next few days by the President. There is no effect on the business pending before the House on adjournment of House *sine die* but as per Rule 335 of the Rules of Procedure and Conduct of Business in the Lok Sabha, on the prorogation of the House, all pending notices, other than notices of intention to move for leave to introduce Bills, lapse, and fresh notices have to be given for the next session.

Lok Sabha continues for five years from the date appointed for its first meeting. Unless sooner dissolved or there is an extension of the term, there is an automatic dissolution of the House by efflux of time, at the end of the period of five years, even if no formal order of dissolution is issued by the President.[17]

Effects of Dissolution

Dissolution marks the end of the life of the existing House and is followed by the constitution of a new House. Once the House has been dissolved, the dissolution is irrevocable. In Lok Sabha, which alone is subject to dissolution under the Constitution, dissolution 'passes a sponge over the parliamentary state'. All business pending before it or any of its committees lapses on dissolution. No part of the records of the dissolved House cane be carried over and transcribed into the records or registers of the new House.

Briefly, the position of various items of business pending before the Lok Sabha at the time of dissolution is as under:

(i) All Bills pending in the Lok Sabha at the time of dissolution whether originating in the House or transmitted to it by the Rajya Sabha, lapse.

(ii) Bills passed by the Lok Sabha, but which have not been disposed of and are pending in the Rajya Sabha on the date of dissolution, lapse.

(iii) Bills originating in the Rajya Sabha, which have not been passed by the Lok Sabha but are still pending before the Rajya Sabha, do not lapse.

(iv) A Bill upon which the Houses have disagreed and the President has notified his intention of summoning a joint-sitting of the Houses for its consideration prior to dissolution, does not lapse, and may be passed at a joint-sitting of both Houses, notwithstanding that dissolution has intervened since the President notified his intention to summon the joint-sitting of the Houses.[18]

(v) Bills passed by both the Houses and sent to President for assent do not lapse on dissolution of the Lok Sabha.

(vi) Bills returned by the President for reconsideration do

not lapse and can be reconsidered by the successive House.

(vii) All other business pending in the Lok Sabha viz. motions, resolutions, amendments, supplementary demands for grants, etc. at whatever stage, lapses upon dissolution.

(viii) Petitions presented to the House which stand referred to the Committee on Petitions also lapse on dissolution.

(ix) Motions for approval or modification of statutory rules passed by the Lok Sabha and transmitted to the Rajya Sabha for concurrence and vice versa also lapse on dissolution of the Lok Sabha.

(x) Pending assurances do not lapse and are considered by the Committee on Government Assurances of the new Lok Sabha.[19]

REFERENCES

1. Representation of the People Act, 1851, Sec. 73
2. Art. 99 and Third Schedule; Dir. 1
3. Art. 85
4. Rule 3
5. Rule 17
6. Rule 18
7. Rule 20
8. Rule 247
9. Rule 7 (1)
10. Rule 7 (2)
11. Rule 7 (3 & 4)
12. Art. 94
13. Rule 12
14. Every member of Parliament, other than a minister is known as private member, irrespective of the party which he belongs to. A minister is a government member.
15. Rule 26
16. Rule 15
17. Subhash C. Kashyap, 'Dissolution of the Lok Sabha', *The Parliamentarian*, LVII, 1 January 1977.
18. Art. 108
19. For special study, see Subhash C. Kashyap, *Parliamentary Procedures*, op.cit.

Annexure 5.1

Sittings of the Lok Sabha
(From the First to the Twelfth Lok Sabha: 1952-1999)

Lok Sabha		No. of Sittings	Duration of Sittings (in hours)
I	(1952-57)	677	3784
II	(1957-62)	567	3651
III	(1962-67)	578	3733
IV	(1967-70)	467	3029
V	(1971-77)	613	4071
VI	(1977-79)	267	1753
VII	(1980-84)	464	3324
VIII	(1985-89)	485	3224
IX	(1989-91)	109	754
X	(1991-96)	423	2527
XI	(1996-97)	125	813
XII	(1998-99)	88	575

Annexure 5.2

Sittings of Lok Sabha and Rajya Sabha
(Yearwise - 1952 to 1999)

Year	No. of Lok Sabha Sittings	No. of Rajya Sabha Sittings	Year	No. of Lok Sabha Sittings	No. of Rajya Sabha Sittings
1952	123	60	1976	98	84
1953	137	100	1977	86	70
1954	137	103	1978	115	97
1955	139	111	1979	68	54
1956	151	113	1980	98	90
1957	106	78	1981	105	69
1958	125	91	1982	92	82
1959	123	87	1983	93	77
1960	121	87	1984	77	63
1961	102	75	1985	109	89
1962	116	91	1986	98	86
1963	122	100	1987	102	89
1964	122	97	1988	102	89
1965	113	96	1989	83	71
1966	119	109	1990	81	66
1967	110	91	1991	90	82
1968	120	103	1992	98	90
1969	120	102	1993	89	70
1970	119	107	1994	77	75
1971	102	89	1995	78	77
1972	11	99	1996	70	64
1973	120	105	1997	65	68
1974	119	109	1998	64	59
1975	63	58	1999	51	48

6

THE SPEAKER

AND OTHER OFFICERS OF THE HOUSES OF PARLIAMENT

If an assembly is to function in an orderly and efficient manner, there must be someone with the authority to regulate its proceedings and working. The Constitution provides for a Speaker and a Deputy Speaker for the Lok Sabha and a Chairman and a Deputy Chairman for the Rajya Sabha. The Vice-President of India is the ex-officio Chairman of the Rajya Sabha. A Deputy Chairman is chosen by the House from among its members. The Speaker and Deputy Speaker of the Lok Sabha are chosen by the Lok Sabha from among its members. In the absence of the Speaker in the House, the Deputy Speaker discharges the functions of the Speaker in the Lok Sabha. Similarly, in the absence of the Chairman, the Deputy Chairman is also appointed in each House. Members of the panel preside over the House in the absence of the Speaker/Deputy Speaker and the Chairman/Deputy Chairman.[1] Next to the two Presiding Officers, an important functionary in each House is the Secretary-General. He is a non-elected permanent officer of the House.

The Speaker

The office of the Speaker evolved through a long period of intense struggle in British constitutional history. In the early days, when the House of Commons was a petitioning rather than a law-making body, the Speaker's main function was to sum up the case of both sides at the end of the debate and to present the views of the House to the Crown. He was the spokesman or the 'Speaker' of the Commons before the King. Paradoxically, the Speaker seldom speaks today. If he speaks, he speaks for the House and not to it. He takes no part in the debate of the House; he presides over the meetings of the House.

Generally speaking, the position of the Speaker in India, more or less corresponds to that of the Speaker of the House of Commons. His office is one of prestige, splendour and authority. He is the head of the Lok Sabha. The smooth and orderly conduct of the business in the House is primarily his responsibility. Within the House and in all matters connected with the House, his word is final.

Independence and impartiality are the two important attributes of the office of the Speaker. This is sought to be ensured in many ways. In the warrant of precedence, the Speaker has been given a very high position. He comes next only to the President, the Vice-President and the Prime Minister. He ranks higher than all Cabinet Ministers other than the Prime Minister himself. His salary and allowances are charged on the Consolidated Fund of India—that is, they do not have to be voted by Parliament. His conduct cannot be discussed except on a substantive motion. He does not vote in the House except when there is an equality of votes.[2] And, when he gives his casting vote in the event of a tie, it is always in accordance with well-established parliamentary principles and conventions. Incidentally, so far there has not been a single instance in India since Independence, when the Speaker was required to make use of his casting vote. The Speaker is politically neutral. Upon his election as Speaker, he dissociates himself from the activities of his party. While he may continue to belong to a party, he ceases to be involved in any party politics.[3] He does not hold any party office, does not participate in any party meetings or functions and keeps away from political controversies and party campaigns.[4]

The Speaker conducts the business and regulates the proceedings of the House. He performs these functions, in accordance with the provisions of the Constitution and the 'Rules of Procedure and Conduct of Business in the Lok Sabha'. He is the final interpreter of the provisions of the Constitution, and the Rule of Procedure within the House. His decision in all parliamentary matters is final. In respect of matters not specifically provided for in the Rules, the Speaker has residuary powers to issue directions.[5] In doing so, he may call upon a member or the government to place before him facts, evidence and information which he may consider necessary in arriving at a decision. But, once after considering all the material, he gives a ruling, it must be accepted as final. A request may be made to him for reconsideration, but his decision cannot be challenged, criticised or questioned.

The Speaker enjoys vast powers to ensure the smooth and orderly conduct of the business of the House.[6] No member may speak unless he "catches the Speaker's eye", a parliamentary term which means that unless a member is called upon or permitted by the Chair to speak, he cannot speak in the House. It is for the Speaker to determine in what order members would speak[7] and how long a member should be allowed to speak. He can order a member to discontinue his speech or to withdraw words or expressions which he feels are unparliamentary or undignified. He may order that anything said by a member without his permission shall not go on record and that anything found unparliamentary shall be expunged.[8] Any word or portions ordered "not to be recorded" or expunged from the proceedings as being unparliamentary, cannot be published by the media or anyone else as there is no unlimited right to the publication of the proceedings of the Houses of Parliament.

The Speaker may ask a member to withdraw from the House for a day or part of a day for disorderly behaviour or may even suspend a member from the service of the House on a proper motion for gross disorderly behaviour. All members alike are subject to his discipline and they have to exercise great care in showing him proper respect and obeying his rulings and decisions. Whenever he intervenes or rises to propose or put questions to make some remarks or to deliver his rulings, he must be heard in silence. He determines whether there is prima facie case for a matter relating to a breach of privilege or contempt of the House,[9] or the conduct of a member being raised or referred to a Committee for investigation. If he withholds his consent the matter does not proceed further. He is looked upon to protect the honour of persons against allegatory, defamatory or incriminatory statements in the House, and unless he has been previously informed of the nature of such statements or the evidence on which they are based, he may stop a member from making such statements.

The Speaker has to be sensitive to the atmosphere in the House. Sometimes when there is excitement, uproar, or continuous interruption in the House, he has to employ great tact, subtle wit and healthy humour to contain the situation, to relieve tension, and to create conditions in which orderly and relaxed debate can proceed. This is a gift which may be either natural or cultivated, but in the hands of a wise and capable Speaker, it is certainly a weapon with a tremendous potential.

While considering the admission or otherwise of various notices of motions, questions, etc. received by him, he always bears in mind his fundamental duty which is that of enabling the House to deliberate and decide on various matters of public importance that arise from time to time. Where in doubt, the Speaker usually acts in favour of giving an opportunity to the House to express itself. He does not so conceive his duties or interpret his powers as to act independently of the House, or to override its authority, or to nullify its decisions. He is a part of the House, drawing his powers from the House for the better functioning of the House. He is in the ultimate analysis, a servant of the House and its master.

Messages on behalf of the House are sent or received with the authority of the Speaker.[10] The Speaker authenticates by his signature that a Bill has been passed by the House before it is presented to the President for assent. He is empowered to correct patent errors in a Bill after it has been passed by the House and to make such other changes in the Bill consequential on the amendments accepted by the House. He receives documents, petitions, messages addressed to the House and all orders of the House are executed through him. He communicates the decisions of the House to the authorities concerned and requires them to comply with the terms of such decisions.

All the Parliamentary Committees of the Lok Sabha are constituted by him or by the House. They function under his control and direction. He appoints the Chairmen of all Committees and issues directions in matters relating to their working and the procedure to be followed by them.[11] All controversial matters are referred to the Speaker for his guidance and his decisions are obeyed. Committees like the Business Advisory Committee, the General Purposes Committee and the Rules Committee work directly under his chairmanship.[12]

The Constitution gives the Speaker a special position in so far as relations between the two Houses in certain matters are concerned. He determines what matters are financial matters which fall within the exclusive jurisdiction of the Lok Sabha. If he certifies a Bill to be a 'Money Bill', his decision is final.[13] Whenever, in the event of disagreement between the Houses on a legislative measure, a joint-sitting is called, he presides over such a joint-sitting and all the Rules of Procedure in such a sitting operate under his directions and orders.[14]

The Speaker is responsible for providing various types

of facilities to members such as library, housing, telephones, payments of salary and allowances, refreshment and retiring rooms in the Parliament House, printing and supply of parliamentary papers, etc. The Speaker regulates the admission of visitors[15] and press correspondents to the Galleries and is responsible for security arrangements in regard thereto. In the event of any breach of his orders, he may award necessary punishment to the visitors under the orders of the House. He can issue summons, if a person is required to appear before the House on a charge of contempt or breach of privilege of the House. He can also issue a warrant of arrest against a member of the House or an outsider, if a motion committing him to prison is adopted by the House.

It is for the Speaker to lay down the guidelines for the recognition of parliamentary parties and to recognise the leader of a party in opposition as the Leader of the Opposition in the Lok Sabha. The Speaker has to be satisfied in regard to the genuineness and voluntary character of a member's letter of resignation before accepting the resignation. If, after an enquiry, the Speaker is satisfied that the resignation is not voluntary or genuine, he may not accept the resignation.[16]

The speaker is available in his chamber to all members. In all questions of disqualification of a member of the Lok Sabha arising on the ground of defection, the Speaker has got the exclusive power to decide the matter. His decision is final. He listens to their views, grievances and suggestions and takes necessary action. All members including ministers are expected to approach the Speaker in his chamber by previous appointments. It is a breach of privilege to reflect upon his impartiality, competence, character or conduct. His decisions cannot be criticised in the House or outside. He must be referred to with respect and held in high esteem. This is essential for preserving and maintaining the dignity of the House.

If a member of the Lok Sabha is arrested on a criminal charge, or is sentenced to imprisonment, or is detained under an executive order, the fact must immediately be reported to the Speaker by the magistrate or the executive authority. Such intimation is also essential in the event of the release of the member. No person can be arrested, nor can a legal process, civil or criminal, be served on him, within the precincts of the House without obtaining the permission of the Speaker.[17]

The Speaker makes obituary references in the House, delivers valedictory address on the expiry of the term of the House and also makes formal references to important national and international events.

The Speaker is the ex-officio President of the Indian Parliamentary Group which in India functions as the National Group of the Inter-Parliamentary Union and the Main Branch of the Commonwealth Parliamentary Association. He nominates, in consultation with the Chairman of the Rajya Sabha, personnel for various parliamentary delegations to foreign countries. He often leads these delegations himself. The Speaker is also the Chairman of the Conference of Presiding Officers of Legislative Bodies in India.

The Lok Sabha Secretariat functions under the direction and control of the Speaker. He enjoys supreme authority over the secretarial staff, the precincts of the House and the Parliament House Estate. He exercises his authority with the assistance of the Secretary-General, Lok Sabha.[18]

In view of the vital and vast responsibilities that a Speaker has to fulfil, Prime Minister Jawaharlal Nehru, while unveiling the portrait of Speaker Patel on 8 March 1958 said:

> The Speaker represents the House. He represents the dignity of the House, the freedom of the House and because the House represents the nation, in a particular way, the Speaker becomes the symbol of nation's freedom and liberty. Therefore, it is right that that should be an honoured position, a free position and

should be occupied always by men of outstanding ability and impartiality.

Prior to 1921, the Governor-General of India used to preside over the sittings of the Legislative Council. The origin of the institution of Speaker[19] in India dates back to 1921 when the Central legislative Assembly was first constituted under the Montague-Chelmsford Reforms. Sir Frederick Whyte was appointed by the Governor-General as the first Speaker of the Assembly on 3 February 1921 for a period of four years.

Shri Vithalbhai J. Patel was the first non-official to be elected as the Speaker of the Assembly on 24 August 1925. He was re-elected on 20 January 1927 and remained in his office till he resigned on 28 April 1930. Shri Patel had the distinction of being the first Indian and the first elected Speaker of the Central Legislature. Shri G.V. Mavalankar was chosen as the first Speaker of the first Parliament constituted after the first general elections after independence. He had, however, held the same office in the Constituent Assembly (legislative) and continued as the Speaker of the Provisional Parliament on the commencement of the Constitution.

Table given in the next page shows the names of the Speakers, or Presidents as they were called till 1947, with their periods of office:

The Deputy Speaker

Whenever the Speaker is absent, the Deputy Speaker presides over the deliberations of the House and so presiding, exercises all the powers of the Speaker in the House under the Rules of Procedure.[23] The Deputy Speaker is the Chairman of the Budget Committee which approves the Budget proposals of the Secretariat before these are sent to the Ministry of Finance for incorporation in the General Budget. Besides this, unlike the Speaker, the Deputy Speaker has no function or responsibilities with reference to the Secretariat

Speakers of the Lok Sabha

Pre-independence Period

Sir Frederick Whyte	– 3 February 1921—24 March 1925
Vithalbhai J. Patel	– 24 March 1925—23 April 1930
Mohammad Yakub	– 9 July 1930—31 July 1930
Ibrahim Rahimtoola	– 17 January 1921—7 March 1933
Sir Sanmukham Chetty	– 14 March 1933—31 December 1934
Abdur Rahim	– 24 January 1935—1 October 1945[20]
Ganesh Vasudev Mavalankar	– 23 January 1946—14 August 1947[21]

Post-independence Period

Ganesh Vasudev Mavalankar	– 17 November 1947—26 January 1950 [Constituent Assembly (legislative)]
	– 26 January 1950—15 May 1952 (Provisional Parliament)[22]
	– 15 May 1952—27 February 1956
Ananthasayanam Ayyangar	– 8 March 1956—16 April 1962
Hukam Singh	– 17 April 1962—16 March 1967
Dr. Neelam Sanjiva Reddy	– 17 March 1967–19 July 1969
Dr. Gurdial Singh Dhillon	– 8 August 1969—1 December 1975
Bali Ram Bhagat	– 5 January 1976—25 March 1977
Dr. Neelam Sanjiva Reddy	– 26 March 1977—13 July 1977
K.S. Hegde	– 21 July 1977—21 January 1980
Dr. Bal Ram Jakhar	– 22 January 1980—18 December 1989
Rabi Ray	– 19 December 1989—9 July 1991
Shivraj Patil	– 10 July 1991—22 May 1996
P.A. Sangma	– 23 May 1996—23 March 1998
G.M.C. Balayogi	– 24 March 1998—3 March 2002
Manohar Joshi	– 10 May 2002

of the Lok Sabha or its officers and staff. The Deputy Speaker is thus a Deputy Presiding Officer but not a Deputy to the Speaker in the latter's capacity as the overall executive or administrative head of the Secretariat or the House.

Deputy Speaker presides over the House for the greater part of a sitting of the House, while the Speaker is busy attending to other parliamentary matters in his chamber. Usually, the Speaker takes the Chair in the forenoon particularly during the Question Hour and the most crucial period following soon after the Question Hour. He may also walk in and preside at other times during the day whenever he finds some matter of special significance under discussion or any special situation necessitating his presence in the House. The Deputy Speaker's rulings are final in so far as the matters under discussion on which they were given are concerned, but the Speaker may for the sake of certainty of procedure and uniformity of practice give general guidance to be followed in future in similar circumstances. Occasionally the Deputy Speaker may reserve a matter for a ruling by the Speaker or may consult him before giving a decision.

Unlike the Speaker, the Deputy Speaker has a right to speak in the House, to take part in its deliberations and to vote on any proposition before the House as a member, but this he can do only when the Speaker is presiding. When himself in the Chair, the Deputy Speaker cannot vote except in the event of equality of votes. When the Speaker is absent from a joint-sitting of the Houses of Parliament, the Deputy Speaker presides and exercises the powers of the Speaker, at such a sitting as is the case when he is presiding over the deliberations of the House.

The Deputy Speaker may take part in the politics of the party to which he belongs, although in practice he, as far as possible, keeps aloof from participation in controversial issues in order to maintain a position of impartiality in the House.

Under the conventions and traditions that have grown round the Deputy Speaker's office, if he is nominated or appointed a member of a Parliamentary Committee, he is also appointed its Chairman. Also, the office of the Deputy Speaker is usually filled by a member of the opposition.

The Office of the Deputy Speaker, Deputy President as it was known till 1947, is as old as the Central Legislature itself. Listed below are the names of the persons (with the year of election or tenure of office) who occupied the office of the Deputy Speaker:

Pre-independence Period	
Sachidanand Sinha	– 3 February 1921
Sir Jamsetjee Jajeebhoy	– 21 September 1921
Diwan Bahadur T. Rangachariar	– 4 February 1924
Sir Muhammand Yagub	– 30 January 1927
H.S. Gour	– 11 July 1930
Sanmukham Chetty	– 19 January 1931
Abdul Matin Chaudhuri	– 21 March 1934
Akhil Chandra Dutta	– 5 February 1936[24]
Sir Mohammad Yamin Khan	– 5 February 1946
Post-independence	
Ananthasayanam Ayyangar	– 30 May 1952—7 March 1956
Sardar Hukam Singh	– 20 March 1956—31 March 1962
Krishnamoorthy Rao	– 23 April 1962—3 March 1967
R.K. Khadilkar	– 28 March 1967—1 November 1969
G.G. Swell	– 9 December 1969—27 December 1970
	– 7 March 1971—18 January 1977
Godey Murahari	– 1 April 1977—22 August 1979
G. Lakshmanan	– 2 February 1980—31 December 1984

Thambi Durai	- 22 January 1985—27 November 1989
Shivraj Patil	- 19 March 1990—13 March 1991
S. Mallikarjunaiah	- 13 August 1991—10 May 1996
Suraj Bhan	- 12 July 1996—4 December 1997
P.M. Sayeed	- 17 December 1998—26 April 1999 and - 27 October 1999—

Panel of Chairmen

If both the Speaker and the Deputy Speaker are absent from a sitting, one of the members of the House out of a panel of six Chairmen, whom the Speaker nominates from time to time, presides. Should a situation arise when none from among the Speaker, the Deputy Speaker and the members of the Panel of Chairmen is present in the House, another member may be chosen by the House to act as the Chairman until one from among the Panel or the Deputy Speaker or Speaker returns to take the Chair.

Like the Deputy Speaker, a Chairman has all the powers of the Speaker in the House during the time he is presiding.[25] A ruling given by the Chairman is final and binding it in the case and on the point it is given in the same way as a ruling given by the Speaker. A Chairman may, however, reserve major issues for decision by the Speaker. It is a contempt of the House to denigrate his conduct while he is in the Chair; he must be shown all respect as is due to a Presiding Officer of the House.

A Chairman is free to participate fully in all discussions in the House and to take active part in the issues, including controversial issues, before the House. He attends the meetings of his party and is usually an active member of his party. The Speaker invariably chooses members on the Panel of Chairmen from both the ruling as well as the opposition parties. The duration of the office of a Chairman on the panel is normally one year, but the same person may be renominated over and over again. The selection is entirely in the hands of the Speaker but he may consult the leaders of political parties in the House before making his choice.

The Secretary-General

The third important officer of the House is the Secretary-General. He is the advisor to the Speaker, to the House and to the members on all parliamentary functions and activities and all matters of procedure and practice. As a permanent officer who heads the Table of the House and is the continuing link between the changing composition of the different Houses and Speakers, the Secretary-General is the custodian of parliamentary conventions and traditions and the repository of the accumulated wisdom and experience of many earlier Houses, presiding officers and his own predecessors.

The Secretary-General discharges in his own right many legislative, administrative and executive functions and renders services and provides facilities to the members. He is the overall incharge of the Watch and Ward Organisation and the security in the precincts of the Parliament Estate. The Parliament Library, Research, Reference, Documentation and Information Services also function under him. He is responsible for the maintenance and upkeep of the buildings and properties of the Parliament. As the overall head of the Parliamentary Museum and Archives, he is the custodian of the heritage of Parliament and the keeper of all parliamentary records and archives. He is the head of the legislative services and the Secretariat of the House and is responsible for its administration, for maintaining discipline and for seeing that the secretarial work of the House and its Committees is organised properly and conducted efficiently and smoothly. He provides secretarial assistance and staff to all the Parliamentary Committees and is available to them for advice. His role is that of a friend, philosopher and guide to the members and the Committees. Members of the various political parties approach him for advice. To a very large extent he has to maintain the same role of impartiality and objectivity as that observed by the Speaker. He must be wide awake and a man of quick decisions. Parliamentary matters require considerable and up-to-date knowledge of national and international events and a proper assimilation thereof. One who occupies the position of Secretary-General, therefore, must be a man of parts and versatile in the manifold functions of the Parliament. The job that is thus entrusted to him is so highly technical and complicated in nature that he has to be assisted by a large number of competent and qualified officials of all grades. The work is organised in such a manner that each unit is concerned with a special subject or aspect of parliamentary life and is staffed by men of caliber who are equipped technically and who discharge their duties efficiently. It is the duty of the Secretary-General to see that adequate personnel is trained to fill the gaps occurring from time to time and that the efficiency of parliamentary life is maintained at a high level always. Much, therefore, depends upon the personality and mind of the occupant of the post of Secretary-General in giving shape and character to the secretarial organisation of the House.

The Secretary-General is unconnected with politics. He is absolutely non-partisan and objective in his approach and perspective. He is chosen from amongst those who have made their mark in the service of Parliament in various capacities in the Secretariat of the House. The Speaker is the authority to choose and appoint him. Once appointed, he remains in his post until he attains the prescribed age of retirement, which at present is 60 years. He is not subject to criticism in the House and his actions are not discussed either inside or outside the House. He is answerable only to the Speaker and sufficient safeguards are provided to give him security of service and independence in order that he may perform his duties zealously, fearlessly, fairly impartially and in the best public interest. The whole Secretariat of the House is completely separate and under the overall control of the Speaker so that the Parliament can get independent advice and its directions are executed properly without any interference from outside quarters or internal pressures.

The Secretary-General issues summons on behalf of the President asking members to attend a session of the House. He authenticates Bills in the absence of the Speaker; sends and receives messages on behalf of the House; receives notices, petitions, documents and papers addressed to or intended for the House; issues summons under his signature to witnesses to appear before the House or Committees thereof, corresponds with members including ministers and others on behalf of the Speaker; issues admission tickets to the galleries; controls the finances and accounts of the House and its Secretariat; circulates lists of business, bulletins and notices of amendments; prepares the journal, minutes and verbatim records of the House; arranges for the supply of information to members on various subjects in which they may be interested; edits and publishes a large number of periodicals and other parliamentary publications—digests, journals, monographs, brochures, factsheets, background briefs, research studies, books, etc. for the benefit of members and others. As the overall head of the Bureau of Parliamentary Studies and Training, he organises many study courses, seminars, training and orientation programmes, etc. in parliamentary institutions and procedures for new members of Parliament and State Legislatures, for probationers of IAS, IFS and several other All India Services, for senior officers of the Government of India, for university teachers, for parliamentary officials from within the country and abroad. As the Secretary of the Indian Parliamentary Group, he also organises the activities of the India Branch of the Commonwealth Parliamentary Association and the Inter-Parliamentary Union. He accompanies parliamentary delegations abroad and attends to numerous other activities of the Parliamentary. When the Commonwealth Speakers' Conference is held in the country, the Secretary-General of Lok Sabha is the ex-officio Secretary-General of the Conference. He is also responsible for preparing and organising the secretarial duties of the Conferences of the Chairmen of various Legislatures and Parliamentary Committees in India and for arranging extra-parliamentary Committees in India and for arranging extra-parliamentary activities such as addresses by foreign dignitaries to members, receptions, the sending of parliamentary goodwill missions abroad or receiving of such missions from foreign countries in India.

Besides these extensive duties that the Secretary-General of the Lok Sabha is charged with and the responsibilities he exercises in his own right, there are many other functions that he discharges and the work that he does on behalf of, and in the name of the Speaker. The relationship between the Speaker and the Secretary-General is very unique, intimate and almost indefinable. The powers of the Speaker that may be exercised by the Secretary-General, for instance, in the matter of allowing or disallowing of various kinds of notices of questions, motions, etc. are not exercised by delegation. In fact, these powers of the Speaker cannot be delegated. The power vests only in the Speaker himself who can be said to be allowing or disallowing various notices, etc. He himself assumes full responsibility for whatever is done in his name, on his behalf and under his general directions.

The Chairman of Rajya Sabha

The Vice-President of India is the ex-officio Chairman of

A view of the Parliament House

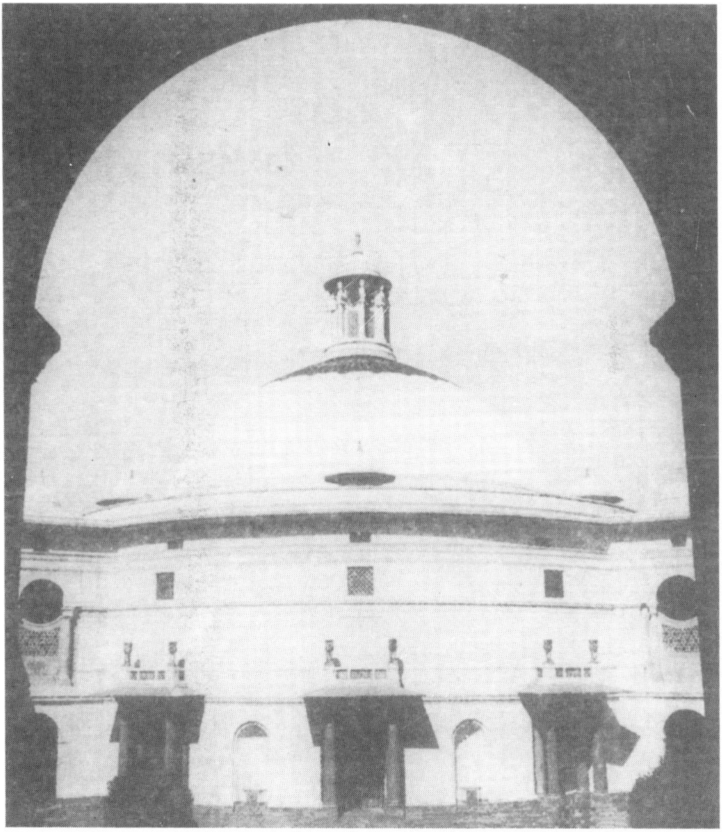

Exterior view of the Central Hall with the dome

A panoramic view of the Central Hall with its high domed ceiling

The then President Shri R. Venkataraman arriving at the Central Hall to address both Houses of Parliament on 22-2-1988

A view of the Rajya Sabha Chamber

A panoramic view of the Lok Sabha Chamber

The Speaker's Chair in Lok Sabha

A view of "Jali" work covering the passage leading to Lok Sabha Gailery

A view of one of the Committe Rooms

The Main Committee Room of Parliament House Annexe

Inner view of Parliament House, Reception Office

the Rajya Sabha. He presides over the Rajya Sabha by virtue of the office of the Vice-President that he holds. When the Vice-President acts as the President or when he discharges the functions of the President, he does not perform the duties of the office of the Chairman of Rajya Sabha. The Vice-President is elected by the members of both Houses of Parliament in accordance with the system of proportional representation by means of single transferable vote and the voting at such elections is held by secret ballot. The Vice-President is not a member of either House of Parliament or of a House of Legislature of any State. He holds office for a term of five years from the date on which he enters office or until he resigns his office or is removed from his office by a resolution of the Rajya Sabha passed by a majority of the members of the House and agreed to by the Lok Sabha.[26]

The functions and duties of the Chairman of the Rajya Sabha as a Presiding Officer and as the overall head of the Secretariat of his House are more or less the same as those of the Speaker in the Lok Sabha.

The names of Vice-Presidents of India who have been ex-officio Chairmen of the Rajya Sabha during 1952-2003 with their tenure of office are as follows:

Dr. S. Radhakrishnan	– 13 May 1952—12 May 1962
Dr. Zakir Hussain	– 13 May 1962—12 May 1967
Shri V.V. Giri	– 13 May 1967—3 May 1969
Dr. G.S. Pathak	– 31 August 1969—30 August 1974
Shri B.D. Jatti	– 31 August 1974—30 August 1979
Shri M. Hidayatullah	– 31 August 1979—30 August 1984
Shri R. Venkataraman	– 31 August 1984—24 July 1987
Dr. Shankar Dayal Sharma	– 3 September 1987—24 July 1902

Shri K. Narayanan	– 21 August 1992—24 July 1997
Shri Krishna Kant	– 21 August 1997—27 July 2002
Shri Bhairon Singh Shekhawat	– 12 August 2002—

The Deputy Chairman

The Deputy Chairman of the Rajya Sabha, who is chosen by the Rajya Sabha from amongst its members, holds office until he ceases to be a member of the Rajya Sabha or he resigns his office or is removed from his office by the Rajya Sabha by a resolution passed by a majority of its members.

The Deputy Chairman, as Presiding Officer of the Rajya Sabha, exercises in all respects, the same duties, functions and powers as the Deputy Speaker of the Lok Sabha.[27]

Panel of Chairmen and Secretary-General

The Chairman of the Rajya Sabha nominates a panel of members called Vice-Chairmen, one of whom presides whenever the Chairman and the Deputy Chairman are absent from the sitting of the Rajya Sabha. The Vice-Chairman and the Secretary-General of the Rajya Sabha perform almost similar functions and duties in relation to the Rajya Sabha as the members of the Panel of Chairmen and the Secretary-General perform, in regard to the Lok Sabha.[28]

REFERENCES

1. Arts 64, 89 and 93; Rule 9
2. Arts. 94, 96, 100 (1) & 112 (3)(b)
3. The only Speaker to have resigned from the party he belonged to was Shri N. Sanjiva Reddy during the years 1967-69.
4. See Subhash C. Kashyap, 'The Role of the Speaker', *The Indian Political Science Review*, March 1969, *Journal of Constitutional and Parliamentary Studies*, October-December, 1968. For a detailed study of the office of the Speaker and the Speakers of Lok Sabha, see Subhash C. Kashyap, *The Speaker's Office*, Shpra, New Delhi, 2001 and *Parliamentary Procedure*, op.cit., Vol. 1, pp. 216-259.

5. Rule 389
6. Rule 378
7. Rule 350
8. Rules 353, 356 & 380
9. Rules 222 & 225
10. Rules 23, 246 and 247; Art. 86 (2)
11. Rules 258 & 283
12. Rules 287, 330 and Appendix II
13. Art 110, Rule 96 (2)
14. Arts 108 and 118 (4), see the Houses of Par (Joint-sittings and Communications) Rules, 1952.
15. Rule 386
16. Art. 101 (3)
17. Rules 229-232
18. See Art. 98 and Dirs. 124 & 1224 (a)
19. Speaker was called President till 1947
20. The tenure of the Fifth Legislative Assembly lasted from 21 January 1935 to 8 February 1945.
21. The Sixth Central Legislative Assembly ceased to exist after 14 August 1947, and the Constituent Assembly of India which had been functioning since 9 December 1946, was empowered to function as the Legislature of the country.
22. Provisional Parliament ceased to exist on 17 April 1952. The President appointed Shri Mavalankar to perform the duties of the Speaker until the first Speaker of the First Lok Sabha was duly elected.
23. Arts 93-95; Rule 10.
24. Since the life of the Assembly was extended from time to time due to war, etc. upto 1945, Shri Dutta remained in office for about a decade.
25. Rules 9 and 10
26. Arts 64, 66, 67 & 89
27. Arts 89-91
28. For a detailed study, see Subhash C. Kashyap, *The Speaker's Office*, op.cit.

7

THE QUESTION HOUR

AND THE SO-CALLED 'ZERO HOUR'

Parliamentary question is a technique of parliamentary surveillance over the administration practiced in all the countries having representative parliamentary democracy. In this system, the government is answerable for all its acts of omission and commission to the Parliament and through the Parliament to the people. This answerability or accountability of the administration is exercised at two levels. The House exercises this power collectively by itself and through its Committees. Individually the members of the House exercise this power *inter alia* through the instrument of parliamentary questions. Members of Parliament are free to ask questions to elicit information on matters of public concern from ministers of the government. Seeking information is an inherent and unfettered parliamentary right available to a private member. A member of Parliament needs information regarding activities of the government to carry out his primary responsibilities as the people's representative. The basic purpose of asking questions, therefore, is to seek information and elicit facts on a matter of public importance. The questions are directed towards the proper implementation of the national and international policies as declared by the government and/or approved by the Parliament. They relate to the whole range of diverse subjects and almost all aspects of administration, therefore, come under their scrutiny.

The first hour of every sitting in both Houses is devoted to asking and answering of questions. It is known as the 'Question Hour'.[1] During this hour, matters concerning the Government of India are raised and problems are brought to the notice of the government to seek their intervention to meet any situation, to redress public grievances or to expose some administrative abuse or excess. The government is thus put on trial during this hour. Besides, the minister's grasp of working of his department is also tested by asking searching, albeit sometimes inconvenient, questions and supplementaries thereon, to expose his weaknesses or inept handling of situations.

Question Hour forms the most interesting part of parliamentary proceedings. No other business evokes as much interest among the public, the Press and the members themselves as the Question Hour. During this hour, the atmosphere in the House is so unpredictable that it may reel from sudden suspense to roars of laughter. The heat generated at times by bitter arguments on a question is completely dispelled by flashes of wit and humour coming either from the members or from the ministers. Several members enliven the Question Hour by their sense of humour from time to time. If the questions relate to important matters of topical interest and are short, succinct and witty, the Question Hour becomes useful, interesting and not infrequently, exciting. This is the reason that not only the chamber but also the public and Press Galleries are always nearly packed to capacity during Question Hour.

Categories of Questions

Questions asked in both Houses of Parliament are normally addressed to the ministers (government members) and can be categorised as Starred Questions, Unstarred Questions and Short Notice Questions. Questions may sometimes be addressed to private members also.

Starred Questions: These questions are to be answered

orally on the floor of the House. Answers to such questions may be followed by supplementary questions by members. Starred questions derive their name from the fact that they are always distinguished by an asterisk.[2]

Unstarred Questions: An unstarred question is so named because it does not carry an asterisk mark. Answer to such a question, unlike a starred question is not given orally, but in a written form. Consequently, no supplementary question can be asked thereon.[3]

Short Notice Questions: A short notice question is one which relates to a matter of urgent public importance and can be asked with notice shorter than the ten days prescribed for an ordinary questions.[4]

It is not that members can ask questions in the House to any minister as and when they want, without a prior notice. In such a case, the ministers may not be in a position to fully satisfy the member's queries. The concerned department needs some time to collect the relevant information form various levels and to prepare to precise answer to be given by the minister in the House. To facilitate this, rules governing the procedure and conduct of business in both the Houses provide that a member may give a notice to the Secretary-General of the concerned House intimating his intention to ask a question. Such notice should be given before not less than 10 days and not more than 21 days keeping in view the date on which the question is desired to be answered.[5]

How Questions are Admitted

Since the questions raised in the Houses of Parliament get wide publicity in the Press and public and they are also taken seriously by the government, it is only logical that every notice of a question by members has to be thoroughly scrutinised before it is admitted. There may be questions based on incorrect information and containing wrong inferences which might cause unnecessary embarrassment either to the government or to a person in his official or private capacity. To avoid this, the rules of the respective Houses have laid down certain conditions governing the admissibility of a question.[6] Questions containing allegations are generally not admitted unless they have a factful basis and concern a class or institution and not an individual, for once an allegation is made publicly whether it is proved or not, it has an effect which cannot be undone. This is especially so if the person against whom an allegation has been made does not have a chance to come before the House and explain his position. In order to ascertain their factual basis, such questions, before admission may be referred to the ministers/departments concerned. Members are also sometimes asked to furnish material in support of the allegations made in the questions.

Besides, if the subject-matter of a question is pending for judgement before any court of law or any other tribunal or body set up under law or is under consideration before a Parliamentary Committee, the same is not permitted to be asked. Questions making discourteous references to foreign countries with whom India has friendly relations are disallowed. Similarly, questions relating to individuals are disallowed, but if a question relates to an individual in a high position or raises an important question of principle or policy, it may be admitted. It should be noted that questions should not relate to a matter which is not primarily the concern of the Government of India. Questions that contain arguments, inferences or defamatory statements or otherwise refer to the character or conduct of any person except in his official or public capacity, and questions which instead of seeking information tend to give information are not admitted.

The distribution of questions between starred and unstarred categories depends upon the conditions provided in the rules. Usually, questions seeking detailed information of statistical nature, concerning matters of local interest, or those of interest to a limited section of the people or which relate to day-to-day administration may be admitted for written answers, that is as unstarred questions. Similarly, questions relating to public importance and in respect of which supplementary questions are likely to arise are put for oral answers as starred questions. It is, however, the discretion of the Speaker to put questions for oral or written answers as he thinks proper.[7]

After the notices of questions have been processed and scrutinised to ensure that questions comply with the Rules of Procedure and do not violate the established parliamentary conventions and usages, the questions are put in separate lists of oral and written answers for the day on which the answer is to be given.[8] Keeping in view the time of the House and other business to be transacted, it has been provided that a member of the Lok Sabha cannot ask more than five questions a day of both the starred and the unstarred category. Further, not more than three starred questions in the Rajya Sabha and not more than one starred question in the Lok Sabha by the same member can be admitted on a single day. The total number of questions in the starred list for a day is not more than 20.[9] The maximum number of questions in the unstarred list for a day is 230 in the Lok Sabha. In the Rajya Sabha there is no such limit but normally the number of unstarred questions listed for a day is less than 200.

For the purpose of answering questions, the ministries and departments of the Government of India have been divided into five groups—A, B, C, D, E—and fixed days have been allotted to these groups of ministries for answering questions on Mondays, Tuesdays, Wednesdays, Thursdays and Fridays, respectively. The grouping is done in such a way that each minister has one fixed day in the week for answering questions in the Lok Sabha and another fixed in the week for answering questions in the Rajya Sabha. The Ministries are supplied with the list of finally admitted questions at least five days before the date fixed for asking questions, in order to provide them sufficient time for preparing the answers.[10]

How Questions are Asked

The member whose question has been admitted as a starred one for a particular day is called by the Speaker or the Chairman, as the case may be, to ask the question. He rises in his place and asks his question just by reading its number in the list and not the text of the question as such.[11] Thereafter, the minister replies to the question.

No debate is permitted during the Question Hour on any question or answer given. However, supplementary or follow-up questions may be allowed to be asked for the purpose of elucidating any matter of fact regarding an answer already given.[12] The member in whose name the question stands is entitled to ask two supplementaries. Thereafter, the Chair, may call other members usually alternating between the government and the Opposition to ask one supplementary question each. By allowing a reasonable number of supplementaries depending upon the merit of a question and selecting members from all sections of the House for asking supplementaries, the Speaker ensures the efficacy of this unique parliamentary device. Besides, during the short span of the Question Hour, he tries to cover as many questions as possible. In order to get answers to more and more oral questions during the Question Hour, the Speaker tries that a starred question should not ordinarily take more than eight minutes. Strictly speaking, if 20 questions are to be covered in 60 minutes, each question should not, on an average, take more than three minutes. If the Speaker/Chairman feels that the matter has been sufficiently dealt with, he calls the member in whose name the next question stands in the list. This process goes on upto 12 noon.

It has been the experience that out of the 20 starred

questions listed for every single day, generally not more than five to seven are actually answered in the House. As for the rest of the questions, written answers are deemed to have been laid on the Table of the House by the Ministers concerned. Likewise, answers to unstarred questions are also laid on the Table at the end of the Question Hour.

Short Notice Questions

A question relating to a matter of urgent public importance may be asked for oral answer with a notice shorter than ten clear days.[13] The member giving notice of such a question has to give brief reasons for asking the question with a shorter notice. If the Speaker/Chairman feels that the matter is of urgent character, the minister concerned is asked whether he is in a position to reply at short notice, and if so, on what date. If the minister agrees to reply to a short notice question, it is fixed on a day indicated by him. If the minister declines to answer the question at a short notice and the Speaker/Chairman is of the opinion that the question is of sufficient importance to be orally answered in the House, the latter may direct that the question may be placed as the first question on the list of questions for oral answers for a day it would become due after satisfying the condition of ten clear days' minimum notice. Only one such question can be placed on the list of questions for a particular day.

At the end of the Question Hour, short notice questions, if any, for that day are taken up and disposed of in the same way as the question for oral answers. The conditions of admissibility of short notice questions are the same as for ordinary questions for oral answers.

Questions to Private Members

A question may be addressed to a private member, provided the subject-matter of the question relates to some Bill, Resolution or any other matter concerned with the business of the House for which that member may have been responsible.[14] Such questions are rarely asked in the Lok Sabha, and for sessions together no such question may be asked. No supplementary query can be asked on such a question. Similarly, no short notice question can be addressed to a private member.

Half-an-Hour Discussions

Half-an-hour Discussion on matters arising out of questions already answered in the House can be held in the Lok Sabha during the last half-an-hour of the sitting on three days in a week, namely—Monday, Wednesday and Friday. In the Rajya Sabha, such discussions can generally be held from 5 p.m. to 5.30 p.m. on any day allotted for the purpose by the Chairman. The subject-matter of such a discussion should be of sufficient public importance, which has been the subject of a recent question, starred, unstarred or short notice, and answer to which needs elucidation on a matter of fact.

A member wishing to raise such a discussion has to give notice in writing at least three days in advance of the day on which he desires to raise the discussion. In his notice, the member is required to specify the point(s) that he wishes to raise. Only one notice of the Half-an-hour Discussion is put down for a sitting. Further, in the Lok Sabha, not more than one such discussion is put down in the name of any one member in a week and no member can raise more than two discussions in the same session. The Speaker/Chairman decides in each case whether the matter needs elucidation on a matter of fact and is also of sufficient public importance to be put down for discussion.

The procedure regarding such a discussion in the House is that after the member, who initiates the discussion has made a short statement, not more than four other members, who have given prior intimation, may ask a question each for the purpose of further elucidating any matter of fact. Thereafter, at the end, the minister concerned replies.

Evaluating the Question Hour

Though the purpose of asking questions, by definition, is to seek information, in actual practice, most of them tend to give information. A member, sometimes, may be having more information on a specific matter than the government is willing to give; the real purpose of such a question, then, may be to pin-point the administrative lapses, to embarrass the government or to extract some inconvenient commitment from the government—commitment for action or to seek some information which he knows but he is interested in its being mentioned on the floor of the House for wide publicity.

Parliamentary questions, on the one hand make it possible for the government to come to know the grievances, problems and expectations of people who provide the material for these questions to their representatives and, on the other, they help to educate the public on the activities and programmes of the government, its policies and stand on various issues and the manner in which the administration is being carried on. Apart from the deterrent effect of parliamentary questions on public functionaries, the questions bring to the notice of the Executive, the way the policies are being implemented in the field and how these affect the common man. Amidst the proliferating machinery of modern government, the political, executive and even the administrative heads should be finding it difficult to keep track of all that is going on in their departments. Looked at from this angle, parliamentary questions are an essential aid to the Executive for they put into focus, areas of vital concern to the public at large.

It may be said with a fair amount of certainty that members have been evincing keen interest in using the right of asking questions. Because of its relative simplicity and ease with which it can be made use of, the question procedure, as compared to other forms of parliamentary procedure, is becoming increasingly popular with members of Parliament. It is evident from the number of questions admitted and answered in all the previous Lok Sabhas (see the Table). While the total number of admitted Questions during the First Lok Sabha was 43,725, it reached 1,02,959 during the seventh Lok Sabha. The number of questions admitted was 98,390 during the Eighth and 21,550 during the Ninth Lok Sabha period. It was 90,695 in the Tenth, 23681 in the Eleventh and 15,579 in the Twelfth Lok Sabha. It has also been observed that out of the number of notices received during the sessions 40 to 70 per cent are admitted, but owing to constraint of prescribed limits on the starred and unstarred questions for inclusion in the lists, merely 33 per cent in the Budget Session and between 30 and 45 per cent in the monsoon and winter sessions can actually get included in the list. The average number of notices of questions received per sitting comes to about 600.

Table 7.1

Period			No. of admitted questions of all the categories
First Lok Sabha		(1952-1957)	43,725
Second	—do—	(1957-1962)	24,631
Third	—do—	(1962-1966)	56,355
Fourth	—do—	(1967-1970)	93,538
Fifth	—do—	1970-1976)	98,606
Sixth	—do—	(1977-1979)	50.144
Seventh	—do—	(1980-1984)	1,02,959
Eighth	—do—	(1985-1989)	98,390
Ninth	—do—	(1989-1991)	21,550
Tenth	—do—	(1991-1996)	90,695
Eleventh	—do—	(1996-1998)	23,681
Twelfth	—do—	(1998-1999)	15,579

The importance of the Question Hour has been very much proved by certain instances when questions closely pursued by vigilant members led to inquiries by the government into matters concerning the violation of statutes, government's policies or misuse of public funds. To mention a few instances, such inquiries include the Jeep Scandal (1951), the Mundhra Deal (1957), Import Licence Case (1974) and the inquiry into the steel deals and the use of beef and tallow in the Vanaspati Case. These facts amply demonstrate the efficacy of the question procedure and utility of the Question Hour.

Zero Hour

The time immediately following the Question Hour in both Houses came to be popularly known as Zero Hour. It is a zero hour in more than one sense. It is a non-existent hour. It starts at 12 noon which is the zero hour of the day. It came to be called an 'Hour' also because very often it continued for one full hour, until the House rose for lunch at 1. p.m. Later, during the Seventh and Eighth Lok Sabha periods, for example, the 'Zero Hour' usually did not consume more than 5 to 15 minutes. The maximum time ever taken by the 'Zero' proceedings during the Eighth Lok Sabha came to 32 minutes. Things, however, changed sharply during the short-lived Ninth Lok Sabha (1989-91) when Speaker Rabi Ray tried to regularise and institutionalise the illegitimate 'Zero Hour'. The result was that it very often continued beyond one full hour. In fact, sometimes it extended to two hours and more to the great discomfiture and uneasiness of the ministers and members waiting for the regular business of the House to start.

Nobody knows what matter might crop up during this period or what kind of attack might be launched against the government. In the rules there is no mention of any 'Zero Hour' at all. It is the Press that gave the name 'Zero Hour' sometime in the early sixties when a practice of raising matters of urgent public importance without any prior notice developed. As soon as the Question Hour is over, several members are on their feet to raise matters which they feel cannot brook any delay even if there are no rules permitting them. The underlying consideration seems to be that rules which come in the way of members raising issues of national importance or serious grievances of the people on the floor of the House, are irrelevant and should yield to the basic concerns and rights of the people's representatives. After all, the Parliament is a political institution consisting of representatives of the people and any attempt to run the House strictly by the Rules Book is likely to be futile. Rules are for general regulations and guidance and could never visualise all eventualities and possible situations that could arise from time to time.

In the eyes of the Rule Book the so called 'Zero Hour' is an irregular affair. Since the matters are raised without any permission or prior notice, it results in loss of precious time of the House and encroaches on the legislative, financial and other regular business of the House. With several agitated members speaking at the same time, the task of the Presiding Officer becomes very difficult. The Speaker and the House, therefore, should not legitimately encourage such interruption of the regular business of the House. But, as things stand, 'Zero Hour' seems to have come to stay. Speaker Patil tried to regulate it and control its duration tactfully and subsequent Speakers have almost legitimised it as an established practice.[16]

REFERENCES

1. Rule 32
2. Rule 36
3. Rule 39
4. Rule 54
5. Rules 33 & 34
6. Rule 41

7. Rule 44
8. Rule 45. List of Questions for oral answers is printed on green paper and that for written answers on white paper.
9. Rule 37 (1)
10. Rule 35
11. Rule 48
12. Rule 46 & 50
13. Rule 54
14. Rule 40
15. Rule 55 (1)
16. For detailed study see Subhash C. Kashyap, *Parliamentary Procedure, op.cit.*, Vol. 1 and *History of Parliament*, 6 Vols., *op.cit.*

8

RAISING MATTERS IN PARLIAMENT

VARIOUS KINDS OF MOTIONS AND OTHER PROCEDURAL DEVICES

It takes more than ten days to get answers to the questions except in the case of Short Notice Questions, which are subject to the consent of the minister concerned. Also, with the exception of the Half-an-hour Discussion, under the question procedure discussions cannot be allowed. Sometimes, a problem may crop up which is sudden and unforeseen. In such a case, it may not be possible to give several days' advance notice to bring it to the notice of the government. For raising urgent matters of public importance requiring immediate attention of the government and the Parliament several additional procedural devices are available to a member of Parliament. These include: Adjournment Motions, Call Attention Notices, Short Duration Discussions and Mentions under Rule 377. Similarly, members may move various Motions and Resolutions to initiate discussions on matters of public interest and draw the attention of the House and the government. The Rules of Procedure of both the Houses contain conditions governing the application of devices for raising urgent matters of public importance and initiating debates in the Parliament.

Adjournment Motions

Usually the House transacts its business according to the agenda paper. It does not take up items not included in the

List of Business without the permission of the Speaker.[1] A matter of urgent public importance, however, can be brought before the House through an adjournement motion by interrupting the regular business, if the Speaker agrees to do so.[2]

The basic object of bringing an adjournment motion is to draw the attention of the House to a recent matter of urgent public importance having serious consequences, and in regard to which moving a motion or resolution with proper notice will be too late. The matter proposed to be raised should be of such a character that something very grave affecting the people and their security has happened and the House is required to pay its attention immediately by interrupting the normal business of the House. The adjournment motion, thus, is an extraordinary procedure which, if admitted, leads to setting aside the normal business of the House for discussing a 'definite matter of urgent public importance'. The following essential elements of an adjournment motion can be delineated:

(a) The matter must be definite.
(b) It should have a factual base.
(c) Issue must be urgent.
(d) It must be of public importance.

Thus the general issues like the political situation in the country, lawlessness, unemployment, railway accidents and air crashes, closure of mills, the international situation in general, are not proper subjects for adjournment motion. Similarly, shortage of transport vehicles, cases of kidnapping, dacoity, explosions, communal tensions have been held not to be appropriate matters for such motions. It should not raise a matter involving a question of privilege; a question which can be raised under a distinct motion; a matter which is *sub-judice*; and a matter which has already been discussed during the same session.[3] The subject matter of the motion must have a direct or indirect relation to the conduct or default on the part of the Government of India. But, if a matter falling under the State jurisdiction concerns the constitutional development in the State or atrocities on Scheduled Castes and Scheduled Tribes or the weaker sections of the society, it may be considered for admission on merit. The following, for example, are some of the subjects on which adjournment motions were admitted and discussed during the Seventh Lok Sabha:

1. Death of eight persons and the illness of several persons due to the consumption of illicit liquor in Delhi and the serious situation arising out of it.
2. Qutab Minar tragedy taking a toll of 45 lives.
3. Serious situation in Punjab arising out of extremist activities and failure of government to settle the issue.

A member wishing to bring an adjournment motion is required to give a notice addressed each to the Speaker, minister concerned and the Secretary-General by 10.00 a.m. on the day on which the motion is proposed to be moved.[4] If the Speaker is satisfied *prima facie* that the matter to be discussed is in order under the Rules, he may give his consent to the moving of the motion. The Speaker, after Question Hour, calls upon the concerned member to ask for leave of the House to move the motion. If objection to leave being granted is raised, the Speaker will request the member in favour of leave being granted to rise in their seats and if not less than fifty members rise accordingly, he will declare that leave is granted.[5]

After the leave of the House to move the motion has been granted, the motion formally stands admitted. The discussion on an admitted adjournment motion normally starts at 4.00 p.m. and continues for two-and-a-half, i.e. till 6.30 p.m. or beyond that.[6] The discussion starts with the motion moved by the mover 'THAT THE HOUSE DO NOW ADJOURN'. After the mover and the other members have spoken on the motion, the minister intervenes and at the end the mover has a right of reply. Thereafter the motion is put to vote. It may be noted that after the discussion on such a motion has started, till the motion is disposed of, the Speaker has no power to adjourn the House because this power vests in the House during that time.

If an adjournment motion is negatived, the House resumes its business which was interrupted by the motion. On the other hand, if the motion is passed, it amounts to censuring the government. Though it does not amount to voting the government out of office, it goes to show that a government which has failed to prevent an adverse vote on an adjournment motion, will not be able to survive a direct 'Motion of No-confidence' in the Council of Ministers. Since the adoption of an adjournment motion involves an element of censure against the government, the Rajya Sabha does not make use of this procedure. It has been seen that the adjournment motion is used very sparingly. During the Seventh Lok Sabha, for example, out of 5762 notices of adjournment motion received, only 149 were brought before the House and finally only 24 of them could be admitted and discussed, and none of them was adopted. In the Eighth Lok Sabha, notices of 1801 adjournment motions were received. Of these 80 notices on four subjects were admitted. In the Ninth Lok Sabha, of the 375 notices, nine on eight subjects were discussed. During the Tenth Lok Sabha, 608 notices were received. Of these four were admitted and discussed. During the Eleventh and Twelfth Lok Sabhas 63 and 83 notices were received respectively. Out of 63 one and of the 83 none was admitted and discussed.

Calling Attention Notices

The provision for the Calling Attention Notices was first made in the year 1954. Prior to this, the need for a precise procedure to raise an important and urgent issue was being felt considerably. The procedure of bringing an adjournment motion which was in the nature of a censure motion against the government, was restricted in its scope in the existing constitutional set-up. It was, therefore, considered that some procedure might be devised whereby members might have an opportunity of bringing urgent matters to the attention of the government.

In the modern parliamentary procedure the idea of introducing Calling Attention Notices in the Rules of Procedure is purely an Indian innovation. It combines the asking of a question for answer with supplementaries and short comments in which all points of view are expressed concisely and precisely, and the government has adequate opportunity to state its case. Sometimes, it gives opportunity to members to criticise the government, directly or indirectly, and to bring to the surface the failure or inadequate action of the government in an important matter.

A member, with the previous permission of the Speaker/Chairman, may call the attention of a minister to a matter of urgent public importance and request him to make a statement on the subject.[7] The minister may make a brief statement or ask for time to make the statement at a later date.

The members' chief source for tabling the Calling Attention Notices is the daily newspapers. Sometimes they may be based on the private information of a member or on the correspondence between him and his constituents.

Notices of Calling Attention have to be given by members in writing by 10.00 a.m. A member can give not more than two calling attention notices for any one sitting. Notices on the same subject may be given by more than one member, but names of not more than five members are shown in the List of Business. All calling attention notices received in a week are kept alive and placed before the Speaker from day-to-day. The Speaker goes through the notices and selects one of them for a statement by the concerned minister at the sitting of the House on a following day. In certain cases, the Speaker may select two such notices to be taken up at one sitting. However, the Speaker may, in his discretion, allow calling attention on the day on which the notice has been given, if he feels the matter is so urgent that the statement should be made by the minister on the same day. The idea behind admitting Calling Attention Notices a day or so in advance is that it would give sufficient time to the minister concerned to gather facts about the matter raised and prepare a statement in time.

Not more than two notices can be taken up at one sitting to call the attention of ministers. There is no debate on such a statement but each member in whose name the matter is listed is permitted to ask a clarificatory question. The main purpose, therefore, of calling attention is to seek an authoritative statement from a minister on a matter of urgent nature. This process does not involve any censure against the government as there is no regular discussion and voting.

The subjects on which ministers have been called upon to make statements have covered matters like disturbances in any part of India, border troubles, railway accidents, shutting down of public undertakings, judgements by law courts in which observations affecting ministries or officers of the Central Government were involved, violations of air space by enemy aircraft, strikes involving the harbours, ports, air companies, railways and other public utility services, position of Indians overseas, a serious food drought or flood situation, etc. It is the discretion of the Speaker to admit a notice to call the attention on any matter, keeping in view the urgency and public importance of the matter.

The procedure of Calling Attention has enabled the Parliament to keep the government on its toes; to call for its explanation immediately on a vital matter of general importance; and to enable the government to state facts or its decision or to deal effectively with the matter with the knowledge and the feeling that it has the support of the House. It is a short and swift method of raising, dealing with, and bringing to a conclusion an important matter in which members, who have given notices, are entitled to take equal part without any party whip and without coming to the painful decisions by dividing on a formal or specific motion. No specific conclusions are recorded. Only the atmosphere is surcharged with feeling on all sides of the House and each member is free to interpret the short discussion in his own light and to come to his own conclusions.

Short Duration Discussions

Yet another device available to the private member to bring to the notice of the House matters of urgent public importance, is to raise a discussion for short duration. Before the year 1953, there was no provision for such discussion except by way of motions and resolutions. Members did not have any option but to resort to an adjournment motion for raising important and urgent matters. Adjournment motion being in the nature of a censure motion could not be used quite often. A convention, therefore, was established in 1953 whereby members could raise discussions on such matters for short duration. This procedure was later incorporated in the Rules of Procedure of both the Houses.

For raising such discussion, a member has to give a notice to the Secretary-General specifying the matter precisely and explaining clearly the reasons thereof. Such notice should also be signed by at least two other members of Parliament.[8]

The Speaker/Chairman decides the admissibility of notices received. If he is satisfied that the matter is urgent and of sufficient importance to be raised in the House at an early date and an early opportunity is otherwise not available for discussing the matter, he may admit the notice.[9] A notice of Short Duration Discussion, to be admissible, should raise a matter which is primarily the concern of the Union Government and is not based on unsubstantial allegations; is not hypothetical; and involves an element of urgency. Only one matter can be raised in a notice.

The Speaker may allot two sittings in a week for short duration discussion and allow such time not exceeding one hour at or before the end of the sitting for such discussion.[10] The date of discussion is fixed on the recommendation of the Business Advisory Committee. Generally such discussions are taken up on Tuesdays and Thursdays. In the Rajya Sabha the Chairman may, in consultation with the leader of the House, fix the date for discussion and allow such time not exceeding two-and-a-half hours.

After the notice has been admitted and a date is fixed for discussion it is included in the List of Business for that day. On that day, the first member in whose name the item stands in the list is called by the Speaker to make a short statement and the Minister replies briefly. Thereafter, other members take part in the discussion. The member who raises the discussion has no right to reply. There is no formal motion nor is there any vote.[11] The purpose of discussion is that members who are in possession of some facts about the matter should apprise the House of the same and the minister clarifies the position for the benefit of the House and the nation.

Mentions Under Rule 377

Any visitor to the public galleries may have witnessed our elected representative trying to raise matters which do not concern interpretation of rules and regulations but which are agitating their minds, and which they feel they must raise at the earliest opportunity. Immediately after the Question Hour, which is euphemistically called 'Zero Hour' by the Press, several members are on their feet to raise such matters creating din and disorder in the House. Presiding Officers of both the Houses, convinced of the need to curb this practice, wanted to devise some method to enable members to raise issues which they felt they should, and which were not the subject matter of a recent question, Adjournment Motions, Calling Attention notices, etc. It was with this view, that the practice of 'Special Mention' in the Rajya Sabha and raising matters under Rule 377 in the Lok Sabha, was started. Recourse to Rule 377, for the first time was taken on 14 may 1966, the matter raised related to ill-treatment meted out to an M.P. by the police. It was a matter which could not have been raised under any other rule.

Matters, which are not points of order or which cannot be raised under the rules relating to questions, Short Notice Questions, Calling Attention Notices, etc. are raised under Rule 377.

A member wishing to raise any matter under Rule 377, gives a written notice to the Secretary-General, giving briefly (ordinarily in not more 250 words) the points proposed to be raised and the reasons thereof. A notice to be admissible should not *inter alia,* raise purely a local issue or of concern to some individual(s) only; a matter which is *sub-judice;* and matters containing allegations, unparliamentary expressions, etc.

A copy of the text as approved by the Speaker is provided to the member concerned on the day on which he is allowed to raise the matter. While raising his point, the member is not permitted to deviate from the approved text of his statement. Normally, the minister concerned does not make statements after a matter has been raised, however, he can do so if he desires. The minister concerned writes to the member directly with regard to matters raised under Rule 377 informing him of the government views and the action taken in the matter. It may be noted that matters so raised are not included in the List of Business.

While prior to the fourth session of the Sixth Lok Sabha, the use of Rule 377 to raise matters in the House was somewhat limited, a more liberal attitude has been adopted thereafter, so that members could raise various matters of public importance particularly those concerning their constituencies at the earliest. It has been seen that the members are increasingly taking recourse to this rule and this procedure has become very popular. While during Fourth Lok Sabha only 36 matters were allowed to be raised under Rule 377, during the Fifth, Sixth, Seventh and Eighth Lok Sabhas such matters numbered 184, 829, 3134, 3180 respectively. The figure for the Ninth Lok Sabha came to 721. During the Tenth, Eleventh and Twelfth Lok Sabhas, this number respectively was 2063, 629, and 667.

Motions

The House takes a number of decisions and expresses its opinion on various matters of public importance. Being an assembly of a large number of people, ascertaining opinion or the will of the House is a difficult task. In order to facilitate this, a member may put a motion in the form of a proposal containing his opinion or the will before the House and, if the House adopts it, it becomes the opinion or the will of the House as a whole. Thus, broadly a 'motion' is a proposal brought before the House for eliciting decision or expressing the opinion of the House. Every question to be decided by the House must, therefore, be proposed by a member as a motion. Since decisions in Parliament are arrived at after full discussion and debate, no discussion on a matter can take place in the House except on a motion made with the consent of the Speaker or the Chairman, as the case may be.[12]

Motions, in fact, are the basis of parliamentary proceedings. Any matter of public importance can be subject matter of a motion. A debate or a motion passes through four stages:

(a) Moving the motion.
(b) Proposing the question by the Speaker/Chairman.
(c) Debate or discussion where permissible, and
(d) Vote or decision of the House

The member moving the motion frames it in the form in which he wants it to be adopted by the House. Now, it is open to the House either to pass it as such or to reject it, or to pass it with certain amendments. Thus, the members who want the motion to be adopted differently can move amendments or substitute motions after the original motion has been proposed by the Presiding Officer.

Motions can be moved by different persons and for different purposes. They may be moved by ministers or by private members. Generally, government motions relate to obtaining approval of the House for some policy or action of the government. Motions moved by private members, on the other hand, generally tend to elicit the opinion or the feeling of the House on a matter. Motions, though they cover a variety of proceedings of the House, fall into three principal categories namely, Substantive Motions, Substitute Motions, and Subsidiary Motions.[13]

Substantive Motions: A substantive motion is a self-contained independent proposal submitted for the approval of the House and drafted in such a way as to be capable of expressing a decision of the House.[14] It neither depends on nor arises out of another motion. The Motion of Thanks on the President's Address, motion for adjournment on a matter of public importance, motion of no-confidence, motions for election or removal of the Speaker, Deputy Speaker of the Lok Sabha or the Deputy Chairman of the Rajya Sabha, privilege motions and also, all resolutions are substantive motions.[15] Further, the Constitution provides for the impeachment of persons in high authority which can be initiated on a substantive motion drawn in proper terms.[16]

Substitute Motions: Motions moved in substitution of the original motion and proposing an alternative to it are called substitute motions.[17] Before the discussion on the original motion has commenced, a member can move a substitute motion which, while conforming to the subject matter of the original motion, is so drawn up as to express an opinion of the House. Discussion is held on both the original and the substitute motions together but vote of the House is taken only on the substitute motion.[18] Further, if adopted, it supersedes the original question which is then not put to vote, while if amendment is adopted, the original question is put as amended.

Subsidiary Motions: They depend upon or relate to other motions or follow up on some proceedings in the House. They, by themselves, have no meaning and are not capable of stating the decision of the House without reference to the original motion or proceedings of the House. Subsidiary motions are further divided into three categories:

(a) Ancillary Motions,
(b) Superseding Motions, and
(c) Amendments.[19]

Ancillary Motions are recognised by the practice of the House as the regular way of proceeding with various kinds of business, e.g., that the Bill be referred to a Select or Joint Committee, or that it be taken into consideration, or that it be passed.

Superseding Motions are moved in the course of debate on another question and seek to supersede that question even though they are independent in form. Any member, in relation to a motion for taking into consideration a Bill, may move a superseding motion seeking recommital of Bill to a Committee or recirculation to elicit further opinion or the adjournment of the debate on the Bill. Most of these motions are dilatory in nature.

Amendment seeks to modify or substitute only a part of the original motion. Amendment may be made not only to motions, resolutions, or to clauses of a Bill but even to an amendment to a clause of a Bill, resolution or motion. It is moved during the course of a debate and if accepted, the original question is put as amended. It is noteworthy, that the substitute motion also seeks to bring before the House a different proposition as an alternative to the original question but is distinct from an amendment inasmuch as it replaces the entire motion.

Notice of motion, like any other notice, is given to the Secretary-General.[20] No period of notice for motions has been prescribed. It may be given either by a minister or a private member. A motion may be admitted or rejected or may be allowed in part by the Chair.[21] Further, the subject matter of a motion, as in the case of questions, should not include, *inter alia*, ironical expressions, defamatory statements, or imputations, and should not raise a question of privilege or a matter which is *sub judice*.[22]

No-day-yet-named Motions: A motion which has been admitted by the Speaker and for the discussion of which no date has been fixed is called a no-day-yet-named motion. These are placed before the Business Advisory Committee which selects the motions for discussion in the House and also allots time for the same.[23]

How a Motion is Moved: On the allotted day, the Speaker calls the member concerned to move the motion and make a speech. Thereafter, the Speaker places the motion before the House. Amendments and substitute motions, if any, are then moved by the members who have given prior notice, and the discussion follows. After the members and the minister have spoken, the mover may again speak expressing his right of reply. At the conclusion of the discussion, the amendments/substitute motions, if any, are put to the vote of the House and disposed of. Therefore, the main motion or the motion as amended, is put to the vote of the House. However, a motion under Rule 342 that a policy or situation or statement or any other matter be taken into consideration is not put to vote. Only substitute motions moved to such a motion are put to vote. A copy of the motion, as adopted by the House, is sent to the minister concerned for appropriate action.

In the Rajya Sabha also, the procedure is the same. At the appointed hour on the allotted day or as the case may be, the last of the allotted days, the Chairman forthwith puts every question necessary to determine the decision of the House on the original question. The mover of the motion has a right of reply. Amendments can also be moved to such a motion.[24]

Resolutions

A resolution is also one of the procedural means available to the members and the ministers to raise a discussion in the House on a matter of general public interest.[25] A resolution is in fact a substantive motion. Unlike motions in general, forms of resolutions have been provided by the Rules of Procedure concerning both the Houses.[26] Accordingly, a resolution to be moved in the Lok Sabha may be in the form so as to record either approval or disapproval by the House of an act or policy of the government or convey a message; or commend, urge or request an action; or call attention to a matter or situation for consideration by the government; or in such other forms as the Speaker may consider appropriate. Similarly, in the Rajya Sabha resolution may be in the form of declaration of opinion by the House or in such other form as the Chairman considers appropriate.

The following resolutions moved in the Lok Sabha will illustrate the general forms and the varied subjects that are dealt with in such resolutions:

(i) Considering that even 34 years after Independence, the lot of a majority of the Scheduled Castes and Scheduled Tribes persons has not improved economically and socially, this House recommends to the Government to draw up plans to provide job guarantee to the educated youths of those communities within next five years.[27]

(ii) This House is of the opinion that the emerging pattern of different linguistic and ethnic groups as distinctive political entities in the body politic of our country necessitates restructuring of financial and other relations between the Centre and the State and, therefore, resolves that the relevant provisions of the Constitution be amended suitably.[28]

Difference Between a Motion and a Resolution: Motions and resolutions cannot be easily distinguished from each other, rather, they have many things in common. The difference between them, in fact, is more of procedure rather than of content. Quite often, both motions and resolutions on the same subject are admitted with some slight change of form. For example, the following motion was admitted for 3 July 1982 in the Lok Sabha:

> That viewing with concern that development work in different fields is not keeping pace with the urges of the nation due to administrative delays in their implementation, this House recommends to the Government, the setting up of a national statutory monitoring body to constantly watch the progress of the different developmental activities at all levels, locate the factors hampering progress and suggest immediate and remedial measures where any projects are held up and delayed.

The following was admitted and moved as a resolution by the same member on 13 August 1982:

> Keeping in view the vital need for speedy implementation of the socio-economic programme of the Government, this House recommends the setting up of a monitoring body under the government to constantly watch the progress of the different developmental activities at all levels, locate the factors hampering the progress and suggest immediate and remedial measures to expedite their implementation.

But there is a difference. All resolutions come in the category of substantive motions, that is to say, every resolution is a particular type of motion. All motions need not necessarily be substantive. Further, all motions are not necessarily put to vote of the House, whereas all the resolutions are required to be voted upon. The substitute motion is not moved to a resolution, on the other hand, such motions can be moved to motions other than substantive.

Types of Resolutions

Resolutions may be classified as Private Members' Resolutions, Government Resolutions, and Statutory Resolutions.

Private Members' Resolution: Resolutions which are moved by private members are called Private Members' Resolutions. They, in fact, enable the government to gauge the feelings of the House with regard to proposals which are still indefinite or may be ahead of public opinion.

The last two-and-a-half hours of a sitting on every alternate Friday are allotted for the discussion on private members' resolutions. A member who wants to move a resolution has to give notice to the Secretary-General informing him of the intentions to move the same. The names of three members in Lok Sabha and five in the case of Rajya Sabha from among those who have expressed their desire to move a resolution are decided by ballot, to allow them to give notice of one resolution each.[29] These resolutions, if admitted, are put down in the private members' List of Business. When called upon by the Chair, the member concerned moves the resolution and makes a speech thereon.[30] Other members and the minister concerned also speak thereafter. Any member, after the resolution has been moved, may, subject to the rules, move an amendment to the resolution.[31] Allocation of time for discussion of private members' resolutions is done by the Committee on Private Members' Bills and Resolutions. Generally, two hours are allotted for discussion on these resolutions. The mover of the resolution has got a right of reply after the minister's speech.

Government Resolutions: Resolutions moved by the ministers are known as Government Resolutions. Ministers also are required to give prior notice to the Secretary-General of their intention to move a resolution. Though no period has been prescribed for this, in actual practice, ministers give such notices several days in advance. These notices are also subject to the same rules of admissibility as the private members' resolutions. After a government resolution has been admitted, time for discussion is allotted by the House on the recommendation of the Business Advisory Committee.[32] The rest of the procedure to dispose them of is same as in the case of the private members' resolutions.

Resolutions tabled by ministers are generally for seeking the approval of the House to international treaties, conventions or agreements to which the government is a party; or for declaring or approving certain policies—national and international—of the government; or for taking the approval to the recommendations of certain committees.

Statutory Resolutions: These resolutions may be moved either by a minister or by a private member. They are so called because they are always tabled in pursuance of a provision in the Constitution or an Act of Parliament.[33] Certain enactments, however, expressly require the government to bring forward a resolution within a specified period of time. There is no specific period of notice for moving a statutory resolution unless the period itself is prescribed in the particular article of the Constitution or in the section of the statute under which it is tabled.[34] Such resolution, after it has been admitted, is discussed for such time as allotted by the House on the recommendation of the Business Advisory Committee from the time allocated for the government business.

A copy of every resolution, whether private members', government or statutory, is forwarded to the minister concerned by the Secretary-General, after it has been passed by the House.

Effect of Motions or Resolutions Adopted by the House: By voting on a motion or a resolution, the House declares its opinion with regard to the subject matter thereof and it becomes an order of the House. As far as their effect is concerned, resolutions passed by the Parliament fall in the following categories:

(i) Resolutions expressing merely an opinion of the House are not binding on the government. As a matter of practice, it rests entirely on the discretion of the government whether or not to give effect to the opinions expressed in these resolutions.

(ii) Resolutions adopted by the House in matters concerning its own proceedings are binding and have the force of law. Their validity cannot be challenged in courts.

(iii) Resolutions having a statutory effect, if adopted, are binding on the government and have the force of law. The Constitution provides for this kind of resolutions to be moved for purposes like impeachment of the President, removal of the Vice-President, Speaker, Deputy Speaker and the Deputy Chairman of the Rajya Sabha; disapproval of an Ordinance promulgated by the President; empowering the Parliament to legislate on a subject in the State List in national interest; creation of All-India Services; and approval of a proclamation of Emergency.[35]

Since the purpose of resolutions is merely to obtain an opinion of the House, there might arise a situation where the Opposition may succeed in getting a resolution passed by the House much against the wishes of the treasury benches. In such a case, should the resolution be treated as amounting to a vote of censure on the government? Should the government resign or advise dissolution of the House? There is no hard and fast rule as to the question of resignation by a government. The only broad principle is that a government is expected to resign office or advise dissolution of the House, if it is defeated on a subject considered to be a major issue or on a specific motion of no-confidence brought forward by the Opposition and adopted by the House.

No-confidence Motion

The Council of Ministers remains in office as long as it enjoys the confidence of the Lok Sabha.[36] The moment it expresses a lack of confidence in the Council of Ministers, the government is constitutionally bound to resign, whether or not the Prime Minister recommends a dissolution of the House. In order to ascertain this confidence, the rules provide for moving a motion to this effect which is called a No-confidence Motion.

There is no express provision in the Constitution regarding the individual responsibility of a minister to Parliament for anything done or not done in his department. This responsibility is collective. Therefore, only a motion expressing want of confidence in the Council of Ministers as a whole is admitted and the one expressing lack of confidence in an individual minister is out of order.[37]

A no-confidence motion need not set out grounds on which it is based, unlike a censure motion. A notice of motion of no-confidence has to be given before the commencement of the sitting on the day it is proposed to be raised. No conditions of admissibility have been laid down in the Rules; the Speaker has the power to decide whether a motion is in order or not.

If the Speaker is of the opinion that the motion is in order, he calls upon the member, after the Question Hour is over, to ask for the leave of the House or the Speaker himself reads the motion to the House and requests those members, who are in favour of leave being granted, to rise in their places and if not less than 50 members rise in their seats, the Speaker declares that leave is granted. Otherwise, it is taken that the member does not have the leave of the House. A motion of no-confidence, once admitted, has to be taken up within ten days of the leave being granted. The Speaker, after ascertaining the views of the government, decides the date for the discussion. If the government so desires, the discussion can even be taken up forthwith. The time for the discussion is usually fixed on the recommendation of the Business Advisory Committee. After the members have spoken, usually the Prime Minister himself replies to charges leveled against the government. The mover has a right to reply. When the debate is concluded, the Speaker puts the question forthwith and ascertains the decision of the House by a voice vote, or a division, if demanded.[38]

Withdrawal of the notice of no-confidence motion by a member may be made when he is called upon by the Speaker to ask for leave of the House. In case, however, the member wants to withdraw his motion after the leave of the House has been granted, he may do so only with the permission of the House. Notice of no-confidence motion can also be withdrawn by members concerned by sending letters of withdrawal signed by all the signatories to the notice before the item is taken up in the House. In that case the item is not mentioned in, or brought before the House.

Rajya Sabha is not empowered to entertain a motion of no-confidence because the government is collectively responsible under the Constitution only to the directly elected House of the People (Lok Sabha).

Censure Motion

A censure motion is distinct from a no-confidence motion. Whereas a motion of no-confidence need not specify any grounds on which it is based, a censure motion must set out the ground(s) or charge(s) on which it is based and is moved for the specific purpose of censuring the government for certain policies and actions.

Censure motion can be moved against the Council of Ministers or an individual minister or a group of ministers for the failure to act or not to act or for their policy, and may express regret, indignation or surprise of the House at the failure of the minister or ministers. The motion should be specific and self-explanatory so as to record the reasons for the censure, precisely and briefly. The Speaker's decision whether the motion is in order or not for any reason is final.

No leave of the House is required to move a censure

motion. It is in the discretion of the government to find time and to fix a date for its discussion. There is no specific provision in the Rules for the moving of a censure motion; such a motion is governed by the rules applicable to motions in general,[39] and can be admitted as a No-day-yet-named Motion.

REFERENCES

1. Rule 31 (2)
2. Rule 56
3. Rule 58
4. Rule 57
5. Rule 60
6. Rules 61 & 62
7. Rule 197
8. Rule 193
9. Rule 194 (1)
10. Rule 194 (2)
11. Rule 195
12. Rule 184 (L.S.) and Rule 167 (R.S.)
13. See Dir. 41 (1)
14. Dir. 41 (2) (1)
15. See Rules, 7, 8, 17, 56, 184, 198, 200, 226 & 328 and see arts 67, 90 (c) & 94 (c)
16. Rule 352 (v) and See arts 61, 121, 124 (4) & (5), 148 (1) and 324 (5)
17. Dir. 41 (2) (ii)
18. Rule 342
19. Dir. 41 (2) (iii)
20. Rule 185
21. Rule 187
22. Rule 186
23. Rules 189 & 190
24. Rules 190-192
25. Rule 172
26. Rule 171
27. This resolution was moved on 28 August 1981 and was withdrawn by leave of the House on 11 September 1981.
28. It was moved on 31 March 193 and was negated by the House on 19 August 1983.
29. Rules 30 (4), 170, Dir. 9
30. Rule 176

31. Rule 177 (1), Dir. 113
32. Rule 288
33. Dir. 9B(1)
34. For example, arts 61, 67, 90 & 94 provide for at least 14 days' notice.
35. Arts 61, 67, 90, 94, 123, 249 and 312.
36. Art. 75 (3)
37. Rule 198 (1)
38. Rule 198
39. Rules 184-189

9

BUDGET IN PARLIAMENT

PROCEDURES FOR FINANCIAL BUSINESS

With the emergence of the Welfare State, governments have come to look after virtually every sphere of man's life. They have to perform manifold functions from maintaining law and order and protecting the territories of the State against foreign aggression, to implementing plans for social and economic betterment of the people. Besides, they provide a variety of social services like housing, education, health and employment to the people. Needless to say, governments need money to discharge these functions. Where is this money to come from? Who is to sanction the funds? The necessary funds are mobilised from the country's resources by way of taxes, loans, etc. to meet governmental expenditures.

It is not as if the government can tax, borrow and spend money the way it likes. Since there is a limit to the resources the State can mobilise, the need for proper budgeting arises to allocate scarce resources to various governmental activities. Every item of expenditure has to be well-thought out and the total outlay worked out for a specific period. Also, there must be the sanction of the people behind all these financial proposals, expressed clearly through their chosen representatives.

It is in this context that the Budget of the Government of India is presented before both the Houses of Parliament every year. The Budget contains the financial statements of the government embodying the estimated receipts and expenditure for one financial year, which at present commences on the 1st of April every year. In other words, it is a proposal of how much money is to be spent on what and how much of it will be contributed by whom or raised from where during the coming year. The Budget gives estimates for the ensuing year and offers an opportunity to the government to review and explain its financial and economic policy and programmes besides enabling the Parliament to discuss and criticise it.

The essential features of the financial procedures followed in India are laid down in the Constitution which ensures the supremacy of the Lok Sabha in financial matters. Constitution provides that no tax shall be levied or collected except by authority of Parliament and that the President shall, in respect of every financial year, cause to be laid before both Houses, the Annual Financial Statement.[1] These two provisions ensure that the government cannot dispense with the Parliament for a period of more than one year because any proposal of expenditure gets the sanction of Parliament for one financial year only. The Constitution provides for a Consolidated Fund of India to which all revenues received by way of loans, advances, etc. are credited.[2] The expenditures are embodied in the Budget as (a) the sums required to meet the items of expenditure described by the Constitution as those *charged on* the Consolidated Fund of India; and (b) the sums required to meet other expenditures *proposed to be made* from the Consolidated Fund of India. Expenditures contained in the first category can be discussed in both the Houses but are not submitted to vote of either House. In other words, they constitute the non-votable part of the Budget. The expenditures charged on the Consolidated Fund of India include the emoluments and allowances of the President, the salaries and allowances of the Chairman, Deputy Chairman of the Rajya Sabha and the Speaker and the

Deputy Speaker of the Lok Sabha. It also includes the salary and other allowances payable to the judges of the Supreme Court and any other expenditure declared by the Constitution or by Parliament by law to be so charged. The expenditure falling in the second category are presented in the form of *Demands for Grants* to the Lok Sabha and are voted by this House. The Lok Sabha has the right to assent or to refuse any such demand or reduce the demand specified therein. No such demand shall be made except on the recommendation of the President.[3] Since these demands are meant to fulfil the programmes and policies of the government, if any demand as a whole is voted down, it tantamounts to a defeat of the government.

No money can be withdrawn from the Consolidated Fund of India except under an Appropriation Act passed by the Parliament.[4]

Stages in Financial Legislation

The procedure adopted in the Parliament while dealing with financial matters, specifically the Budget, involves many stages:

(a) ***Presentation of the Budget***: The Budget in our Parliament is presented in two parts, namely, the Railway Budget, pertaining to railway finance and the General Budget. The primary idea behind presenting a separate Budget for the railways is to secure stability for civil estimates by providing for an assured contribution by the railways and also to introduce flexibility in the administration of railway finance.

While the Railway Budget is presented to the Lok Sabha by the Minister of Railways sometimes in the third week of February every year, the General Budget is presented by the Minister of Finance on the last working day of February usually at 5 p.m. There is, however, no binding rule that the Budget must be presented only at 5 p.m. or on the last working day of February. The Budget for 2002-2003 was presented at 11 a.m. Earlier, the last annual Budget of the 20th century was presented at 11 a.m. and on 27 February 1999 which was a Saturday. The Budget for 1984-85 was presented on 29 February 1984 which was a parliamentary holiday on account of *Maha Shivaratri*. The Budget for 1985-86 was presented on 16 March 1985. There have been other instances also of such variation.

The Budget is presented with a 'Budget Speech' which is, in fact, one of the most important speeches in Parliament. This speech is in two parts: Part A contains 'a general economic survey' of the country and Part B 'the taxation proposals' for the ensuing financial year. A copy of the Budget is laid on the Table of the Rajya Sabha at the conclusion of the speech of the Finance Minister in the Lok Sabha. Soon after, the Minister introduces the Finance Bill which contains the taxation proposals made by the government.[5] The House rises thereafter, and there is no discussion of the Budget on the day on which it is presented.[6]

(b) ***Discussion on the Budget***: The Parliament is primarily a deliberative body. The passage of the Budget is marked by deep and thorough discussions in both Houses of the Parliament. The discussion on the Budget starts after a few days of its presentation.[7] It gives members the necessary time to go through the text of the Budget and to discuss the financial proposals among themselves. Budget is discussed in two stages—the 'General Discussion' followed by a detailed 'discussion and voting on the demands for grants'. Besides, opportunity for further discussion on financial proposals arises during consideration and passing of Appropriation Bill and the Finance Bill.[2]

(i) *General Discussion*: Discussion on the Budget starts from a general debate spread over three or four days in both the Houses of Parliament. Convention is that at this stage, members deal with only the general aspects of fiscal and economic policy of the government and do not go into details of taxation and expenditure. The general debate thus offers an occasion for each House to express its mood. The government may also get an idea as to how a particular proposal will be taken at the subsequent stages. It may be noted that the Rajya Sabha by virtue of its power, has no business with the Budget beyond the general discussion. Voting on demands is the exclusive preserve of the Lok Sabha.

(ii) *Discussion on Demands for Grants*: The next stage in the procedure is discussion and voting of demands for grants. Generally, separate demands are made for the grants proposed for each ministry. These 'demands' are related to the expenditure part of the Budget and are in the nature of request made by the Executive to the Lok Sabha for grant of authority to spend the amount asked for. Demands are required to be made in the form of a motion but in practice, they are assumed to have been moved and are proposed by the Chair to save the time of the House.

During the discussion on demands which is lively, the policy and the working of the ministry comes in for close scrutiny. Time is allotted to each ministry for discussing demands relating to that particular ministry. It is open to members to disapprove a policy pursued by the ministry or to suggest measures for economy in the administration or to focus attention of the ministry to specific local grievances. The members can do so by moving a subsidiary motion to the main motion for demands for grants. These subsidiary motions are called, in parliamentary parlance, 'Cut Motions'.[8] Three types of Cut Motions are familiar. The most drastic is the *Disapproval of Policy Cut* which says "that the amount of demand be reduced to Re.1". It implies that the mover disapproves of the policy underlying the demand. Then there is the *Economy Cut* which seeks to reduce the demand by a specific sum with a view to effect economy in the expenditure. The form of this motion is "that the amount of the demand be reduced to Rs. ..." (a specified sum). And lastly the *Token Cut* which says "that the amount of the demand be reduced by Rs. 100". The object of this motion, which is the most widely used form of Cut Motion, is to voice a particular grievance for which the Government of India is responsible.

For the sake of convenience, usually the main motion for demand and the Cut Motion relating to it are put and discussed together in the House. Cut Motion, thus is a device to initiate discussion on demands for grants. After discussion, first the cut motions are disposed of and thereafter, the demands for grants are put to vote of the House. Cut Motions have, in fact, only symbolic value, for they have no chance of being carried unless the government loses the support of the majority in the House. Cut Motions are generally moved by members from the opposition, and if carried, amount to a vote of censure against the government. In such event the government has to consider whether it should continue in office.

The Business Advisory Committee fixes a time limit for voting a particular demand and for all the demands for grants included in the Budget. As soon as the time limit for a demand is over, 'Closure' is applied and the demand is put to vote. Likewise, on the last day allotted for all the demands, demands not disposed of so far, are put to vote whether they have been discussed or not. This process is known as *Guillotine.* With this, the discussion on demands for grants is concluded.[10]

(iii) *Scrutiny by Departmentally Related Standing Committees:* Experience had shown that year after year demands for grants of only a few ministries—sometimes only two or three—got discussed on the floor of the House before the Guillotine was applied, and demands for grants of all other ministries and departments of the government were voted without any parliamentary scrutiny or debate. Now, the 17 departmentally related Standing Committees of Parliament are *inter alia* charged with the task of considering the demands for grants of the concerned ministries and departments, and report to the House before voting on the demands. From 1994-95 every year, after demands for grants are presented, both the Houses are adjourned for a period of about one month to enable the respective Standing Committees to examine and discuss them. The committees present reports on demands for grants.

(c) ***Appropriation Bill:*** Under the Constitution, no money can be withdrawn from the Consolidated Fund of India without enactment of law by the Parliament. In pursuance of this, a Bill incorporating all the demands for Grants voted by the Lok Sabha, along with the expenditures charged on the Consolidated Fund, is introduced in the Lok Sabha. This Bill is known as the Appropriation Bill. The Bill, as the name itself suggests, intends to give legal authority to the government to appropriate expenditure from and out of the Consolidated Fund.

Appropriation Bill is considered and passed in the same manner as any other Bill except that the debate is restricted to those matters only which were not covered during the debate on demands and that no amendments can be proposed.[11] After the Bill is passed by the Lok Sabha, The Speaker certifies it as a Money Bill and transmits it to the Rajya Sabha. The latter House has no power to amend or reject the Bill, but has to give its concurrence. The Bill, thereafter, is presented to the President for his assent.

(d) ***Finance Bill***: All the financial proposals of the Government for the following year are incorporated in a Bill known as the Finance Bill which is ordinarily introduced in the Lok Sabha every year immediately after the Budget is presented. It gives effect to the financial proposals of the government as also to supplementary financial proposals for any period.[12]

The motion for leave to introduce the Finance Bill cannot be opposed and it is forthwith put to vote.[13] Discussion on the Bill covers matters relating to general administration and local grievances within the sphere of responsibility of the Union Government.[14] While general criticism of the policy of the government is permitted, discussion on the details of particular estimates is not. In short, the whole administration comes under review but questions which have already been discussed cannot be reopened. This Bill has to be considered and passed by the Parliament and assented to by the President within 75 days after it is introduced.[15]

Vote on Account

In a democratic set-up, the government endeavours to provide the Parliament full opportunity to discuss the budgetary provisions and the tax proposals. The passage of the Budget beginning with its presentation and ending with discussion and voting of demands for grants and adopting Appropriation and Finance Bills, generally goes beyond the start of the current financial year. It is necessary that the government should keep enough finance with it to run the administration of the country, until the demands are voted by the Parliament. A special provision, therefore, has been made for what is called the Vote on Account, which empowers the Lok Sabha to make any grant in advance for a part of any financial year, pending the completion of the budgetary process.[16]

Normally, the vote on account is taken for two months for a sum equivalent to one-sixth of the estimated expenditure for the entire year under various demands for grants. During an election year, the vote on account may be taken for a longer period, say, three to four months, if it is anticipated that the main demands and the Appropriation Bill will take longer than two months to be passed by the House. As a convention, vote on account is treated as a formal matter and passed by the Lok Sabha without discussion. Vote on account is passed after the general discussion on the Budget is over and before the discussion on demands for grants is taken up. In the case of the Railway Budget which is passed before 31 March, no vote on account is taken except, if necessary, in an election year.

Supplementary and Excess Demands for Grants[17]

No expenditure in excess of the sums authorised by the Parliament can be incurred without its sanction. If the amount sanctioned for a particular service is found to be insufficient for the purposes of that year or when a need arises during the current financial year for supplementary or additional expenditure upon some 'new service' not contemplated in the Budget for that year, the President causes to be laid before both the Houses of Parliament another statement— Supplementary Demands for Grants—showing the estimated amount of that expenditure.

If any money has been spent on any service during a financial year in excess of the amount granted for that year, the President causes to be presented to the Lok Sabha a demand for such excess. All cases involving such excesses are brought to the notice of the Parliament by the Comptroller and Auditor General through his report on the Appropriation Accounts. The excesses are then examined by the Public Accounts Committee which makes recommendations regarding their regularisation in its report to the House.

The Supplementary Demands for Grants are presented to and passed by the House before the end of the financial year, while the demands for excess grants are made after the expenditure has actually been incurred and after the financial year to which it relates, has expired.

The discussion on the Supplementary Demands for Grants is confined to the items constituting the same and no discussion can be raised on the original grants nor on the policy underlying them.[18] In respect of schemes already sanctioned in the main Budget no discussion on any question of principle or policy is allowed. As regards demands for which no sanction has been obtained, the question of policy has to be confined to the items of expenditure on which the vote of the House is sought. General grievances cannot be ventilated during discussion on a supplementary grant. A member can only point out whether the supplementary demand is necessary or not.

During discussion on Excess Demands for Grants, members can point out how money has been spent unnecessarily or that it ought not to have been spent.

Beyond this, at this stage, there is no scope for general discussion or for ventilation of grievances.

Vote of Credit and Exceptional Grants[19]

On account of some national emergency, the government may require funds to meet an unexpected demand for money for which it may not be possible to give detailed estimates. In such a case, the House might grant lumpsum money without details through a Vote of Credit.

An Exceptional Grant is made for a particular and special purpose which does not form part of the ordinary expenditure of the financial year. In that case, the House may separately grant funds for that special purpose. However, no such demands have so far been presented to the Parliament.

Besides, the Budgets of Union Territories and States under President's Rule are also presented to the Lok Sabha. The procedure in regard to the Budget of the Union Government is followed in such cases with such variations or modifications, as the Speaker may make.[20]

REFERENCES

1. Arts 112, 113, 265 & Rule 204. The term Budget does not appear in the Constitution. It is the popular name for the 'Annual Financial Statement'.
2. Art. 226. Besides, there is a Contingency Fund also, placed at the disposal of the President to meet urgent and unforeseen expenditures pending authorisation by Parliament (Art. 267).

3. Art. 113
4. Art. 114 (1)
5. Rule 219
6. Rule 205
7. Rule 207
8. Rule 209
9. Rule 362
10. Rule 208
11. Rule 218
12. Rule 219 (1)
13. Rule 72 (Second Proviso)
14. Rule 219 (5)
15. Vide the Provisional Collection of Taxes (Amendment) Act, 1964.
16. Art. 116 (1) (a) & (b)
17. Art. 115
18. Rule 216.
19. Art. 116.
20. See Subhash C. Kashyap, 'A case for Budget Committees' *National Herald*, 16 November 1990;—'Budget and Parliament—need for Innovations', *Economic Times*, 3 March 1991; and for details *Parliamentary Procedure*, op.cit., Vol. 2, chapter 24, pp. 1418-1553.

10

THE LEGISLATIVE PROCESS

HOW LAWS ARE MADE

Law in essence, refers to the results or products of legislation which define the norms of conduct. It may prohibit or permit people to do certain things or may prescribe the manner in which the same ought to be done. Every law should have the sanction of the Parliament because the Parliament alone represents the general will of the people. In order to fulfil its obligations towards the people, it has to legislate on the matters which reflect their social and economic needs and seek to fulfil their hopes and aspirations.

Law-making is still deemed to be the predominant function of the Parliament even though today it is not the only function it performs nor is the Parliament the only actor in the drama of law-making. Now-a-days only a small portion of the time of the Legislature is devoted to the business of law-making and initiative in law-making lies mostly with the Executive.[1] In actual practice, the government makes legislative proposals and the Parliament, after discussion and debate, puts its seal of approval. It performs this function through a series of processes.

All legislative proposals are initiated in the Parliament in the form of Bills. A Bill is the draft of a legislative proposal. It can be initiated either by the government or by any private member in either House of Parliament. Bills, thus, broadly fall into two categories (a) Government Bills and (b) the Private Members' Bills. However, as things stand, most laws that find their way to the Statute Book are through the government Bills. Although the Private Members' Bills that become law are few and far between, they also serve a good purpose in as much as they bring to the attention of the government and the public the need to amend an existing law in the light of the changing conditions or to enact a needed piece of legislation.

The volume of legislation passed by the Parliament during the First to the Twelfth Lok Sabha period yearwise is given in Annexure 10.1 at the end of this chapter.

On the basis of their content, the Bills can further be classified into:

(i) Original Bills embodying new proposals, ideas and policies;
(ii) Amending Bills seeking to modify or amend existing Acts;
(iii) Consolidating Bills intending to consolidate the existing laws in an area;
(iv) Bills seeking to continue the expiring Acts;
(v) Bills to replace Ordinances issued by the President; and
(vi) The Constitution (Amendment) Bills.

Besides, the Bills can broadly be categorised as:

(i) Ordinary Bills
(ii) Money Bills based on their provisions regarding financial matters; and
(iii) Constitution Amendment Bills.

Ordinary Bills

All Bills which are not Constitution Amendment Bills and Money Bills, are Ordinary Bills, i.e. draft proposals for ordinary legislation.

Legislative Procedure Regarding Ordinary Bills

Drafting of Bills: As soon as a legislative proposal is conceived, the ministry concerned works out its political, administrative, financial and other implications. If other ministries or the State governments are also involved, their advice is obtained. The Ministry of Law and the Attorney General of India are consulted in respect of legal and constitutional aspects. Professionals and various interest groups such as business, labour, agriculture and industry, if considered necessary, are also consulted. After the proposal has been thoroughly examined from all points of view, it is submitted to the Cabinet for approval, when the Cabinet has approved the proposal, the government draftsman, assisted by departmental experts and officials, gives it the shape of a Bill. The Bill is, then, examined in detail by the administrative machinery in consultation with all other authorities concerned and given a final shape.

When this has been done, the Bill is ready to be brought before the House. It can be introduced in either of the two Houses by the minister concerned. For this, a minister is required to give seven days notice, to move for leave to introduce the Bill.[2] Simultaneously, two duly corrected copies of the Bill are sent to the Secretary-General of the House in which it is sought to be introduced. After the Bill has been found complete in all respects by the Secretariat, it is included in the List of Business on a date selected by the Speaker or the Chairman as the case may be. Normally, copies of the Bill are made available to the members at least two days before the date on which it is proposed to be introduced.[3]

The Three Readings: A Bill has to pass through different stages in the Parliament before it becomes an Act. Each Bill undergoes three readings in each House, i.e. First Reading, Second Reading, and Third Reading.

(i) *First Reading:* It is necessary to ask for leave of the House to introduce a Bill. After the Question Hour on the appointed day, the minister incharge of the Bill on being called upon by the Speaker, rises in his seat and says "Sir, I beg to move for leave to introduce the Bill...". Generally, the leave is granted by a voice vote and is opposed rarely. The Minister rises again to say "Sir, I introduce the Bill...".

Usually, the 'introduction' which is the 'first reading' of a Bill is only a formality and by convention there is no discussion at this stage. But, if introduction of a Bill is opposed on the ground that the proposed legislation is outside the legislative competence of the Parliament, the Chair may permit a full discussion in which the Attorney-General also may participate.[4] The question is put to vote of the House thereafter. There being no restriction on the number of Bills to be introduced on a particular day, a minister may introduce as many Bills as he wants.

After a Bill has been 'introduced' in the House, it is published in the Gazette of India.[5] Even before introduction, a Bill can be published in the Gazette with the permission of the Speaker/Chairman. In such a case, leave of the House to introduce the Bill is not necessary.[6] In other words, the Bill does not have to go through the introduction stage.

(iii) *Second Reading:* Second Reading forms the most elaborate and vital stage in the life of a Bill because it is at this stage that it receives detailed and minute examination. The second reading or the consideration stage consists of two steps which may be called as the First Stage and the Second Stage.

The First Stage: The first stage involves the general discussion on the Bill as a whole where only the principle underlying the Bill is discussed and not the details of the Bill.[7] At this stage, it is open to the House to refer the Bill either to a Select Committee of the House or to the Joint Committee of the two Houses or to circulate it to elicit opinion thereon or straightaway take it into consideration.[8]

Reference to Committee: A Bill may be referred to a Select Committee or a Joint Committee. The members of the Select Committee are drawn from among the members of the House where the Bill has originated. In the case of a

Joint Committee, members from Lok Sabha and Rajya Sabha, in such a case, will be 2:1. The Chairman of the Joint Committee is appointed by the Presiding Officer of the House in which the Bill was introduced.[9] These are *ad hoc* Committees which are appointed to consider particular Bills referred to them.

Bills may also now be referred by either House or its Presiding Officer to the new departmentally related Joint Standing Committees of the two Houses in accordance with the subject matter of each Bill.

The Committee considers the Bill clause by clause just as the House does. Amendments can be moved to various clauses by members of the Committee.[10] The Committee can also take evidence of experts, associations or public bodies who are interested in the measure.[11] Procedure for consideration of a Bill is the same as it is in the House.[12] After clauses, Schedules, etc. have been individually considered and adopted by the Committee, the Lok Sabha Secretariat prepares a report for presentation to the House(s)[13] which, in its turn, considers the Bill as reported by the Committee.

Eliciting Opinion: If a motion for circulation of the Bill for the purpose of eliciting opinion thereon is adopted, the Secretariat of the House circulates letters to all the State governments and Union territories asking them to publish the Bill in their Gazettes for inviting opinions of local bodies, associations, individuals or institutions concerned with the Bill. The period for eliciting opinion is generally specified in the motion for circulation of the Bill, but where no date has been specified, the State governments are asked to send opinions within three months of the adoption of the motion.[14] After the opinions have been received, these are laid on the Table of the House followed by a motion for reference of the Bill to a Select/Joint Committee.[15] It is not ordinarily permissible at this stage to move a motion for consideration of the Bill. The Bill again passes through the

Committee stage and the Bill as reported, is presented to the House

After the report of the Select or Joint Committee on a Bill has been presented to the House, the minister may make any one of these motions—that the Bill as reported, be taken into consideration or that the Bill, as reported, be committed to the same Committee or to a new Committee or that the Bill be circulated or recirculated, as the case may be, for the purpose of eliciting opinion or further opinion thereon.[16]

In case the minister prefers to move the motion that the Bill, as reported, be taken into consideration, a debate is allowed. The scope of the debate is confined to the Bill as reported by the Committee and the principle of the Bill is not open to discussion again, because the House, in effect, commits itself to the principle of the Bill when a motion to refer the Bill to a Committee is adopted.

The Second Stage: After the motion that the Bill or the Bill as reported by the Select/ Joint Committee, be taken into consideration has been adopted, the Bill is taken up for consideration clause by clause. Each clause is placed before the House separately for discussion. Immediately after a clause is placed before the House, amendments thereto can be moved subject to the conditions of admissibility.[17] The clause by clause consideration is often long and laborious as each clause is normally discussed separately and each amendment (except those withdrawn by the mover) is also be discussed, adopted or rejected by the House. Amendments, if accepted, become a part of the Bill.

(iv) *Third Reading:* When all the clauses and schedules, if any, of the Bill have been considered and voted upon by the House, the Minister can move that the Bill be passed.[18] At this stage, discussion is confined to arguments either in support of the Bill or for its rejection without referring the details thereto further than is absolutely necessary.[19] Only verbal, formal and consequential amendments are allowed to be moved at this stage.[20] Since the general principles of the Bill have already been agreed to and its details have also been examined, the third reading is seldom the occasion for a lengthy debate.

In passing an ordinary Bill, a simple majority of members present and voting is required. In a parliamentary system with the government enjoying majority support in the Lok Sabha, a government Bill, therefore, has got nearly full guarantee of easy passage.

Bill in the Other House: After the Bill has been passed by the originating House, it is transmitted to the other House for its concurrence with a message to that effect.[21] Here, again, it goes through all the three stages. The House which receives the Bill can take either of the following courses:[22]

(a) It may reject it altogether giving rise to a deadlock between the two Houses.

(b) It may pass the Bill as it is or with amendments. If it passes it as transmitted by the originating House, it goes to the President for his assent. If, on the contrary, it is passed with amendments, the Bill is returned to the first House. There the amended Bill is laid on the Table of the House. After two days, the minister concerned may move that the amendment(s) as proposed by the other House, be taken into consideration. If the House agrees to the amendments(s) proposed by the other House, the Bill is deemed to have been passed, as amended, by both the House. If, however, the originating House does not agree to the amendments proposed by the other House, the Bill is sent again to the latter to get its concurrence. If this House continues to insist on its amendments, the result is a deadlock.

(c) It may take no action on the Bill, i.e. keep it lying on its Table. In such a case, if more than six months elapse from the date it receives the Bill, a deadlock is deemed to have taken place.

Joint-sitting of the Two Houses: In case of a deadlock due to disagreement between the two Houses on a Bill, an extraordinary situation arises which is resolved by both the Houses sitting together. The Constitution empowers the President to summon a 'joint-sitting' of both the Houses for the purpose of deliberation and voting on the Bill; unless the Bill has already lapsed due to the dissolution of the Lok Sabha. Such a joint-sitting is presided over by the Speaker who is assisted by the Secretary-General, the Lok Sabha.[23] The joint-sitting is governed by the Rules of Procedure of the Lok Sabha.[24] At the joint-sitting, only such amendments can be proposed which become necessary due to the delay in the passage of the Bill. The decisions at such sittings are taken by the majority of the total number of members of both the Houses present and voting. Thus, Lok Sabha, due to its numerical superiority may have a decisive advantage. So far only three bills, the Dowry Prohibition Bill, 1961, the Banking Service Commission (Repeal) Bill, 1978, and the Prevention of Terrorism Bill 2002, have been passed at joint-sittings.

Assent to Bills: When a Bill has been passed by both the Houses either singly or at a joint-sitting, the Bill is presented to the President for his assent. If the President withholds his assent, there is an end to the Bill. But since the President is a constitutional head who must act on the advice of the Council of Ministers, he would normally not withhold assent against the advice of his ministers but he may seek information, clarification or even reconsideration of the advice and for this purpose send the Bill back to the government [Arts 74(2) and 78 (b)]. This is presumably what President Zail Singh did in case of the Postal Bill and President Venkataraman in case of a Bill *inter alia* seeking to give pension to members of Parliament after just one year's service.[25]

If the President gives his assent, the Bill becomes an Act from the date of his assent. Instead of refusing or giving his assent he may return the Bill with a message for reconsideration by the two Houses. If, however, the Houses pass the Bill a second time, with or without amendments, and the Bill is presented again to the President for his assent, he shall have no power to withhold his assent to the Bill.

Money Bills

The Constitution provides an elaborate definition of a Money Bill in Art. 110. According to this article, a Bill is deemed to be Money Bill if it contains only provisions dealing with all or any of the matters relating to:

(a) the imposition, abolition, remission, alteration of any tax;
(b) the regulation or borrowing of money by the government;
(c) the payment of moneys into or withdrawal of moneys from the Consolidated or the Contingency Funds of India;
(d) declaring a new item to be expenditure, charged on the Consolidated Fund; and
(e) any matter incidental to any of the matters specified in sub-clauses (a) to (f) of Art. 110(1).

But a Bill shall not be deemed to be a Money Bill by reason only if it provides for the demand or the payment of fees for licence or fees for service rendered or by reason that it provides for imposition, abolition and regulation, etc. of any tax by a local authority or body for local purposes. It may be remembered that in case any question arises whether a Bill is a Money Bill or not, the decision of the Speaker will be final.[26]

A Money Bill cannot be introduced in the Rajya Sabha.[27] It can be introduced in the Lok Sabha only on the recommendation of the President.[28] After a Money Bill has been passed by the Lok Sabha, it is passed on to the Rajya Sabha for its recommendations with a certificate by the Speaker that it is a Money Bill. The Rajya Sabha cannot reject a Money Bill nor can it amend it by virtue of its own powers. It must, within a period of 14 days from the date of receipt of the Bill, return the Bill to the Lok Sabha with its recommendations. The Lok Sabha may thereupon either accept or reject all or any of the recommendations of the Rajya Sabha. If the Lok Sabha accepts any of the recommendations of the Rajya Sabha, the Money Bill shall be deemed to have been passed by both the Houses with the amendments recommended by the Rajya Sabha and accepted by the Lok Sabha. If the Lok Sabha does not accept any of the recommendations of the Rajya Sabha, the Bill shall be deemed to have been passed by both the Houses in the form in which it was passed by the Lok Sabha (before the amendments recommended by the Rajya Sabha). Further, if a Money Bill passed and transmitted to the Rajya Sabha for its recommendation is not returned to the Lok Sabha within the said period of 14 days, it shall be deemed to have been passed by both the Houses at the expiration of 14 days. There is no chance of any disagreement between the two Houses in regard to Money Bills as in the case of an ordinary Bill, where the Rajya Sabha enjoys a co-equal power with the Lok Sabha. Hence, there is no provision of a joint-sitting in the case of a Money Bill. The approval of a Money Bill by the Rajya Sabha is, in effect, only formal and routine.

Financial Bills

The Constitution distinguishes Money Bills from the Financial Bills.[29] Generally speaking, a Financial Bill may be any Bill which relates to revenue or expenditure. These, besides providing for any of the matters specified in the Constitution for a Money Bill, also provide for other matters. Let us, for the sake of convenience, divide the Financial Bills into two categories:

Category A: Those Bills which make provisions for any of the matters specified in Art. 110 for the Money Bill but do not contain solely those matters, e.g. a Bill which contains a taxation clause, but does not deal solely with taxation.

Category B: Bills containing provisions involving expenditure from the Consolidated Fund.

Difference Between Money Bill and Financial Bill

The difference between a Money Bill and a Finance Bill, as provided in the Constitution, is merely technical. Accordingly, all Finance Bills are not Money Bills. Only those Finance Bills may be Money Bills which contain solely the matters specified under Art. 110 and which are, above all, certified by the Speaker to be Money Bills.

Besides, there is a slight procedural differences as far as the passage of Money Bills and Financial Bills through both the Houses is concerned. A Money Bill can be introduced only in the Lok Sabha on the recommendation of the President and the Rajya Sabha has no power to withhold its concurrence. A Financial Bill of category A, that is to say, any Bill which contains any of the matters specified for a Money Bill but does not exclusively deal with such matters, has two features in common with a Money Bill, viz., (a) that it cannot be introduced in the Rajya Sabha and also (b) that it cannot be introduced except on the recommendation of the President. But, if not being a Money Bill, the Rajya Sabha is fully empowered to reject or amend it as it does in the case of an ordinary Bill. Subject to the limitation that an amendment other than for reduction and abolition of tax cannot be moved in either House without the President's recommendations, such a Bill has to go through all the stages in the Rajya Sabha as an ordinary Bill and in case of a disagreement between the two Houses, the provision of joint-sitting is resorted to for resolving the deadlock. It may be repeated that the provision for joint-sitting is not applicable in the case of a Money Bill.

Further, a Financial Bill of Category B containing,

inter alia, a proposal or proposal which involves expenditure from the Consolidated Fund of India and also does not include any matter specified in Art. 110, is treated as an ordinary Bill and hence can be introduced in either House and the Rajya Sabha has full power either to reject or amend it. It does not require the recommendation of the President for its introduction. However, the recommendation of the President is essential for its consideration by either House. In other words, the President's recommendation is not a condition precedent to its introduction as in the case of the Money Bill and the Financial Bill of Category A, but in this case unless such recommendation has been received, neither House can pass the Bill. In all other respects, such a Bill is governed by the same procedure as an ordinary Bill, including the provision of a joint-sitting in case of disagreement between the two Houses.

Constitution (Amendment) Bills

The procedure for amendment of the Constitution of India has been laid down in Art. 368. The Constitution does not provide for a separate constituent body; the power to amend the constitution is vested in the Parliament. An amendment of the Constitution may be initiated by introduction of a Bill for the purpose in either House of Parliament. Such a Bill may be brought forward by the government or by a private member. Generally, Constitution (Amendment) Bills brought forward by ministers are introduced in the Lok Sabha. A Constitution (Amendment) Bill initiated by a private member, apart from being subject to the normal rules applicable to a private member's Bill, has also to be examined and recommended for introduction in the House by the Committee on Private Members' Bills and Resolutions.[30]

Articles of the Constitution have been classified into three categories for the purposes of amendment:

(a) articles amendable by simple majority;

(b) articles which require special majority for their amendment; and
(c) articles which require a special majority as well as ratification by the legislatures of not less than one-half of the States.

Amendment by Simple Majority: A bill seeking to amend the following provisions of the Constitution requires only simple majority and such Bill is not deemed to be a Constitution (Amendment) Bill under Art. 368 of the Constitution:
(a) admission or establishment of new States, formation of new States and alteration of areas, boundaries or names of existing ones (Art. 2, 3 & 4);
(b) creation or abolition of Legislative Councils in a State (Art.169);
(c) administration and control of Scheduled areas and Scheduled Tribes (para 7 of the Fifth Schedule), and
(d) administration of Tribal areas in the States of Assam, Meghalaya and Mizoram (para 21 of the Sixth Schedule).

A Bill providing for the formation of new States and for the alteration of areas, boundaries or names of existing States, can be introduced in either House of Parliament only on the recommendation of the President. Before he makes his recommendation, the President shall refer the Bill to the concerned States for eliciting their views within the period specified by him. He, however, is not bound by the Views so ascertained.[31]

The Parliament may pass a law to provide for the abolition or creation of a Legislative Council in a State, if the Legislative Assembly of the State passes a resolution to that effect by a majority of not less than two-thirds of the members of the Assembly present and voting.[32] The Parliament may approve or disapprove of such resolution or it may not take any action thereon.

Amendment by Special Majority: A Bill seeking to

amend any other part of the Constitution has to be passed by a special majority, i.e. a majority of the total membership of that House and by a majority of not less than two-thirds of the members of that House present and voting. Strictly speaking, the special majority is required only for voting at the third reading stage of the Bill but by way of abundant caution the requirement for special majority has been provided for in the Rules of the Houses in respect of all the effective stages of the Bill.[33]

Amendment by Special Majority and Ratification by States: A Bill seeking to amend the following provisions of the Constitution has to be passed by a special majority of both Houses of Parliament and has also to be ratified by the legislatures of not less than one-half of the States by resolutions to that effect passed by those Legislatures before such a Bill is presented to the President for assent.[34]

(a) the election of the President (Arts 54 & 55);
(b) the extent of the executive power of the Union and the States (Arts 73 &162);
(c) the Supreme Court and the High Courts (Art. 341, Chapter IV of Part V, and Chapter V of Part VI of the Constitution);
(d) distribution of legislative powers between the Union and the States (Chapter I of Part XI and the Seventh Schedule of the Constitution);
(e) representation of States in Parliament; or
(f) the procedure for amendment of the Constitution itself (Art. 368).

The Constitution does not provide for any time limit within which the States must signify their ratification of a Constitution (Amendment) Bill, referred to them for this purpose.

Private Members' Bills

In order to give opportunity to the people's representatives to express their views on various issues of public importance and persuade the government to formulate programmes and policies, parliamentary rules and procedures provide for initiation of legislation by private members also.

Discussion on Bills initiated by private members affords an opportunity to the House to come to grips with a problem and to discuss it in all its aspects. All shades of opinion of the House are made known to the government, it does not matter whether the Bill is finally passed or not. The purpose of focusing the attention of both the government and the public on the particular proposals contained in the Bill is attained. The government takes a policy decision on the subject of the Bill and presents its views before the House. The discussion helps the government to bring a comprehensive Government Bill on the Subject, if necessary.

Two-and-a-half hours are allotted on every alternate Friday during a session for transaction of business relating to Private Members' Resolutions.

So far as the stages of a Private Member's Bill in the House and the general procedure are concerned, there is no difference between the Government Bills and the Private Members' Bills. There are, however, some special procedural features concerning Private Members' Bills in respect of the period of notice for introduction, restriction on number of Bills which can be introduced in a session by a member, Bills seeking amendment to the Constitution, relative precedence for discussion, etc.

A member who wants to introduce a Bill has to give one month's notice unless the Speaker or the Chairman, as the case may be, allows introduction at a shorter notice. The notice is to be accompanied by a copy of the Bill and an explanatory Statement of Objects and Reasons. Where a Bill, if enacted, is likely to involve expenditure from public funds, a financial memorandum giving an estimate of the expenditure involved is appended to the Bill by the member. In case the Bill contains proposals for delegated legislation, a memorandum regarding delegated legislation is also appended to the Bill.[35]

All the Bills due for introduction on a particular day allotted to Private Members' Bills are included in the List of Private Members' Business for that day.[36]

In the Lok Sabha, however, bills seeking to amend the Constitution, apart from being subject to the normal rules applicable to Private Members' Bills, have also to be examined by a Committee of the House, namely, the Committee on Private Members' Bills and Resolutions[37] and only those Bills which have been recommended by the Committee are put down in the List of Business for introductions.

By convention, a motion for leave to introduce a Private Member's Bill is not opposed. If a motion is opposed, the Presiding Officer may permit brief statements by the member who opposed the motion and the member who moved the motion and thereafter put the motion for decision of the House. Where a motion for introduction is opposed on the ground that the Bill initiates legislation outside the legislative competence of the House, the Chair may permit a full discussion thereon and thereafter put the motion for the decision of the House. If the motion is adopted, the member in-charge of the Bill introduces the Bill. Ordinarily, a member can introduce four Bills in a session.

In the Lok Sabha, after a Bill has been introduced and before it is taken up for consideration in the House, the Committee on Private Members' Bills and Resolutions classifies the Bills according to their nature, urgency and importance into two categcries i.e., category 'A' and Category 'B'. The time for their discussion is also allocated by the Committee. Bills classified in category 'A' have precedence over Bills classified in category 'B' for the purpose of consideration in the House. In Lok Sabha, the relative precedence of Bills in a particular category is determined by ballot. The Bills are included in the List of Business in the order of priority determined by the ballot.[38] In other respects, the stages through which a Bill passes are the same as in the case of a Government Bill.

During the last 33 years, not a single Private Members' Bill has become law. The 14 Bills in this category that got to the Statute book in the first 18 years of the two Houses of Parliament (1952-1970) were:

i. The Muslim Wakfs Bill 1952 (Passed in 1954)
ii. The Indian Registration (Amendment) Bill 1955 (Passed in 1956)
iii. The Proceedings of Parliament (Protection of Publication) Bill 1956 (Passed in 1956)
iv. The Code of Criminal Procedure (Amendment) Bill 1953 (Passed in 1956)
v. The Women's and Children's Institutions (Licensing) Bill 1954 (Passed in 1956)
vi. The Code of Criminal Procedure (Amendment) Bill 1957 (Passed in 1960)
vii. The Salaries and Allowances of Members of Parliament (Amendment) Bill 1964 (Passed in 1964)
viii. The Hindu Marriage (Amendment) Bill 1963 (Passed in 1964)
ix. The Supreme Court (Enlargement of Criminal Appellate Jurisdiction) Bill 1968 (Passed in 1970)
x. The Ancient and Historical Monuments and Archaelogical Sites and Remains (Declaration of National Importance) Bill 1954 (Passed in 1956)
xi. The Hindu Marriage (Amendment) Bill 1956 (Passed in 1956)
xii. The Orphanages and other Charitable Homes (Supervision and Control) Bill 1960 (Passed in 1960)
xiii. The Marine Insurance Bill 1959 (Passed in 1963)
xiv. The Indian Penal Code (Amendement) Bill 1963 (Passed in 1969).

Of the above, the first nine were introduced in Lok Sabha and the other five in Rajya Sabha.

Subordinate Legislation

The complexities of modern civilisation and rapid industrialisation of necessity made the State to shift its emphasis from the concept of laissez-faire to that of social welfare. As a result, the State has become more and more an instrument of social and economic change. The legislation that a government has to undertake is so vast and varied that it must touch every aspect of human endeavour. Moreover, law-making is becoming increasingly complicated and technical, it is no longer a simple affair. In this situation, the Legislature has neither enough time to deliberate upon, discuss and approve all the necessary laws nor the requisite expertise to work them out in procedural and technical details. Though the Parliament normally meets for six to seven months in a year, a large volume of legislation always remains in arrears. It is, therefore, provided that the Legislature may delegate some of its power of legislation to subordinate agency. Consequently, the Legislature frames laws in general terms and leaves it to the government to make detailed rules and regulations within the limitations specified, and to carry out the objects of the legislation and to meet new situations not foreseen by the Legislature while enacting laws. Such rules and regulations made by a subordinate agency within the purview of the authority delegated by the Legislature, is called 'subordinate legislation'. It is sometimes described as 'delegated legislation' also.

In India, this power of delegation is a constituent element of the legislative power as a whole. The Legislature is not competent to delegate to the Executive or any other body its essential legislative functions namely, the determination of legislative policy and its formulation as a rule of conduct. It is permissible only when legislative policy and principle are adequately laid down and the delegate is only empowered to carry out the subsidiary policy within the guidelines laid down by the Legislature.

In other words, it can only utilise the other bodies or authorities to work out details within the essential principles laid down by it.

Subordinate legislation is sometimes denounced vehemently on the ground that it enables the administration to usurp the legislative powers of the Parliament and this leads to a 'new despotism' of civil servants who are not responsible to the Parliament or to the people directly. Such a blanket authority could obviously enable the bureaucracy to do anything it liked. On the other hand, today it is impossible to completely avoid subordinate legislation. What is most essential, therefore, is continuous parliamentary surveillance and control over the exercise of the power of subordinate legislation.

Certain safeguards have been provided against the possible abuse of this power. For example, it is laid down that a "Bill involving proposals for the delegation of legislative power shall further be accompanied by a memorandum explaining such proposals and drawing attention to their scope and stating also whether they are of normal or exceptional character.[39] It has been further provided that regulations, rules and bye-laws framed in pursuance of the legislative functions delegated by the Parliament to a subordinate agency, is laid before the House where amendments may also be moved. Thus Parliament exercises scrutiny and control by asserting itself at these stages. Besides, all such rules and regulations are subject to examination by Courts on the plea of utra vires to the provisions of the Constitution. Above all, there is a 'Committee on Subordinate Legislation' in each House of the Parliament consisting of its members to see and report to either House whether powers delegated by Parliament have been properly exercised within the statute delegating such powers. It is the Committee on Subordinate Legislation which, in fact, appropriately guards against the possible assumption of arbitrary powers by the administration. It has all along endeavoured to see that all rules and regulations so framed, are not only laid before the Parliament without delay but Parliament has also the statutory right of annulling and modifying them.[40]

REFERENCES

1. See Chapter 3
2. Dir. 19 A
3. Dir. 19 B
4. Rule 72
5. Rule 73
6. Rule 64
7. Rule 75
8. Rule 74
9. Rule 258
10. Dir. 77
11. Rule 302
12. Rule 300 (2)
13. Dir. 68
14. Dirs 20 (1) & (3) and 21
15. Dirs 24 and 26
16. Rule 77
17. Rules 79 & 80
18. Rule 93 (1)
19. Rule 94
20. Rule 93 (3)
21. Rule 96 (1)
22. Art. 108 (1)
23. Art. 118 (4) and the Houses of Parliament (Joint-Sitting and Communications) Rules, Rule 2
24. *Ibid.*, Rule 7
25. Art. 111 and Rule 128. See Subhash C. Kashyap, 'M.P.s and their Pensions', *Hindustan Times*, 5 April 1991,—'Return the Pension Bill', *Financial Express*, 7 April 1991;—'Return of the M.P.s' Pension Bills', *Hindustan Times*, 2 April 1992.
26. Art. 110
27. Art. 109
28. Art. 117 (1)
29. Art. 117
30. Rule 294
31. Art. 3
32. Art. 169

33. Rules 157, 158 & 159
34. Art. 368 (2)
35. Rules 65, 69 and 70
36. Rule 27 (1)
37. In Rajya Sabha, there is no Committee on Private Members' Bills and Resolutions.
38. Dirs 3 & 7
39. Rule 70
40. For further analysis and precedents, see Subhash C. Kashyap, *Parliamentary Procedure,* op.cit., Vol. 1, Chapter 15, pp. 817-1103.

Annexure 10.1

Volume of Legislation from the First to the Twelfth Lok Sabha (1952-1999)

Year	Number of Acts Passed	Year	Number of Acts Passed
1952	82	1976	118
1953	58	1977	48
1954	54	1978	50
1955	60	1979	32
1956	106	1980	72
1957	68	1981	62
1958	59	1982	73
1959	63	1983	49
1960	67	1984	73
1961	63	1985	92
1962	68	1986	71
1963	58	1987	61
1964	56	1988	71
1965	51	1989	38
1966	57	1990	30
1967	38	1991	63*
1968	67	1992	44
1969	58	1993	75
1970	53	1994	61
1971	87	1995	45
1972	82	1996	36
1973	70	1997	35
1974	68	1998	29
1975	57	1999	27

* excluding the Salary, Allowances and Pension of Members of Parliament (Amendment) Bill 1991 which did not get President's assent.

11

PARLIAMENTARY COMMITTEES

STRUCTURE, FUNCTIONS AND IMPACT

In a parliamentary system, the Legislature has to lay down governmental policies, make laws and oversee administration. But the enormous range and complexity of legislation and administrative functions of a modern State make it almost impossible for the Legislature to adequately scrutinise legislative proposals and oversee administrative action. While the government has vast and highly sophisticated administrative machinery and organisation manned by experts, specialists and seasoned civil servants at its disposal to undertake its complex tasks, the Legislature finds itself severely handicapped in this regard. Through the parliamentary devices like questions and debates it is not able to exercise more than a sporadic supervision of administration. In order to make parliamentary surveillance more effective and meaningful, the Parliament needs an agency of its own in which the whole House has confidence. This, among other things, the Parliament seeks to achieve through Parliamentary Committees composed of a small number of their members. This is specially so in India.

The review of administrative action and the examination of numerous and complicated legislative proposals and subordinate legislation require expertise and close scrutiny that are not possible in the Lok Sabha consisting as it does of 545 members. *Second,* the work load is enormous. It does not have the time to undertake detailed investigations or even to discuss every matter at length. The Committees while ensuring a fuller and more comprehensive examination of technical and other matters, result in saving the time of the House for discussion of important matters and prevent the Parliament from getting lost in details and thereby losing hold on matters of policy and broad principles. *Third*, matters dealt with by Committees are often such as need to be considered in greater depth, with care and expedition, away from the glare of publicity, in a calmer and, so far as possible, non-partisan atmosphere. Accommodating different views and effecting compromises through give-and-take are accomplished more easily in committee atmosphere than in the House itself where, by and large, members operate on the basis of party loyalties and are naturally concerned with building a public image. *Fourth*, since there is not much difference in the actual composition of the two Chambers in the Indian Parliament, the Rajya Sabha has become almost a parallel Chamber. Even if this were not so, the Rajya Sabha could hardy be considered to be the traditional "cooling" or revising Chamber, or the house of elders or experts, guarding against hasty or faulty legislation. Under the circumstances, the Select Committees and the Joint Committees on Bills may *inter alia* perform the role of the traditional Second Chamber. *Fifth*, in a party system like that in the Indian Parliament with one very large party and several small groups, some of the Committees perform functions that would otherwise belong to the Opposition in that they keep the Executive on its toes and prevent its becoming arbitrary. The Opposition members also, despite their actual strength, find it easier to make their impact felt much more in the Committees than on the floor of the House. Moreover, in Committees the government may willingly concede a point or two and accept constructive suggestions from Opposition members. While all sections of the House are generally represented in the Committees, the proceedings in the latter are less formal and the procedure is more flexible than in the former. This also leads to a more comprehensive and judicious consideration of the issues entrusted to the Committees. *Last,* Committees provide useful forums for the utilisation of experience and ability that may otherwise remain untapped. They also constitute a valuable training ground for future ministers and presiding officers. They train a large number of members not only in the ways in which administration is carried on, but also make them aware of the problems that the administrators have to face in their day-to-day functioning.[1]

An important aspect of our committee system is that the Committees act as a liaison between the Parliament and the people on the one hand and between the government and the people on the other. They enable the general public, institutions and in some cases even individual citizens to participate more directly and effectively in the consideration by the Parliament of issues directly affecting the people. This kind of public participation in the work of Parliament is made possible by the Committees inviting written memoranda and representations from experts and bodies, organisations or interests affected by the measures under consideration of the Committees, hearing oral evidence from the representatives of the parties concerned and undertaking study tours for on-the-spot study of the issue under their consideration. This procedure helps in educating the public in the functioning of the parliamentary system and focusing their attention on important public issues.

The Constitution of India does not make any specific provision in regard to Parliamentary Committees, but these are mentioned in several articles.[2] It is obvious that the framers of the Constitution took Parliamentary Committees for granted and left it to the House to make provisions for them under their Rules Procedure. Under the Rules of the Lok Sabha, not every Committee consisting of members of Parliament is a Parliamentary Committee *suo motu.* A

Parliamentary Committee may be defined as one that:

(a) is appointed or elected by the House or nominated by the Speaker/Chairman;
(b) works under the direction of the Speaker/Chairman;
(c) presents its report to the House or to the Speaker/Chairman; and
(d) has a Secretariat provided by the Lok Sabha/Rajya Sabha Secretariat.

There are other Committees which may consist of members of Parliament or may include members of Parliament, but they are not Parliamentary Committees because they do not fulfil the aforesaid conditions. For example, Consultative Committees attached to various ministries and departments consist entirely of members of Parliament but they are neither appointed by the Speaker/Chairman nor elected by the House(s); staff for them is not provided by the Secretariat of the House(s) and they do not report to the Speaker/Chairman. In fact, Consultative Committees do not report to anybody, but merely provide a forum for informal exchange of views between the ministers and members of Parliament interested in their departments. As such, they are not Parliamentary Committees.[3]

In all, there are 45 Standing Committees of the two Houses of Parliament. Of these, 24 are joint standing committees of the two Houses. Besides, there are 21 single House Standing Committees—9 of the Rajya Sabha and 12 of the Lok Sabha. Of the 17 Departmentally related Standing Joint Committees, 11 are serviced by the Lok Sabha Secretariat and 6 by the Rajya Sabha Secretariat. The latest joint standing committee is the Women's Empowerment Committee.

So far as the 21 single House Committees are concerned, their functions in the two Houses are generally similar. During the Twelfth Lok Sabha period, two new ad hoc Committees of the two Houses were constituted, viz.

(1) Members of Parliament Local Area Development Scheme Committee, and (2) Joint Select Committee on the Essential Commodities (Amendment) Bill.

Types of Committees

There are two types of Parliamentary Committees in India, viz. (1) Standing Committees and (2) ad hoc Committees. Standing Committees are those which are elected by the House or nominated by the Speaker/Chairman every year or from time to time, as the case may be, and are permanent in nature, whereas ad hoc Committees are those constituted by the House or by the Speaker/Chairman, to consider and report on specific matters and become functus officio as soon as they have completed their work on these matters.

Standing Committees: Standing Committees in each House (and certain Joint Committees) may be categorised in terms of the nature of their functions as follows:

(i) Financial Committees (e.g. Committee on Estimates of the Lok Sabha, Committee on Public Accounts and Committee on Public Undertakings);

(ii) Departmentally related Standing Joint Committees of the two Houses;

(iii) House Committees, i.e. Committees relating to the day-to-day business of the House (e.g. Committee on Absence of Members from Sittings of the House, Business Advisory Committee, Committee on Private Members' Bills and Resolutions and Rules Committee);

(iv) Enquiry Committees (e.g. Committee on Petitions and Committee on Privileges);

(v) Scrutiny Committees (e.g Committee on Government Assurances, Committee on Subordinate Legislation, Committee on Papers Laid on the Table and Committee on the Welfare of Scheduled Castes and Scheduled Tribes);

(vi) Service Committees, i.e. Committees concerned with the provision of various services and facilities to members (e.g. General Purposes Committee, House Committee,

Library Committee and Joint Committee on Salaries and Allowances of Members of Parliament).

Ad hoc Committees: Such Committees may be broadly put into two categories:

(a) The Select or Joint Committees on Bills which are appointed to consider and report on particular Bills. These Committees are distinguished from the other ad hoc Committees inasmuch as they are concerned with Bills and the procedure to be followed by them is laid down in the Rules of Procedure and Directions by the Speaker/Chairman.

(b) Committees which are constituted from time to time either by the two Houses on a motion adopted in that behalf, or by the Speaker/Chairman to inquire into a report on a specific subject. For example, a Committee was constituted in 1951 to go into the conduct of a member Shri H.G. Mudgal, on a motion adopted by the Lok Sabha. Railway Convention Committee is appointed from time to time, Joint Committee on Offices of Profit and any other Committee appointed by the House or by the Speaker or Chairman for some specific purpose, are also other examples of such Committees. More recently, important Joint Committees of the two Houses have been constituted on matters like the salary, allowances and pension for members, the Bofors Gun Deal and the Bank Securities Scam.

Constitution of Committees

The members of Parliamentary Committees are *appointed* or *elected* by the House on a motion, or *nominated* by the Speaker or Chairman, as the case may be.[4] Select or Joint Committees on a Bill are appointed on a motion adopted by the House. Members of all Financial Committees (Public Accounts Committee, Estimates Committee, Committee on Public Undertakings), the Committee on Welfare of Scheduled Castes and Scheduled Tribes and the Joint

Committee on Offices of Profit are elected every year by members, according to the system of proportional representation by means of single transferable vote. Rest of the Committees are nominated by the Presiding Officer of the House concerned.

While some of the Committees are constituted by each House separately, others are constituted jointly by both the Houses. As in the case of Joint Committees, members of the Committee on Public Accounts, Committee on Public Undertakings, Committee on the Welfare of Scheduled Castes and Scheduled Tribes and the Committee on Government Assurances, are drawn from both Lok Sabha and Rajya Sabha.

As far as possible, different parties and groups are represented on Parliamentary Committees in proportion to their respective strengths in the House(s). Usually the Committees are reconstituted every year on the basis of names of members suggested by leaders of parties/groups for consideration of, and selection by, the Presiding Officers.

The Chairman of a Parliamentary Committee is appointed from amongst the members of the Committee by the Presiding Officer of the House to which it belongs. If the Presiding Officer himself is a member of the Committee, he is invariably its Chairman. Where he is not a member, but his Deputy is, then the latter is appointed the Chairman.

Terms of Committees

A Parliamentary Committee holds office for a period not exceeding one year or for a period specified by the Speaker or until a new Committee is nominated. The Business Advisory Committee, Committee on Petitions, Committee on Privileges and the Rules Committee continue in office till re-constituted whereas other Standing Committees hold office for a period not exceeding one year. If no term is specified by the Speaker/Chairman in regard to an ad hoc

Committee, it continues in office till the completion of work and presentation of report, if any.[5]

Committee Procedure

Committees hold their meetings in the Parliament House or in the Parliament House Annexe, but in special cases with the permission of the Speaker/Chairman, meetings may be held outside also. A Committee has the power to take oral or written evidence. It may send for persons, papers and records provided that if any question arises whether the evidence of a person or the production of a document is relevant for the purposes of the Committee, the question is referred to the Speaker whose decision is final. Sub-committees may also be appointed by the main Committee to examine matters referred to them. The report of the Sub-committee is submitted to the main Committee.[6]

The sittings of a Committee are held in camera. There are no public hearings. The proceedings in Committees are largely conducted in the same manner as in the House but in a more intimate and informal atmosphere and on non-party lines. When a Committee is deliberating, a member can speak more than once on a question under the consideration. All questions are determined by a majority of votes of the members present and voting. In case of an equal division of votes on any matter, the Chairman has a second or casting vote. The Committee drafts a report thereafter, on the basis of the minutes of the sittings of the Committee containing the substance of deliberations of the Committee together with the recommendations. Reports may be either preliminary or final. It may make a special report on any matter that comes to light in the course of its work which it may consider necessary to bring to the notice of the Speaker or the House, even if such matter does not fall within the terms of reference.[7]

The report of a Committee is presented to the House by the Chairman of the Committee or any member of the

Committee so authorised. Until a report is presented to the House, it is treated as confidential; it becomes a public document only after its presentation to the House.[8]

(i) Financial Committees

It is the responsibility of the Parliament to examine and approve the proposals for taxation and estimates of expenditure made by the government. Although nearly two months of the 'Budget Session' are devoted for this purpose, discussions are neither very extensive nor intensive. In its anxiety to cover the whole field, the observations and criticism by the Parliament have tended to be general, repetitive and formal. As the time available is short, often demands relating to a number of ministries/departments are not discussed at all and the 'guillotine' is applied. It is here that the Financial Committees of Parliament endeavour to undertake the task of detailed scrutiny of governmental spending and performance, thereby securing the accountability of the administration to the Parliament in financial matters.

Implementation of a policy is more important than mere formulation. The former if not carried out properly may defeat the very purpose of the policy. The policy may fail to achieve the desired goals either because of inefficiency or due to lack of proper organisation of the machinery available to implement it. It is always, therefore, necessary to have a body which should examine the policy in action and bring the governmental organisation, their procedures and practices under scrutiny. Their very performance has to be assessed with reference to their efficiency and economy for both are interdependent. Further, no administrative system can perhaps be 100 per cent free from problems like misuse of power, negligence, delay, indifference, nepotism, etc. It is not possible to arrive at facts in regard to these aspects of administration without research based study, methodical enquiry and thorough examination of the officials of the ministry or undertaking concerned.

The Financial Committees are said to play a very important role as the watch dogs of the Parliament. They are unique because whereas accountability of the administration to the Parliament is not direct and is exercised through ministers, in the Committees, the civil servants come face to face with the Committees. Thus the control exercised by these Committees is continuous, thorough and direct, employing all the means of scrutiny by way of issuance of questionnaires, calling of memoranda from representative non-official organisations and knowledgeable individuals, on-the-spot study of organisations and informal discussions and oral evidence of non-officials and officials.

The three Financial Committees bring to light inefficiencies, waste and indiscretion in the implementation of policies and programmes approved by the Parliament. Their recommendations are intended to tone up the administration for economic, efficient and speedy execution of these policies and programmes. The relentless crusade of the Financial Committees to this end keeps the administration on its toes. Reports of these Committees have earned for them considerable respect from all sections of the society—both official and non-official. A measure of the regard in which these Committees are held by the government can be understood from the fact that a very high percentage of their recommendations are accepted by the government. Each recommendation is carefully analysed and processed and the administration always endeavours to esche and avoid the faults and lapses pointed out by the Committees and to regulate its conduct in accordance with the recommendations made by the Committees.

The Financial Committees have developed adequate procedures to ensure that their recommendations ar. given due consideration by the government and where they are not accepted, the Committees are apprised of the reasons. The progress in the implementation of the recommendations as well as any unresolved differences between the Committees and the government are brought to the notice of the House by way of 'Action Taken Reports'. The elaborate and effective procedure for follow-up of the recommendations made by these Committees is essentially an Indian innovation to the parliamentary procedures prevalent elsewhere.

All the three Financial Committees are elected by the House for one year. Ministers can neither become members of these Committees, nor can they be asked to appear before them for the purpose of giving evidence. Their Chairmen are nominated by the Speaker. They can frame their own internal Rules of Procedure subject to the approval of the Speaker. They normally do not go into questions of policy in pursuance of the fact that policy formulation is the exclusive privilege of the Parliament and a Committee is not supposed to sit in judgement on a policy already approved by the Parliament. Another noticeable common feature of all the three Financial Committees is that they examine the administration *ex post facto.* In order to avoid possible interference in day-to-day administration, the Committees examine only those acts which have already been done or not done which otherwise ought to have been done.

The recommendations of the Committees have neither the power to direct the government nor do they have any binding force—that is the reason why the findings of the Committees are in the form of recommendations only. But by virtue of their constitution and authority behind them, no minister or official can disregard or ignore them.

The Estimates Committee: The Estimates Committee consists of 30 members of the Lok Sabha.[9] Unlike the Public Accounts Committee and the Committee on Public Undertakings, the members of the Rajya Sabha are not associated with it. The Committee acts as the 'continuous economy committee' and its criticisms and suggestions act as a deterrent on extravagance in public expenditure. It makes a detailed examination of the annual budget estimates in order to:

(a) report what economics, improvements in organisation, efficiency or administrative reform, consistent with the policy underlying the estimates, may be effected;
(b) suggest alternative policies in order to bring about efficiency and economy in administration;
(c) examine whether the money is well-laid-out within the limits of the policy implied in the estimates; and
(d) suggest the form in which the estimates shall be presented to the Parliament.[10]

To elucidate, we may recall that matters of policy approved by the Parliament cannot be questioned by the Committees. The position of the Estimates Committee is slightly different from the other two Financial Committees in this regard. In this case a distinction has been drawn between "policy laid down by Parliament by means of statute or by specific resolutions" and all other policies not so laid down. In the latter case, the Committee considers itself free to examine any matter which may have been settled as policy by the government in the discharge of its executive duties. The Committee can examine the working of the policy and not the policy as approved by the Parliament. Thus, where it is found that a particular policy is not going in the desired direction and will lead to waste, it is considered the duty of the Estimates Committee to point out the defects and bring to the notice of the Parliament, the need for change in policy.

The Public Accounts Committee: The Public Accounts Committee, popularly known as PAC, is the oldest Financial Committee. It consists of 22 members (15 from the Lok Sabha and 7 from the Rajya Sabha). As a matter of practice, since 1967, a member of Opposition is being appointed as the Chairman of the Committee.[11]

The Public Accounts Committee is sometimes described as the 'twin-sister' of the Estimates Committee in the sense that the works of these two Committee are complementary. While the Estimates Committee deals with the estimates of public expenditure, the Public Accounts Committee examines mainly the accounts showing the appropriation of sums granted by the House for the expenditure of the Government of India in order to ascertain whether the money has been spent as authorised by the Parliament and for the purpose for which it was granted. If any money has been spent on any service during a financial year in excess of the amount granted by the House for that purpose, the Committee examines the circumstances leading to such excess, and makes such recommendations as it may deem fit. Such excesses are required to be brought up before the House by government for regularisation.[12]

The Committee is interested not merely in discovering technical irregularities but also in bringing out any evidence of waste, corruption, inefficiency or operational deficiency in the conduct of the nation's financial affairs. It might also record its opinion in the form of disapproval or pass strictures against the extravagance or lack of proper control by the ministry/department concerned.

The basic material from which the Committee draws its subjects for examination are the audit reports of the Comptroller and Auditor General of India relating to the accounts of the Union which are laid before each House of the Parliament. The Committee is assisted by the Comptroller and Auditor-General of India who participates in its meetings.[13]

The Committee functions under two broad limitations—one, that it is not concerned with the question of policy and two, its findings are ex post facto. In other words, the Committee can point out irregularities only after they have taken place and the damage has been done. However, the investigations of the Committee are taken very seriously by officials. The very fact of the existence of such a Committee has a deterrent effect on a possible administrative waste and extravagance. The recommendations of the Committee, by pointing out administrative lacunae in policy implementation, have led to valuable improvements in the financial machinery.

The Committees on Public Undertakings: The planned economic development which the country opted for, necessitated setting up of numerous enterprises—industrial, agricultural, commercial, etc., controlled and managed by the Government of India. Several corporations and government companies, commonly called 'public undertakings', involving large sums of money, have thus come into existence. Since the money invested in them are appropriated from the Consolidated Fund of India, it becomes the responsibility of the Lok Sabha to have adequate control over their affairs. For this purpose a Committee on Public Undertakings consisting 22 members—15 elected from the Lok Sabha and 7 from the Rajya Sabha—has been constituted by Parliament. The Chairman of the Committee is appointed by the Speaker from among the members of the Committee drawn from the Lok Sabha.

The functions of the Committee are to examine the reports and accounts of the public undertakings specified in the Rules of Procedure and the reports of the Comptroller and Auditor-General thereon, if any, and to examine, in the context of the autonomy and efficiency of the public undertakings, whether the affairs of the public undertakings are being managed in accordance with sound business principles and prudent commercial practices. The Committee may also examine such subjects or matters which may be specifically referred to it by the House or by the Speaker. The Committee is, however, barred from examining and investigating matters of major government policy as distinct from business or commercial functions of public undertakings or matters of day-to-day administration or matters for the consideration of which machinery is established by any special statute under which the particular undertaking is established.[14]

The examination by the Committee is generally in the nature of an evaluation of the undertaking covering all aspects like production, contribution to general economy, generation of employment, development of ancillaries, safeguarding of consumer interests, etc. The Committee, in the past, has undertaken horizontal studies covering various aspects like project planning, management in all its spheres, control systems, foreign collaboration and their role and achievement, etc. The studies have brought to the notice of the Parliament and the public heavy expenditure incurred by the undertakings on township and office buildings, guest houses, entertainment and on foreign tours undertaken by the officials.

(ii) Departmental Committees

The Rules Committee of the Lok Sabha in 1989 approved the proposal of setting up three subject-based/departmentally related Standing Committees to cover the area of Agriculture, Environment and Forests, and Science and Technology. The three committees were first set up with effect from 18 August, 1989. During the Ninth Lok Sabha period (1989-91) the Rules Committee recommended a full-fledged system of Standing Subject Committees to ensure parliamentary oversight over the entire gamut of administration. In addition to the three Committees set up earlier, seven more committees were proposed. During the Tenth Lok Sabha period, the three subject committees set up in 1989 grew into a full-fledged system of 17 departmentally related Standing Committees covering amongst them all the ministries and departments of the Government of India. Their functions include:

(i) to consider the demands for grants of respective ministries/departments,
(ii) to examine Bills referred by the Chairman, Rajya Sabha/Speaker, Lok Sabha,
(iii) to consider annual reports of ministries, and
(iv) to consider any policy documents referred by the Chairman/Speaker.

Departmental Committees and their areas of responsibility are as follows:

Departmental Standing Committees

S.No.	Name of the Committee	Ministries/Departments
1.	Committee on Commerce	(1) Commerce (2) Textiles
2.	Committee on Home Affairs	(1) Home Affairs (2) Law, Justice and Company Affairs (3) Personnel, Public Grievances and Pensions
3.	Committee on Human Resource Development	(1) Human Resource Development (2) Health and Family Welfare
4.	Committee on Industry	(1) Industry (2) Steel (3) Mines
5.	Committee on Science and Technology, Environment and Forests	(1) Science and Technology (2) Electronics (3) Space (4) Ocean Development (5) Biotechnology (6) Environment and Forests
6.	Committee on Transport and Tourism	(1) Civil Aviation (2) Surface Transport (3) Tourism
7.	Committee on Agriculture	(1) Agriculture (2) Water Resources (3) Food Processing

8.	Committee on Communications	(1) Information and Broadcasting (2) Communications
9.	Committee on Defence	Defence
10.	Committee on Energy	(1) Coal (2) Non-Conventional Energy (3) Power (4) Atomic Energy
11.	Committee on External Affairs	External Affairs
12.	Committee on Finance	(1) Finance (2) Planning (3) Programme Implementation
13.	Committee on Food, Civil Supplies and Public Distribution	(1) Food (2) Civil Supplies, Consumer Affair and Public Distribution
14.	Committee on Labour and Welfare	(1) Labour (2) Welfare
15.	Committee on Petroleum and Chemicals (3)Fertilisers	(1) Petroleum and Natural Gas (2) Chemicals and Petrochemicals
16.	Committee on Railways	Railways
17.	Committee on Urban and Rural Development	(1) Urban Development (2) Rural Development

(iii) House Committees

Business Advisory Committee: In each House, there is a Business Advisory Committee. In the Lok Sabha, the Committee consists of 15 members including the Speaker who is the ex officio Chairman of the Committee. In the Rajya Sabha it consists of 11 members, including the Deputy Chairman. The Chairman of the Rajya Sabha is the *ex-officio* Chairman of the Committee. The Speaker/Chairman, nominates the Committee which continues in office till reconstituted.

The function of the Committee is to recommend the

time that should be allocated for the transaction of such legislative and other business as initiated by the government. In the Rajya Sabha, however, the Committee also recommends the time that should be allocated for the discussion of Private Members' Bills and Resolutions. The Committee discharges such other functions as may be assigned to it by the Speaker/Chairman, Rajya Sabha, as the case may be, from time to time. The Committee, on its own initiative, may recommend to the government to bring forward any particular subject for discussion in the House and recommend allocation of time for such discussion.

The role the Committee plays in assisting the House in allocating time for various types of business has always been of considerable significance. At the sittings of the Committee, the atmosphere is cordial and the spirit of give and take between the government and the Opposition has been very prominent. Though all shades of opinion in the House are generally represented on the Committee, the decisions have all along been unanimous in character and have generally been agreed to by the whole House.

Committee on Private Members' Bills and Resolutions: This Committee of Lok Sabha consists of 15 members with the Deputy Speaker as its Chairman. The functions of the Committee are to allot time to Private Members' Bills and Resolutions, to examine Private Members' Bills where the legislative competence of the House is challenged. The Committee thus performs the same function in relation to Private Members' Bills and Resolutions as the Business Advisory Committee does in regard to government business. There is no such Committee in the Rajya Sabha.

Committee on Absence of Members from the Sittings of the House: The Constitution provides that if a member of either House keeps himself absent from all meetings of the House for a period of 60 days without permission, the House may declare his seat vacant. To facilitate matters, the Lok Sabha constituted a Committee consisting of 15 members, to consider requests from members seeking leave of absence from the House. In the Rajya Sabha such matters are considered by the House itself.

The functions of the Committee are (i) to consider matters of procedure and conduct of business in the House; and (ii) to recommend any amendments or additions to the Rules that may be deemed necessary. Suggestions for amendments or additions to the Rules can be made by any member of the House, minister or the Committee itself.

(iv) Enquiry Committees

Committee on Petitions: In a parliamentary democracy like ours, it is the inherent right of the people to present petitions to the Parliament with a view to ventilating grievances and seeking redressal thereof and offering constructive suggestions on matters of public importance. This right is exercised through the mechanism of a Committee on Petitions.

Each House of Parliament has a Committee on Petitions. In the Lok Sabha, the Committee consists of 15 members, while in the Rajya Sabha, it has 10 members. The function of the Committee on Petitions is to examine every petition which, after presentation to the House, stands referred to the Committee. The Committee reports to the House on specific complaints made in the petitions after taking such evidence as it deems fit. The Committee suggests remedial measures, either on the specific case under review or in a general way to prevent such cases in future.

The Committee also considers representations, including letters and telegrams received from various individuals and associations which are not covered by the rules relating to petitions, and gives directions for their proper disposal. This Committee has already made its mark in affording parliamentary support to the common man in the matter of redressal of his just grievances. It has proved to be a real boon to those wronged and oppressed citizens for whom no remedy or relief is available elsewhere. The Committee, thus, acts as an Ombudsman or Public Grievances Committee.

Committee on Privileges: Each House of Parliament and its committees collectively and its members individually enjoy certain privileges which entitle them to some rights and immunities without which the House, its committees and its members cannot discharge their functions effectively and smoothly. Whenever a question of breach of privilege arises, even though the House is competent to deal with it, it is generally referred to the Committee of Privileges existing in either House for examination, investigation and report.

The Committee of Privileges is constituted usually every year by the Presiding Officers of the respective Houses. In the Lok Sabha, it consists of 15 members while in the Rajya Sabha, it has 10 members.

The functions of this Committee are of a semi-judicial nature and it is vested with wide powers. Although its findings are subject to the ultimate decision of the House, it enjoys the latter's confidence and its recommendations are seldom rejected. The Committee performs a vital role in safeguarding the powers and prestige of the Parliament and its members.

(v) Scrutiny Committees

Committee on Government Assurances: While replying to questions in the House or during discussions on Bills, Resolutions, etc. ministers often give an assurance, promise or undertaking, either to consider a matter or to take action or to furnish the House with fuller information later. In order to watch the implementation of such assurances each of the Houses of Parliament has constituted a Committee on Government Assurances. While the Committee of the Lok Sabha consists of 15 members, the Committee of the Rajya Sabha has 10 members.

The functions of the Committee are to scrutinise the assurances so given by ministers on the Floor of the House and to report to the House, the extent to which such assurances have been implemented and, where implemented, whether such implementation has taken place within the minimum time necessary for the purpose.

Committee on Subordinate Legislation: The Parliament seeks to have a close vigil and check over the way the legislative powers delegated to a subordinate agency or to an executive office are exercised. To ensure an effective and continuous check on a possible abuse of such power by the administration each House of Parliament has its own Committee on Subordinate Legislation. The Committee of each House consists of 15 members nominated by the Speaker/Chairman. Normally, the Committee is reconstituted every year.

The main function of the Committee is to scrutinise and report to the House whether the powers to make rules, sub-rules, regulations, bye-laws, etc. conferred by the Constitution or delegated by the Parliament by statutes have been properly exercised within such conferment or delegation, as the case may be. The Committee also examines all Bills, which seek to delegate powers of legislation to a subordinate authority with a view to seeing whether suitable provisions for laying of rules or orders on the Table of the House have been made therein. While examining rules or orders passed under the authority so delegated, the task of the Committee is to ensure, *inter alia*, that the rules or orders do neither intend to impose any tax nor involve any expenditure from the Consolidated Fund; that they do not directly or indirectly bar the jurisdiction of Courts; and that there has been no unjustifiable delay in their publication or in laying them before the Parliament.

If the Committee comes to the conclusion that the provisions contained in the Bill delegating legislative powers should be annulled wholly or in part or should be amended in any respect, it may make a report to the House before the Bill is taken up for consideration. The Committee keeps a regular watch to ensure implementation of its recommendation by the government.

Through its reports, the Committee has tried to control and regulate the vast discretionary powers enjoyed by the administration with the main objective of protecting the citizens against any excess or abuse of authority. Late Shri G.V. Mavalankar, the First Speaker of Indian Parliament, held that the Committee on Subordinate Legislation is the 'custodian of the duties of Parliament' and keeps the administration within bounds intended by Parliament.

Committee on Papers Laid on the Table: At every session, the government lays before the Parliament a number of statements, reports and papers either in pursuance of constitutional/statutory provision[15] or in reply to questions or suo moto to inform the members of Parliament on various matters. While some of these reports/papers stand referred to different parliamentary committees, including the Committee on Subordinate Legislation, a bulk of them remain to be examined in detail by the *Committee on Papers Laid on the Table* which is constituted by either House of Parliament. The Committee in the Lok Sabha consists of 15 members and in the Rajya Sabha of 10 members.

The Committee examines all papers laid on the Table of the House and reports to the House any defaults in compliance with the provisions of the Constitution, Act, Rule or Regulation under which the papers have been laid or if there has been any unreasonable delay in the laying of such papers before the Parliament. Thus, the Committee seeks in general to enforce parliamentary control over the administration in areas where it was non-existent till it was constituted in 1975.

Committee on Welfare of Scheduled Castes and Scheduled Tribes: The Constitution of India provides several safeguards for the Scheduled Castes and Scheduled Tribes as also the machinery to watch their implementation. The Commissioner for Scheduled Castes and Scheduled Tribes makes regular reports in this regard to the President, which are subsequently placed before the Parliament to ensure effective implementation of the recommendations made by the Commissioner for Scheduled Castes and Scheduled Tribes, a Committee on Welfare of Scheduled Castes and Scheduled Tribes is set up.

The Committee consists of 30 members, 20 from Lok Sabha and 10 from Rajya Sabha, elected by the respective Houses of Parliament from amongst their members.

The functions of the Committee are mainly to consider the Report of the Commissioner for Scheduled Castes and Scheduled Tribes and report to the Parliament as to the measures taken or required to be taken by the government thereon. The Committee in fact examines and reports on all matters pertaining to the welfare of the Scheduled Castes and Scheduled Tribes including their representation in the different services, working of their welfare programmes, etc. It also ensures the effective implementation of the constitutional safeguards for these backward communities.

(vi) Service Committee

There are also a few Committees of the Parliament which look into various kinds of facilities and services provided to the members and other matters connected with the functioning of the members of the Houses of Parliament. These are the General Purposes Committee, the House Committee, the Library Committee and the Joint Committee on Salaries and Allowances of Members of Parliament.

General Purposes Committee: In each House there is a General Purpose Committee. The Presiding Officer of the concerned House is the *ex officio* Chairman of the Committee. It consists of the Deputy Speaker or Deputy Chairman as the case may be, members of Panel of Chairmen,

Chairmen of all the Standing Committees belonging to that House, leaders of recognised parties/groups and such other members as may be nominated by the Presiding Officer.

The Committee is constituted to advise on such ad hoc matters concerning the affairs of the House and its members as do not appropriately fall within the purview of any other Parliamentary Committee and which may be referred to it from time to time.

House Committee: Each House of Parliament has a House Committee mainly to deal with questions relating to the residential accommodation of members and other facilities such as food, medical aid, etc.

Library Committee: The Library Committee which is a joint committee of the two Houses consists of six members of Lok Sabha (including the Deputy Speaker) nominated by the Speaker and three members of the Rajya Sabha nominated by its Chairman. It is constituted every year. The main function of this Committee is to help the members in the use of the library and its allied services, viz. reference, research and documentation. It advises the Speaker on matters pertaining to the selection of books, framing of library rules and its future planning, etc.

The Joint Committee on Salaries and Allowances of Members of Parliament: The Joint Committee was constituted to frame rules under the Salaries and Allowances of Members of Parliament Act, 1954. It consists of ten members from Lok Sabha and five from Rajya Sabha.

The functions of the Committee are to make, after consultation with the Government of India, rules to provide for matters like medical, housing, telephone and postal facilities to members of the two Houses and generally for regulating the payment of their daily and traveling allowances, etc.

Conclusion

Notwithstanding the fact that the Joint Parliamentary

Committee Report on the Bofors Gun Deal did not carry conviction with the Opposition and that the Action Taken Report on the Report of the JPC on the Securities Scam generated fierce controversies, generally the government views recommendations of Parliamentary Committees with deference and accepts most of them. Committee Reports instil fear and respect in the administration. The possibility of a close scrutiny by a Parliamentary Committee, in itself exercises a salutary effect on the administration. Many an act of negligence, nepotism, and waste are not committed for the simple fear that they may be looked into and exposed to public gaze by a Committee of Parliament. Reports of Committees have been of great educative value for members as well as the general public.

There is no doubt that the Committees of Parliament have proved a helpful adjunct to the Indian political system. By their constant vigilance and fair and constructive appraisals of the functioning of government departments, the Committees have made a distinct contribution to the effective working of the Parliament and have played a significant role in generally strengthening parliamentary institutions in the country.

For quite some time, there was a feeling in different quarters that the Committee System of the Indian Parliament should be improved in keeping with the growing complexities of the modern Welfare State. Until 1989, Indian Parliament had nothing like subject-based or ministry/department-based specialist Committees, as elsewhere, embracing the entire spectrum of administration for an indepth and continuous scrutiny of administrative performance. The establishment of such Committees could provide the Parliament with the means of keeping governmental activities under constant and continuous scrutiny besides examining all the proposals emanating from the executive within their subject-areas. Now that 17 Departmental Standing Committees have been finally set up, it may become an important landmark in the annals of our Parliament and result in the emergence of a new dimension in the structure and process of administrative accountability and parliamentary surveillance. Without weakening the parliamentary system, the concept of ministerial responsibility or the position of the Parliament and its existing Committees, an integrated system of Departmental Committees could strengthen even the government by providing valuable insights into its own working, by providing to the Parliament sharper and more effective surveillance tools, restoring the balance between the Parliament's legislative and deliberative functions and its role of a representational body, and above all by saving valuable parliamentary time to the mutual advantage of both the Parliament and the government.

Working away from the glare of publicity, in a truly corporate sense, free from the normal partisan spirit that often characterises the debates in the House, such an integrated system of Committees could provide a potent mechanism for a meaningful multilateral dialogue between the government and the members of Parliament enabling a proper appreciation of each other's views, reasonable accommodation of varying viewpoints and harmonisation of conflicting interests. However, the success of such a Committee system and its efficiency as an accountability mechanism would, in the ultimate analysis, depend upon the quality of the members, the willingness of the government to provide timely, factual and full information and the orientation, independence, objectivity and research expertise of the Committee itself.

The 17 Departmental Committees cover the entire gamut of governmental activities. More importantly, these new structures constitute significant improvements in the existing instrumentalities for ensuring scrutiny of the government. They are indicative of the potential for effective change in our parliamentary system. It is hoped that in the times to come, these Committees would fulfil their intended role and make parliamentary surveillance a living reality.

A matter which needs to be clarified in regard to these Committees concerns their nature and role *vis-à-vis* the executive government. There is a serious misapprehension in some quarters that establishment of these Committees would have the effect of diluting the position and power of the ministers, creating new or rival centres of power in the form of Committee Chairmen thereby weakening the system of parliamentary democracy with its concept of ministerial responsibility. Nothing can be farther from the truth. The whole purpose of these committees is to strengthen the system of ministerial responsibility and parliamentary polity and not to weaken them in any way.

While bringing about further reforms in India's Parliamentary Committee system, the foremost thing to be remembered is that in a parliamentary polity, Committees are not intended to be and should never be conceived as strong or separate independent centres of power *vis-à-vis* the Legislature or the Executive. Their role is supplementary and complementary and that of a friendly critic or internal management auditor. The Committees examine and oversee the implementation of policies by the administration, i.e. by the bureaucracy. In other words, Committees scrutinise the working of the administration and not of the Executive. They do not sit on judgement over what the ministers have done or not done but what the administration has done. The Committees are an additional supervisory or overseeing authority, alongwith the minister and on behalf of and representing Parliament like the minister himself. Committee reforms should seek to make our Committees more effective in this task assigned to them.[16]

REFERENCES

1. See Subhash C. Kashyap, 'Committees in Indian Lok Sabha' in John D. Lees & Malcolm Shaw (ed) *Committees in Legislature: A Comprehensive Study*, 1979, pp. 297-300.
2. See Arts 88 & 105
3. Kashyap, *op.cit.* p. 297
4. Rule 254
5. Rules 256 and 258
6. Rules 267, 270 and 263 and Dir. 50(1), 56 and 57
7. Rules 266, 268, 261, 276 and 277
8. Rule 279 (1) and Dir. 68(1), 71(A) (1-3), 55 and 65(1)
9. Rules 309, 311 and 312B, and Dir. 99(1)
10. Rule 310 and Dir. 98
11. The Committee was first set up in 1921, under the *Montague-Chelmsford Reforms 1919*. Before 1954-55 it consisted 15 members drawn from Lok Sabha only.
12. Rule 308
13. Rule 308 (3)
14. Fourth Schedule to the Rule 312A and Proviso (i-iii) to Rule 312-A.
15. Annual Reports of autonomous and statutory bodies, Reports of Committees and Commissions appointed from time to time, Ordinances promulgated by the President, statutory rules and orders are some of the categories of papers laid on the Table.
16. For further study, see Subhash C. kashyap, 'A New Parliamentary Initiative—Subject-based Standing Committees of Parliament', *Economic and Political Weekly*, 6 October 1990; 'Budget and Parliament: Need for Innovations', *Economic Times*, 3 March 1991; 'A case for Budget Committees', *National Herald*, 16 November 1990; 'Committees must Vet Demands for Grants', *Times of India*, May 1992, 'Subject-based Parliamentary Panels 1 & 2', *Financial Express*, 2-3 October 1992.

12

SERVICING OF PARLIAMENT

SECRETARIATS OF THE HOUSES OF PARLIAMENT

The Legislature of a country, as we know, does not participate in the execution of the policies approved by it, or in the administration thereof. Yet, as a representative body of the people, it is the trustee of their sovereignty. It has to keep a watch on their interests and do all that may be necessary to ensure that the administration acts within the ambit of the Constitution.

If members of the country's Legislature have to exercise their rights and discharge their responsibilities without fear or favour, they must have the liberty of seeking exposure, of any governmental lapses, thus bringing the policies and performance of the government to the limelight of public scrutiny. The Legislature and the Legislators can discharge this function effectively and in a competent manner, only if they have a Secretariat of their own unconnected with and independent of the control of the Executive. This independence of the Secretariat is essential if parliamentary democracy is to function in the best interests of the people, since it is in the Legislature that members question and discuss government policies and it is the Presiding Officer who, with the assistance of the Secretariat, decides whether a question or a discussion should be admitted or not. If the decisions of the Presiding Officer were to be influenced by the Executive, then the very basis of parliamentary democracy would be in danger.

The idea of a separate Secretariat for the Legislature of India, "independent of and unconnected with the government", was mooted as early as January 1926, when the Conference of Presiding Officers of Legislative Bodies in India, convened by Vithalbhai Patel, adopted a resolution proposing the creation of a separate office for the Central Legislative Assembly. This was followed by a resolution moved in the then Central Legislative Assembly by no less a person than Motilal Nehru and seconded by another illustrious leader, Lala Lajpat Rai on 22 September 1928, seeking the constitution of a separate Assembly Department. This resolution was adopted and in fact became "the source of the creation and the authority of the Assembly Department". As a result, a separate self-contained department known as 'Legislative Assembly Department' was created on 10 January 1929, in the portfolio of the Governor-General with the President of the Legislative Assembly as its *de facto* head.[1]

Position after Independence

The name of the department continued to remain the same until 26 January 1950, when with the coming into force of the Constitution of India and the creation of the Provisional Parliament, it was changed to 'Parliament Secretariat'. Even after the creation of two separate Houses—the Council of States (Rajya Sabha) and the House of the People (Lok Sabha)—in 1952 under the new Constitution, the Secretariat of the House of the People continued to be called the 'Parliament Secretariat', while a new Secretariat called the 'Council of States Secretariat' was set up for the Council of States. Their names were changed to 'Lok Sabha Secretariat' and 'Rajya Sabha Secretariat', respectively, in 1954 in keeping with the Hindi nomenclature.

Constitutional Provisions

The underlying object of establishing separate and

independent Secretariats for the two Houses has been to ensure an effective and unimpaired exercise of the concepts of executive responsibility and the administrative accountability to the Parliament. In fact, the Constitution of India itself has recognised this paramount need. While Arts 74 and 75 ordain that the Council of Ministers with the Prime Minister at its head shall be collectively responsible to the Lok Sabha, Art. 98 (clause 1) provides for separate staff for each House and also allows the creation of posts common to both. Clause 2 of this Article authorises the Parliament to make laws regulating the recruitment and conditions of service of the Secretariat staff of the two Houses. And clause 3 provides that until such laws are made by the Parliament, the President may, after consultation with the respective Presiding Officers, make rules regulating their recruitment and conditions of service. No legislation has been passed by the Parliament so far, under clause 2 of Art. 98 of the Constitution. But on 1 October 1955, in pursuance of clause 3 of Art. 98, Lok Sabha Secretariat (Recruitment and Conditions of Service) Rules, 1955, were framed and promulgated by the President in consultation with the Speaker. Similar rules in respect of the Rajya Sabha Secretariat were framed and promulgated by the President in 1957, in consultation with the Chairman.

Separate Recruitment and Terms of Service

Recruitment and conditions of service of persons appointed to the Secretariats of Parliament are regulated by the aforesaid Rules. They do their own recruitments through competitive examinations. The Secretariats, thus, function as independent entities under the ultimate guidance and control of the Chairman/Speaker, as the case may be. According to well-established conventions the orders issued by the Government of India to its ministries and departments in regard to conditions of service of their staff do not, automatically, apply to the officers and staff of the Lok

Sabha and Rajya Sabha Secretariats. All these government orders are examined, and if found suitable, it is decided to extend the provisions thereof *in toto*, to the officers and staff of the two Secretariats, adoption orders are issued in the form of Recruitment and Conditions of Service Orders without consulting the government. Where, however, any modification or alteration, etc. in a financial order is considered necessary, the adoption order is issued after consulting the Ministry of Finance. If the staff of the Legislature Secretariat were to depend upon the Home Ministry, the Finance Ministry or any other department of the government for career prospects, promotions, pay scales, etc. it is obvious that they could not be independent vis-à-vis the Executive.[2]

Budget of the Two Houses of Parliament

The position of independence is maintained also in the field of expenditure incurred in respect of salaries and allowance of, and amenities to, members and officers of the Parliament. These expenses are met from the Consolidated Fund of India. As in the case of other ministries of the Government of India, separate demands for grants in respect of the Rajya Sabha and the Lok Sabha are also laid before both the Houses of Parliament. The Parliament sanctions the expenditure through the Appropriation Act every year. No cut motions or any discussion relating to the demands of the two Houses and their Secretariats is allowed on the floor of the House.

The Budget estimates of the Lok Sabha, for instance, are compiled by the Lok Sabha Secretariat and after approval by the Secretary-General, are placed before an *ad hoc* Committee appointed by the Speaker and consisting of the Deputy Speaker and the Chairmen of the Financial Committees. These are then submitted to the Speaker for his approval, along with the recommendations, if any, of the Committee. The estimates approved by the Speaker are forwarded to the Ministry of Finance for incorporation in the Central Budget as a matter of course. These are not subject to any examination by any Departmental Committee of the Ministry of Finance or any other Committee of the Parliament.

Broad Division of Work on Functional Basis

Keeping the need of independence and efficiency of the Secretariats in view, the Speaker of the Lok Sabha and the Chairman of the Rajya Sabha, in consultation with each other, appointed a Committee of Parliament in August 1973, to advise them on the revision of pay and other conditions of service of parliamentary staff, especially in the light of the recommendations of the third Pay Commission set up by the Government of India, which had submitted its report in the same year. In their deliberations, the Committee took into consideration the independent character of the two Secretariats and the specialised nature of their functions and responsibilities. The Committee recommended a rational reorganisation of both the Secretariats to make them more efficient and economical. Consequent upon this, the Secretariats were functionally reorganised into the following services:

(i) The *Legislative Service* for dealing with the work connected with the business of the House such legislation, questions, preparation of List of Business, etc;

(ii) The *Financial Committee Service* for rendering secretarial assistance and attending to all works connected with the three Financial Committees and the Railway Convention Committee;

(iii) The *Executive* and *Administrative Service* to deal with administrative and general matters and to look after the payment of salaries, allowances and other amenities to members and staff;

(iv) The *Library, Reference, Research, Documentation* and *Information Service* to keep the members of Parliament well-informed of the day-to-day developments in India and abroad, by maintaining an up-to-date and well-equipped library and efficient research and reference services to provide reference material on legislative measures and other matters coming up before the two Houses—Lok Sabha and Rajya Sabha—so as to enable the members to participate effectively in the debates of their respective Houses;

(v) The *Verbatim Reporting, Personal Secretaries* and *Stenographic Service* for the reporting of parliamentary proceedings and those of the Committees and for provision of stenographic assistance to officers;

(vi) The *Parliamentary Interpreters Service* with responsibility for simultaneous interpretation of proceedings in the Lok Sabha as well as its Committees;

(vii) The *Printing, Publications, Stationery, Sales, Stores, Distribution Service* covering (a) printing, rota-printing, and bindery works, (b) stationery and stores, record-keeping (c) sales, and (d) receipt and distribution;

(viii) The *Editorial* and *Translation Services* for editing of debates and preparing synopsis of debates, translation of debates, reports and parliamentary papers;

(ix) The *Watch and Ward, Doorkeeper* and *Sanitation Service* to look after security measures inside and outside the Parliament House and to ensure proper maintenance of the premises;

(x) *Clerks, Typists, Record Sorters* and *Daftries Service,* and

(xi) The *Messenger Service* to function as supporting staff required by all the other services.

The entire structure of the two Secretariats, thus, is functional, keeping the hierarchy and levels of supervision to the minimum and organising the work, wherever possible, on a more or less desk-officer system so that the work units in the Secretariats are small and compact and geared to quick and quality turn-out of work without diffusion of responsibilities.

Similarly, after the fourth Pay Commission submitted its report, a Parliamentary Pay Committee was appointed in July 1986 by the Chairman, Rajya Sabha and the Speaker, Lok Sabha to advise them in regard to the structure of pay, etc. of the officers and staff of the Rajya Sabha and Lok Sabha Secretariats. Following the recommendations of the Committee as accepted by the Presiding Officers of the two Houses, employees of the Secretariats of the Parliament have been given, in several cases, scales of pay somewhat better than those admissible to their counterparts in the government. In deciding various pay scales, the effort of the Committee was "to see that all categories of staff and officers have as far as possible equal opportunities to get promotions and there is uniformity in benefits commensurate with their qualifications, merit and experience and the duties and responsibilities of their respective posts." Also in view of the specialised and arduous nature of their duties, certain other functional facilities were provided. The position has since been further improved after the fifth Pay Commission Report as adopted for the employees of the two Secretariats.

As at present, the number of employees in the Lok Sabha Secretariat is nearly 2000 while the Rajya Sabha Secretariat has about 1000. If other functionaries connected with serving Parliament and stationed in its precincts e.g. those in the Medical Centre, Para Military Forces, Public Works Department, Canteen, etc. are included, the number of public servants engaged in the service of Parliament during session periods would add up to about 5,600. During non-session periods, it may work out around 4,400.

Parliament Library and Information Service

The Parliament of India may easily claim to have one of the best libraries with every efficient information service. Functionally known as the Parliament Library and Reference, Research, Documentation and Information Service (LARRDIS) its primary objective is to keep the members of Parliament well-informed of the day-to-day developments in India and abroad, by maintaining an up-to-date and well-equipped library and efficient research and reference services.

The size of the present holdings of the library is over one million volumes. Two hundred Indian and foreign newspapers and 665 periodicals in English and in Indian languages are received regularly in the library. It possesses a rich collection of rare books, art books, etc. The earliest printed book available dates back to 1671. By far, the most precious possession of the library, however, is the original calligraphed copy of the Constitution of India, as adopted by the Constituent Assembly and signed by its members.

From time to time, and on specific occasions, the Parliament Library organises Book Exhibitions on themes of interest. The Reference and Documentation Division has been fully equipped to handle *inter alia* references received from members of Parliament. As against the 700 references received and handled by the Reference Wing in 1970, the number rose up to 3,627 during 1980 and 5,167 during 1990. During 1995, 1996, 1997, 1998 and 1999, their number came to 4302, 3891, 4194, 4487 and 3808 respectively.

The Research and Information Division assesses in advance the information requirements of the members of Parliament, and constantly endeavours to keep them informed of current developments, both national and international, in various fields by timely issue of objective information material like brochures, information bulletins, background notes, fact-sheets, etc.

The Press and Public Relations Wing looks after all the press and public relations work of the Lok Sabha Secretariat involving, in the main, continuous liaison with the Press, governmental publicity organisations, and the media. It also deals with all matters concerning the Press Gallery of the Lok Sabha including the issue of press releases on various parliamentary events and activities.

To keep pace with the advances in information

technology, the Parliament Library Information System (PARLIS) made a beginning in the field of computerised information service with the establishment of the Computer Centre in 1987. Since then the entire Secretariat has computerised its work by setting up Computer Centres in Parliament House and Parliament Library Building. Members of Parliament have also been supplied the latest computer hardware.

PARLIS database was designed to cater to instant reference needs of the members of Parliament, officers of Parliament, Committees, the research and references personnel and other staff. The information stored in the computers and data available for on-line retrieval covers subject index references to question-answers and debates in the two Houses of Parliament, Bills, bio-data profiles of members, Constituent Assembly debates, socio-economic background of members, Parliamentary Committees, Speaker's decisions and observations, etc. Data relating to some parliamentary activities contained in the PSRLIS database are also available on request to State Legislatures. Some State Legislatures have already made arrangements to access some PARLIS data through linkage of their computers NECS-1000 of NIC through NICNET (National Informatics Centre Network). PARLIS has been connected to NICNET and can correspond with the District Information Centres under the system all over the country. Also, it has direct access to some international databases.

The Documentation Service is mainly responsible for locating, collecting and subject-classifying/cataloguing of books, reports, periodicals, press clippings and documents of all kinds received and maintained in the library, and then abstracting/making available the relevant material for the use of members of Parliament in their day-to-day parliamentary work. Documentation cards are also prepared on all important subjects and filed in card catalogue cabinets and fed in the PARLIS database as well. The Documentation Service brings out a fortnightly periodical, *Parliamentary Documentation*.

As an important aid to reference and research work, this service maintains an exhaustive collection of editorial comments, articles and important news items from selected newspapers, both in English as well as in Hindi. These press clippings are kept in a chronological sequence in separate folders and can be consulted or referred to by members in the library.

New Library Building: For a long time, faced with acute shortage of space—like all libraries anywhere—the Parliament Library now has a large new building equipped with very modern state-of-the-art infotech and other facilities. It is christened 'Sansadiya Gyanpeeth'. Its foundation was laid on 15 August 1987 and this name was also given then.

Bureau of Parliamentary Studies and Training

Parliamentary democracy has developed some highly sophisticated procedures and processes which can neither be imbibed nor understood overnight. The policy makers, the legislators, the administrators and different functionaries at various levels involved in the functioning of the democratic set-up, therefore, need to be trained in the tenets, tools and operational mechanics of parliamentary institutions. Also their attitudes have to be oriented to the needs and responsibilities and the tenor and temper of parliamentary democracy. The task of carrying on the necessary studies and imparting the required orientation and training primarily falls on the Parliament itself.

The Bureau of Parliamentary Studies and Training, set up in 1976 as an integral division of the Lok Sabha Secretariat, is designed to meet the long-felt need to provide the legislators and officials with institutionalised opportunities for problem-oriented studies and systematic training in the various disciplines of parliamentary institutions, process and procedures.

The Bureau's activities thus include holding of seminars and orientation programmes for members of Parliament and of State Legislatures, training and refresher courses for officers of the Secretariats of Parliament and of the State Legislatures, appreciation courses for senior and middle-level officials of the Government of India and probationers of the IAS, IFS, IPS and several other All-India and Central Services. Organising model Parliaments for university students all over India and training university teachers for the purpose, arranging study visits by the members of State Legislatures and government officials, students and others, and attachments of parliamentary and legislature officials from India and foreign Parliaments also form part of the Bureau's activities. Two of the latest regular courses of the Bureau, mainly for participants from abroad, are the Parliamentary internship programme for parliamentary officials and the international course in legislative drafting.

Parliamentary Museum and Archives

India has all along attached utmost importance to parliamentary institutions. Of late, efforts are being made to harness all necessary resources towards salvaging, collecting and preserving for the present and future generations, the country's rich heritage in this area. A beginning was made in 1976 when the Lok Sabha Secretariat set up a Parliamentary Archives of Photographs and Films to preserve an authentic, comprehensive, complete and up-to-date pictorial record of the history of the institution of Parliament, its activities and personalities. A proposal for setting up a Parliamentary Museum and Archives was approved by the General Purposes Committee of the Lok Sabha on 1 August 1984.

The basic aim of the Parliamentary Museum and Archives is to preserve the past and the present for the future by protecting from ravages of time and neglect all the precious records, historic documents, and articles connected with the Constitution and Parliament and through them to make the history and growth of Parliamentary institutions and the political system better understood. In the current phase of its growth, it is concentrating on acquisition and building of comprehensive collections, proper preservation of all its holdings and display of selected items. In due course, it proposes to undertake other tasks devoted to dissemination of information on parliamentary institutions and the projection of a proper image of, and the encouragement of a healthy respect for Parliament by stimulating interest in its growth, activities and achievements.[3]

Hall of National Achievements

The General Purposes Committee of the Lok Sabha, on 1 August 1984, approved a proposal for the establishment of a Hall of National Achievements which should present an overall picture of the progress the nation had achieved in diverse fields particularly since independence. It was proposed to present through exhibitions, models, photographs and other visual materials a panoramic view of India's achievements. The underlying idea was to project through audio-visual means an integrated and healthy image of the country to members of foreign parliamentary delegations, visiting dignitaries, students, tourists and others coming to Delhi. Unfortunately, progress in this direction has been tardy and slow in recent years.

Role of Parliamentary Officials

With the latest technological advances and the widening scope and complexities of governmental business, some attention has been paid in recent years to the need for better equipped and suitably trained professional staff to man the Secretariats of the House of our Parliament. That each

Legislature requires efficient and adequate staff cannot be overemphasised.

The nature of the responsibilities of their officers and staff requires a high degree of quality and promptness, while ensuring at the same time economy, efficiency and specialisation coupled with mobility and diversification of experience. The officers and staff of the two Houses, serving members of Parliament, as they do, have to be persons of high caliber, impeccable integrity, requisite qualification and training. They have to use all their competence, tact and experience in discharging their onerous responsibilities.

The ultimate aim of the secretarial staff of the Parliament is to assist the members in performing their function as legislators as effectively and efficiently as possible. A parliamentary official's first and foremost duty is to serve and assist the House and to be objective, fair and impartial in all matters. He has to make sure that factual information supplied to the Speaker is correct in every respect, that all the relevant rulings and precedents pertaining to an issue are placed before the Chair to facilitate right decisions being taken. As far as advice to members is concerned, parliamentary officials are not expected to offer it gratuitously. It is only when a parliamentary official is specifically asked for advice on a matter relating to parliamentary work that he may furnish factual information and not advance opinions.

A parliamentary official has no concern with the political affiliations or the ideologies of the members. For him every member, whatever his party, qualifications, or station in life may be, is an honourable representative of the people with whom he is expected to deal with reverence and patience. As a servant of the House, a parliamentary official must treat all members as equal. Remembering always that all members are entitled to equal and impartial assistance from him, he has to render efficient service to everyone of them, who seek his help in connection with his parliamentary duties.

In order to perform his duties, the official has to be an expert in his line of work. He must have thorough knowledge of the relevant rules and practices and a clean grasp of the intricacies and nuances of procedures. He must also keep himself abreast of developments in all the important matters and sensitive issues so that, as often happens, he is not taken unawares and is able to meet promptly and sufficiently if he is suddenly faced with a situation or a difficult problem. Speed and accuracy in the disposal of work are thus the key ingredients in the operational dynamics of parliamentary officials.[4]

It is necessary to instil among the parliamentary staff the norms of our parliamentary culture and a spirit of inquiry and questioning. Some of the guiding norms may be summed up as follows:

(i) respect for the institution of Parliament and for the representatives of the people;
(ii) unfailing commitment to the service of members irrespective of their party affiliations;
(iii) dedication, courtesy, self-control, patience, coolness and tolerance in dealing with members and others;
(iv) precision and accuracy and the habit of placing before the Speaker full facts and rendering impartial advice;
(v) promptness in taking decisions and in the disposal of work—a work culture which does not allow postponement of any item for tomorrow;
(vi) presence of mind, the quality of being a listener with a smile;
(vii) non-partisan, objective approach—a parliamentary official has to learn to be in the midst of it all and yet out of it; and
(viii) an ability to find solutions which are not merely theoretically correct but are also practical and feasible.

The Secretariats of Parliament are dynamic, developing institutions requiring constant attention to keep pace with the growing and changing needs of parliamentarians. The officers and staff of the Secretariats have to be on their toes all the time, constantly thinking of improvements in the ways of serving the members and parliamentary institutions. In the service of parliamentary institutions, the journey's end never comes.

Thanks to the training procedures and facilities, the Parliament in India can take legitimate pride in having done well. It hopes to do better in the years to come.[5]

REFERENCES

1. The Speaker of the Central Legislative Assembly was then called "President"
2. For a detailed discussion see the keynote paper presented by Dr. Subhash C. Kashyap on *Recruitment and Training of Parliamentary Staff* at the meeting of Society of clerks-at-the-Table in Commonwealth Parliaments at Saskatoon, Canada, in October 1985. Also published in *The Parliamentarian,* LXVII, No.3, July 1986, pp.134-36
3. Subhash C. Kashyap, *Parliamentary Museum and Archives,* L.S.S., New Delhi 1985.
4. See Kashyap, *Recruitment and Training of Parliamentary Staff,* op.cit.
5. *Ibid*

13

PARLIAMENTARY ETIQUETTE

CODE OF CONDUCT FOR MEMBERS

Every House has a personality of its own, but there are some rules of etiquette, customs and conventions which are common to each House. The Legislature is not just another club. The conduct of its members has, therefore, to be characterised by a high standard of dignity, grace, mutual respect and courtesy, as befits the place where all the competing forces in the polity are brought face-to-face for organised interaction. For the orderly, smooth and efficient dispatch of business and for the accommodation of all shades of opinion in the House, the atmosphere in the nation's supreme deliberative forum must be solemn and dignified. Outside the House as well, a member is expected to observe a standard of conduct consistent with the dignity of his office.

In the day-to-day functioning of the Parliament, the observance by members of certain rules regarding personal behaviour or etiquette is very important not only for the smooth and decent conduct of the business of the House but also for upholding the dignity of the Parliament and its members. These rules are based on the Rules of Procedure and Conduct of Business in both the Houses and have been gradually evolved from conventions and rulings given by the Presiding Officers from time to time.[1]

Behaviour in the House

When the sitting Begins: The first rule to be observed by the members in their behaviour towards the House when it is in session is that they should be present in their seats a few minutes before the scheduled time of the commencement of a sitting and its re-assembly after lunch-break. Thereafter when the Marshal announces the arrival of the Speaker and the Speaker enters the Chamber, members should stop all conversation, rise in their places and bow to the Chair in response to the Speaker himself bowing to either side of the House. Members who enter the House at that time, should stand silently in the gangway till the Speaker takes the Chair. This is by way of elementary respect to the House as well as to the Chair.

Once the sitting of the House commences, every member should enter and leave the Chamber with decorum and in such a manner as not to disturb the proceedings in the House. A member should bow to the Chair while entering or leaving the Chamber, and also when taking or leaving his seat.[2] This respect is to the whole House and not to an individual occupying the Chair. The Speaker represents the House to all outside bodies and authorities. Regard for the authority of the Chair as the symbol of the corporate personality of the House, is the basic norm of Parliamentary conduct.

While Speaking: A leading principle is that at any point of time only one member should speak or ask questions and the Chair is given the power to call upon members to speak one by one. When a member wants to speak he should rise in his place to attract the attention of the Chair. Waving of hands to attract the attention of the Chair is not considered to be the normal parliamentary practice. No member should speak unless he has caught the Chair's eyes and has been called upon by the Chair to speak.[3]

A member should not use his right of speech for obstructing the business of the House. The practice of exchanging arguments by members between themselves or of indulging in a sort of running commentary on another member's speech or minister's statement has been deprecated by the Speaker. A member addressing the House had to resume his seat when any other member has interposed in the course of the debate to raise a point of order, or to offer a personal explanation with the permission of the Chair.

If a member desires to make an observation on a matter before the House or to ask a question from another member who is speaking, either to obtain clarification or for the purpose of any explanation about a matter which is under consideration of the House, he has to address the question through the Chair. Members are to speak from their allotted seats and rise while speaking. A member disabled by sickness or infirmity is, however, permitted by the Speaker to speak while sitting.[4]

A member must not address individual members of the House while speaking, but he should always address the Chair and make remarks to other members through the Chair.[5] This may appear to be a mere formality, but it is sought to be practiced assiduously so that debates are prevented from developing into dialogues between members. It has been ruled that members should address each other in third person. Similarly, ministers have to be referred to by their official designation and not by name.

If the Presiding Officer feels that a member while speaking is persistently irrelevant or is indulging in tedious repetition of his own arguments or those advanced by other members who had preceded him, he may direct that member to discontinue his speech.[6] It has been ruled quite often that while speaking, members should not repeat arguments, except when it is absolutely necessary to give emphasis to a point. If a member continues to speak in defiance of the Chair's observation, it may direct that his remarks would not form part of the record.

In their speeches, members cannot refer to matters which are *sub judice*. It, however, does not apply to matters of privilege or where disciplinary jurisdiction of the House with respect to its own members is concerned. In such cases, the Chair and the House consider each case on its merits.

No member is expected to use offensive expressions about the conduct or proceedings of either House of Parliament or of any State Legislature. They are not expected to cast reflections on any decision of the House except on a motion for rescinding such decision.[7] Members are not allowed to make allegations of a defamatory or incriminatory nature against other members or ministers unless previous intimation has been given to the Speaker and also the minister concerned.[8] Members should not make personal references by way of imputation of motives or questioning the *bona fides* of any member. Members should not refer to government officials by name—they are not there to defend themselves. Members are also not expected to make allegations against or cast aspersions on persons in high authority except on a substantive motion drawn in proper terms.[9]

The language which the members use should be parliamentary and words and expressions used must not be treasonable, seditious or defamatory. Although there is no bar to criticism of the government, yet the members are expected not to use this right for the purpose of obstructing the business of the House.

Members should not make use of expressions which are offensive, or attribute motives to the Chair. Propriety, decency and good taste require that members should not use ironical, derogatory or unbecoming words or expressions while speaking. If certain words and phrases are defamatory, indecent, unparliamentary or undignified, they can be ordered to be expunged by the Presiding Officer.

A member except when making a maiden speech is not to read his speech, though he may refresh his memory by a reference to notes. Also, when a member is quoting figures, he may read from his notes. This rule against written speeches is for maintaining the cut and thrust of debate.

Debate is a discussion in which ideas battle with ideas and arguments wrestle with arguments. Set speeches prepared beforehand would be without reference to what has been spoken in the House. To have a lively debate without repetitions, and with arguments addressed only to the points raised, the written speeches have to be barred. This, however, does not apply to ministers who may make policy statements from written texts and also read prepared speeches as and when they consider it necessary.

When Another Member is Speaking: For an effective debate, the behaviour of those who listen to the speeches is as important as the conduct of those speaking, and there are, therefore, rules in this regard also.

Tolerance of the opposite viewpoint is the spirit of parliamentary ethos. The House discusses subjects that are generally complex and sometimes contentious. It would be neither natural nor desirable that there should not be occasional disagreement. The deliberations must, therefore, be animated by a spirit of mutual concession. A member should not interrupt any member who is speaking, by disorderly manner. Witty or otherwise relevant comments are often overlooked. Occasional interruptions are allowed to clear a point or seek information through the Speaker, to follow the tenor of a speech or to challenge mildly a statement, but frequent interruptions disturb the line of argument of the member speaking and introduce disorderliness in the proceedings. Also, interruptions by heckling are not permissible parliamentary practice and have been deprecated by the Chair. Continuous interruptions mar the proceedings and dignity of the House as a whole. If the member having the floor does not give way, he should not be interrupted. Any point about his speech can be raised after he has finished his speech. Members should not normally converse among themselves in the Chamber but, if it becomes absolutely necessary, they may do so in a very low voice, so as not to disturb the proceedings. Members are also not to talk or crack jokes with each other.[10] A member should not read any book, newspaper or letters except in connection with, or necessary for the business of the House.[11] A member should not sit or stand with his back to the Chair. A member should not cross the floor or pass between the Chair and any member who is speaking. Breach of this rule is strongly taken objection to by the Chair.[12]

The temptation to listen only to one's own voice all the time is great but a good parliamentarian makes it a point to listen to others. Also, every member should maintain silence in the House when he himself is not speaking.

Visitors and Galleries: References to the presence of strangers in the Visitors' Gallery have been held to be out of order. But, in appropriate cases, the Chair may make references to the presence of distinguished foreign visitors in the Special Box of the House and on such occasions, members can cheer those visitors by thumping their desks. Ordinarily, however, members should not applaud when a distinguished visitor enters any of the Galleries, or the Special Box. No member should speak to the Gallery from inside the House nor should he make any reference or appeal to it.[13]

General Conduct in the House: Resort to hunger-strike, *dharna* or any type of demonstration or performance of any religious function in the precincts of the Parliament is not permissible. Besides, in keeping with parliamentary conventions, members are forbidden to bring arms inside the House; to enter the Chamber with a coat hanging on the arm; to place their caps, coats, jackets or shawls on the desks in the House; to carry walking sticks into the Chamber unless permitted under such exceptional circumstances as old age or physical infirmity; to smoke in the Chamber; to raise any slogans or special terms of exclamation or anything of the kind in the House; to display flags or emblems on their seats in the House; to bring a tape-recorder into the House or play it there; to stand in the gangway and talk to other members; to produce exhibits during debate or make demonstration in the House; to distribute within the precincts of the Parliament House, any literature, questionnaire or pamphlets, etc. not connected with the business of the House, unless a permission has been obtained in writing in advance, and to indulge during debate in any frivolity or in jokes with a barb or sarcasm in them. Members should not approach the Chair personally. They may send chits to the Officers at the Table, if necessary. Also, members should not leave the Chambers immediately after delivering their speeches. It is not decent parliamentary behaviour. Every member is expected to hear what other members have to say with reference to his speech. In particular, when any member offers a criticism of another member or minister, the latter is entitled to expect that the critic should be present in the House to hear his reply. To be absent when the latter is replying is a breach of parliamentary etiquette.

In the interests of decorum and dignity of the House members are required not to indulge in any flippancy. Lady members are expected to desist from knitting in the House.

When the Speaker Rises: Whenever the Speaker rises to address the House, members are enjoined to hear him in silence and any member who is then speaking or offering to speak is required to sit down.[14] It is a well-recognised parliamentary convention that every member should resume his seat as soon as the Speaker rises to speak or calls out 'order' and addresses the House. Members should not rise on a point of order when the Speaker is addressing the House. Members are not to cross the floor, walk, stand, enter or leave the Chamber when the Speaker is addressing the House.

Member's Pecuniary Interest

A member having a personal, pecuniary or direct interest in the matter to be decided by the House is expected, while taking part in the proceedings on that matter, to declare his interest. This is to ensure objectivity in deliberations and avoid any objection being taking to the vote of the member on ground of personal, pecuniary or direct interest. Similarly, in case a member of a Committee has any such interest in a matter which is to be considered by the Committee, he should state his interest in the matter to the Speaker.[15]

Customs and Conventions

Besides the rules of legislative etiquette which the members are expected to observe while in the House, there are a number of customs and conventions which are equally important for the maintenance of proper standards in parliamentary life and the dignity of the House and its members. Members of Parliament are, therefore, expected to observe a certain standard of conduct not only inside the House but also outside it.[16] The conduct of members should not be contrary to the usage or derogatory to the dignity of the House or in any way inconsistent with the standard which the parliament is entitled to expect from its members.

The extent and amplitude of the words "conduct of a member" have not been defined exhaustively, and it is within the powers of the House in each case to determine whether a member has acted in an unbecoming manner or has acted in a manner unworthy of a member of Parliament. Thus even though the facts of a particular case do not come within any of the recognised heads of breach of privilege or contempt of the House, the conduct of a member may be considered by the House as unbecoming and derogatory to the dignity of the House.

The House has the right to punish its member for their misconduct. It exercises its jurisdiction of scrutiny over its members for their conduct whether it takes place *inside* or *outside* the House. It also has the power to punish a member for disorderly conduct and other contempts, whether committed *within* the House or beyond its walls.

Some of the more important customs and conventions are:[17]

(i) Rulings given by the Chair should not be criticised, directly or indirectly, inside or outside the House. As the authority to conduct the proceedings of the House is conferred on the Chair by the House itself, the Chair's interpretation of the rules and practices of the House has to be obeyed, howsoever dissatisfied a member may be or howsoever contrary to the individual inclinations of a member the interpretation may be.

(ii) A member should not give publicity in the Press to the discussions held by him with the Speaker in his Chamber.

(iii) A notice should not be given publicity until it has been admitted by the Speaker and circulated to members. A notice of a question should not be given any publicity until the day on which the question is answered in the House.

(iv) Information given to members in confidence or by virtue of their being members of Parliamentary Committees should not be divulged to anyone nor used by them directly or indirectly in the profession in which they are engaged, such as in their capacity as editors or correspondents of newspapers or proprietors of business firms.

(v) Members should not take action on behalf of their constituents on some insufficient or baseless facts or without verifying the veracity of facts nor should they allow themselves to be used as ready supporters of individual grievances. The legislator should normally write or speak to the minister concerned regarding the grievances of his constituents. In case of a grievance of general character he may take up the matter at question time or raise it in the House by other means. But individual cases cannot be brought before the House. If the legislator feels that the cause is just and legitimate but the normal channels would get delayed justice, he can approach the civil servant concerned and bring the matter to his notice, but with decorum and in a manner not in any way amounting to pressurising or exercising undue influence.

(vi) Members should not give certificates which are not based on facts, make profit out of government residences allotted to them by sub-letting the premises, or unduly influence government officials or ministers in cases in which they have direct or indirect financial interests.

(vii) A member should not receive hospitality of any kind for any work he desires or proposes to do from a person or organisation on whose behalf the work is to be done by him.

(viii) A member should not write recommendatory letters or speak to government officials for employment or business contracts for any of his relations, or other persons in whom he is directly or indirectly interested.

(ix) A member should not elicit any official information in an unauthorised manner by inducting a government employee to give information to him which in the course of his normal functions he should not give, nor encourage any such person to speak to him against his senior officials on matters of public importance and policy.

(x) A member should not unduly influence the government officials or the ministers in a case in which he is interested financially, either directly or indirectly.

(xi) A member should not try to secure business from the government for a firm, company or organisation with which he is directly or indirectly concerned.

(xii) A member should not in his capacity as a lawyer or a legal adviser or a counsel or a solicitor appear before a minister or an executive officer exercising quasi-judicial powers.

(xiii) Conduct of a member involving corruption in the execution of his office as a member is treated by the House as a breach of privilege. Thus, acceptance of any fee, compensation or reward in connection with the promotion of or opposition to any Bill, resolution or matter submitted or proposed to be submitted to the House or any Committee thereof is a breach of privilege. It would also be a breach of privilege of misconduct on the part of a member to enter into an agreement with another person for any reward to advocate and prosecute in the House the claims of such person.

Unfortunately, of late there has been a widespread feeling of decline in the levels of conduct and etiquette followed by the members both inside and outside the Houses of Parliament. When day after day, the Houses are adjourned after scenes of pandemonium and without transacting any business, one wonders whether the institutions are not becoming dysfunctional despite their high costs to the public exchequer. It is also found that many of our elected representatives in their personal conduct, relationships and dealings with the people do not follow the basic norms of their code of conduct. In a democracy nothing can be sadder and cause for greater concern than the erosion in the respect for the representatives.[18]

REFERENCES

1. Subhash C. Kashyap, *Ministers and Legislators,* New Delhi, 1982, pp. 44-50
2. Rule 349 (iii)
3. Rule 350, Dir. 115A (2)
4. Rule 351
5. Rule 349 (vi)
6. Rule 356
7. Rule 352 (iii & iv)
8. Rule 353
9. Rule 352, (ii & v)
10. Rule 349 (viii)
11. Rule 349 (1)
12. *Ibid* (iv)
13. *Ibid* (x & xi)
14. Rule 361 (1)
15. Rule 371
16. Kashyap, *op.cit.*, pp. 139-140
17. *Handbook for Members* (Eighth Edition)
18. For further study, see Subhash C. Kashyap, *Parliamentary Procedure, op.cit.*, Vol.2, Chapter 35, pp.2332-2502.

14

PARLIAMENTARY PRIVILEGES

MEMBERS' SALARIES AND PERKS

(A) Privilege Law and Procedure

'Privilege' means a special or exceptional right or freedom or an immunity enjoyed by a particular class of persons or some individuals. It is 'special' in the sense that it is a right or freedom which is not available to the rest of the people. In its legal sense it means an exemption from some duty, burden, attendance or liability to which others are subject. Privilege can also be defined as a right which others do not have. Parliamentary privileges are not the privileges of Parliament inasmuch as while the Parliament consists of the President and the two Houses, parliamentary privileges extend only to the two Houses, their Committees and their members. Parliamentary privileges are those special rights belonging to each House of Parliament, its members and Committees, without which they cannot perform their functions in the manner they are expected to. The privileges are granted with a view to maintaining the independence of action and the dignity of the position of the Houses of Parliament, their Committees and members and to enable them to function without any let or hindrance. The privileges, in practice give rise to certain powers, immunities and exemptions. It does not, however, imply that the privileges belonging to members place them on a footing different from that of an ordinary citizen in the eyes of law unless there are good reasons in the interest of the Parliament itself to do so. Members, apart from being representatives of the people, are also ordinary citizens as far as applicability of laws is concerned. The basic law is that all citizens including members of Parliament should be treated equally before the law. They have the same rights and liberties as ordinary citizens except when they perform their duties in Parliament. The privileges are available to the members only when and to the extent that they are functioning as representatives of the people in the Parliament and discharging their parliamentary responsibilities. The privileges do not, in any way, exempt the members from their normal obligations to society which apply to them as much, and perhaps more closely in that capacity, as they apply to others.

Thus, the privilege against assault or molestation is available to a member only when he is obstructed or in any way molested while discharging his duties as a member of Parliament. In cases, when members were assaulted while they were not performing any parliamentary duty, it was held that no breach of privilege or contempt of the House had been committed. Similarly, privilege of the Parliament will not be attracted if a libel or a reflection upon a member of Parliament does not concern his character or conduct in his capacity as a member of the House, and is not based on matters arising in the actual transaction of the business of the House. Further, a member does not enjoy any exemptions from the operation of the ordinary laws of the land and it has been held in a typical case that a member does not enjoy any special privilege in regard to the censoring of mail and tapping of telephone authorised by law equally applicable to all citizens.

Constitutional Provisions: The more important of the privileges, namely freedom of speech in the Parliament and immunity of members from any proceedings in courts in respect of anything said or any vote given by them in Parliament, are specified in Art. 105 of the Constitution (corresponding provision for the States being Art. 194).

Some of them are specified in certain statutes and Rules of Procedure and Conduct of Business in the Lok Sabha, while some others are based on precedents and conventions which have grown in this country.

Article 105 of the Constitution reads as under:

(i) Subject to the provision of the Constitution and to the rules and standing orders regulating the procedure of Parliament, there shall be freedom of speech in Parliament.

(ii) No member of Parliament shall be liable to any proceedings in any court in respect of anything said or vote given by him in the Parliament or any committee thereof, and no person shall be so liable in respect of the publication by or under the authority of either House of Parliament of any report, paper, votes or proceedings. (Tej Kiran v. Sanjiva , AIR 1970 SC 1573; Gatish v. Harisadhan (1956) 60CWN 971, AIR 1961 SC 613).

(iii) In other respects, the powers, privileges and immunities of each Houses of Parliament, and of the members and the committees of each House, shall be such as may from to time be defined, shall be those of that House and of its members and committees immediately before the coming into force of section 15 of the Constitution (Forty-Fourth Amendment) Act, 1978.

(iv) The provisions of clauses (1), (2) and (3) shall apply in relation to persons who by virtue of this Constitution have the right to speak in, otherwise to take part in the proceedings of a House of Parliament or any committee thereof as they apply in relation to members of Parliament.

The provisions of the Constitution as originally enacted provided that the privileges of members of Parliament were to be the same as those of the British House of Commons, its members and Committees at the commencement of the Constitution until our Parliament defined them in whole or in part, by law. In other words, if Parliament enacted any provision relating to any particular privilege at any time, the British precedents could not to that extent be applicable to our Parliament. This clause (clause 3) was, however amended in 1978, to provide that in respect of privileges other than those specified in the Constitution, the powers, privileges and immunities of each House of Parliament, its members and Committees shall be those of that House, its members and Committees immediately before the coming into force of the Constitution Forty Fourth Amendment Act, 1978 (w.e.f. 20 June 1979). This amendment has in fact made only verbal changes by omitting all references to the British House of Commons but the substance remains the same. In other words, each House, its Committees and members in actual practice shall enjoy the powers and privileges (other than those specified in the Constitution) that were available to the British House of Commons as on 26 January 1950.

As stated by the then Law Minister while replying to the discussion on the Constitution (Amendment) Bill, the purpose of the amendment to Art. 105 (3) was "That the original provision—there was no escape from it—had referred to the British House or Commons. Now a proud country like India would like to avoid making any reference to a foreign institution in its own solemn constitutional document... Therefore, this verbal change is being introduced by this clause so that there may not be any reference to a foreign institution."

Main Privileges: Lists of parliamentary privileges can be drawn and have in fact been drawn. No such list, however can be exhaustive. The important privileges of each House of Parliament, its members and Committees may said to be:

(i) Freedom of speech in Parliament (Art. 105 (1) of the Constitution);

(ii) Immunity to a member from any proceedings in any court in respect of anything said or any vote given by him in Parliament or any Committee thereof [Article 105 (2) of the Constitution];

(iii) Immunity to a person from proceedings in any court in respect of the publication by or under the authority of either House of Parliament of any report, paper, votes or proceedings [Art. 105 (2) of the Constitution];

(iv) Prohibition on the courts to inquire into proceedings of Parliament (Article 122 of the Constitution);

(v) Freedom from arrest of members in civil cases during the continuance of the session of the House and 40 days before its commencement and 40 days after its conclusion (Section 135 A of the Code of the Civil Procedure);

(vi) Exemption of members from liability to serve as jurors;

(vii) Right of the House to receive immediate information of the arrest, detention, conviction, imprisonment and release of a member (Rules 229 and 230 of the Rules of Procedure and Conduct of Business in Lok Sabha, Sixth Edition);

(viii) Prohibition of arrest and service of legal process within the precincts of the House without obtaining the permission of the Speaker (Rules 232 and 233 of the Rules of Procedure and Conduct of Business in Lok Sabha, Sixth Edition);

(ix) Prohibition of disclosure of the proceedings or decisions of a secret sitting of the House (Rule 252 of the Rules of Procedure and Conduct of Business in Lok Sabha, Sixth Edition);

(x) Members or officers of the House are not to give evidence or produce documents in courts of law, relating to the proceedings of the House without the permission of the House. (First Report of Committee of Privileges of the Second Lok Sabha, adopted by Lok Sabha on 13 September 1957);

(xi) Members or officers of the House are not to attend as witness before the other House or a Committee thereof or before a House of State Legislature or a Committee thereof without the permission of the House and they cannot be compelled to do so without their consent

(Sixth Report of the Committee of Privileges of the Second Lok Sabha, adopted by Lok Sabha on 17 December 1958);

(xii) All Parliamentary Committees are empowered to send for persons, papers, and records relevant for the purpose of the inquiry by a Committee. A witness may be summoned by a parliamentary Committee who may be required to produce such documents as are required for the use of a Committee (Rules 269 and 270 of the Rules of Procedure and Conduct of Business in Lok Sabha, Sixth Edition);

(xiii) A Parliamentary Committee may administer oath or affirmation to a witness examined before it (Rule 272 of the Rules of Procedure and Conduct of Business in Lok Sabha, Sixth Edition);

(xiv) The evidence tendered before a Parliamentary Committee and its report and proceedings cannot be disclosed or published by anyone until these have been laid on the Table of the House (Rule 275 of the Rules of Procedure and Conduct of Business in Lok Sabha).

In addition to the above mentioned privileges and immunities, each House also enjoys certain consequential powers necessary for the protection of its privileges and immunities. These powers are as follows:

(i) to commit persons, whether they are members or not, for breach of privilege or contempt of the House;

(ii) to compel the attendance of witnesses and to send for papers and records;

(iii) to regulate its own procedure and the conduct of its business; (Art. 118 of the Constitution);

(iv) to prohibit the publication of its debates and proceedings (Rule 249 of the Rules of Procedure and Conduct of Business in Lok Sabha, Sixth Edition);

(v) to exclude strangers from the House (Rule 248 of the Rules of Procedure and Conduct of Business in Lok Sabha, Sixth Edition).

The most important of parliamentary privileges is that of freedom of speech while performing parliamentary duties. Article 19 also gives a citizen the right of free speech but Arts 105 and 194 lay special emphasis on the right of free speech of members of the legislatures. Under article 19, the right of free speech is subject to reasonable restrictions, for instance, the law of libel. An ordinary person who speaks something libellous is liable to be proceeded against but a member of Parliament speaking in the House or in one of its Committees is immune from any attack on the grounds that his speech was libellous or defamatory.

Members have to give expression to public grievances and raise various matters of public importance. In doing this, members should not suffer any inhibition and they should be able to speak out their mind and express their views freely. Inside the House or Committees of the Parliament, a member is absolutely free to say whatever he likes subject only to the internal discipline of the House or the Committee concerned; no outside authority has any right to interfere. Freedom of speech is absolutely necessary for a member to function freely without any fear or favour in the Committees and in the Houses of Parliament. Unless whatever a member says enjoys immunity from legal action, he cannot be expected to speak freely and frankly. The Constitution provides, therefore, that no action can be taken against a member of Parliament in any court or before any authority other than the Parliament in respect of anything said or a vote given by him in the Houses of Parliament or any Committee thereof. It is also a breach of privilege to molest a member to take any action against him on account of anything said by him in the Parliament or a Committee thereof. Likewise, it would be a breach of privilege to institute any legal proceedings against a member in respect of anything said by him in Parliament or in a Committee thereof.

A member cannot also be questioned in any court or

by any agency outside the Parliament for any disclosure he may make in the Parliament. It has been held by the Supreme Court in the *Searchlight case* that the freedom of speech conferred on members under Art. 105 is subject only to those provisions of the Constitution which regulate the procedure of Parliament and to the rules and standing orders of the House, but is free from any restrictions which may be imposed by any law made under Art. 19 (2) upon the freedom of speech of an ordinary citizen. Any investigation outside the Parliament in respect of anything said or done by members in the discharge of their parliamentary duties would amount to a serious interference in the members' rights. Even though a speech delivered by a member in the House may amount to contempt of Court, no action can be taken against him in any Court. Court being an outside authority, does not have the power to investigate the matter. Article 122 specifically forbids any inquiry by Courts into the proceedings of the Parliament.

The immunity from external influence or interference, however, does not mean an unrestricted licence of speech within the walls of the Parliament. It is subject to the constitutional provisions. For example Art. 121 provides that no discussion shall take place in the Parliament with respect to the conduct of any judge of the Supreme Court or of a High Court in the discharge of his duties except upon a motion for presenting an Address to the President praying for the removal of the judge. Rules 352 and 353 of the Rules of Procedure of the House *inter alia* prohibit making of unwarranted allegations against a person and provide for remedial measures for incorrect statements made by ministers or members of the House. When a member violates any of the restrictions, the Speaker may direct him to discontinue his speech or order the defamatory, indecent, unparliamentary or undignified words used by the member to be withdrawn or expunged from the proceedings of the House. In extreme cases, he may even direct the member to withdraw from the House, and/or initiate the process for suspension of the member from the service of the House.

A member cannot be arrested not only when the House to which he belongs is in session or when a parliamentary Committee of which he is a member, is meeting or during joint-sitting of both the Houses, but also during 40 days before and 40 days after the session of the Parliament or when he is coming or going from the House. It would be a breach of privilege even if that molestation or obstruction is caused to him at a place outside New Delhi while he is on his way to New Delhi to attend any business of Parliament or a Committee thereof.

The object of this privilege is to ensure the safe arrival and regulate the attendance of members in the Parliament. Although the members have immunity from arrest only in civil cases and it does not apply to arrests in criminal cases or under the law of Preventive Detention, the House has a right to receive immediate information of the arrest, detention, conviction, imprisonment and release of a member. It is the duty of the concerned authority to intimate the Speaker immediately of every arrest, detention or imprisonment of a member of the Lok Sabha. The failure on the part of authorities to do so, constitutes a breach of privilege of the House. The information has to be given at the earliest possible moment. The member arrested may be in any part of the country; the information must be sent telegraphically and later confirmed by a letter.

It has been laid down that no summons—no legal process, civil or criminal—can be served and no member of Parliament can be arrested within the precincts of Parliament, without the permission of the Speaker/Chairman. This immunity is available even to a private person inside the precincts of the Parliament. Thus, nobody can be arrested inside the Parliament House without the permission of the Speaker/Chairman because within the precincts of the Parliament, only the writ and orders of the House of Parliament or of the Speaker/Chairman prevail and not of any other governmental authorities or local administration. Even Section 144 cannot be applied to the precincts of the Parliament. If the authorities ever sought to so extend it, it would be a breach of privilege and contempt of the House. It is another matter that within the precincts of the Parliament there may be in operation an order of the Speaker that may be similar to the provision of Section 144.

Members are free from the liability to serve as jurors in criminal cases. Though it is the duty of every citizen to serve as a juror whenever the system of jury prevails, the members of Parliament and State Legislatures have been exempted.

An officer of the Legislature Secretariat or other person cannot be compelled to give evidence or produce documents which relate to the proceedings of a House without the permission of the House. Similarly, there cannot be any compulsion for appearance as a witness before the other House without the permission of the House of which he is a member.

All Parliamentary Committees have the power to send for persons, papers and records. The following types of conduct of a witness before a Committee would constitute a breach of privilege and contempt of the Committee:

(i) Refusal to answer questions;
(ii) Prevarication or willfully giving false evidence or suppressing the truth or misleading the Committee;
(iii) Trifling with the Committee and returning insulting answers;
(iv) Destroying or damaging a material document relating to the enquiry by the Committee.

The Committees of the Parliament are entitled to the same respect as the Parliament itself. Therefore, if anybody casts reflections on the decisions or conduct of a Parliamentary Committee it is treated as a breach of privilege and contempt of the House.

Also, as a part of the privilege law, a member under custody enjoys the right to communicate without any hindrance with the Speaker/Chairman of a Parliamentary Committee. A communication so addressed by the member in custody cannot be withheld by the administrative authorities.

When a matter is under consideration of a Parliamentary Committee and the Committee is holding its sitting day to day for that purpose, no person including a member of Parliament should make or publish a statement or comment about that matter. Making public comments on a matter which is being considered by a Parliamentary Committee is highly improper and may even amount to a contempt of the House. The publication of the proceedings or of any documents or papers which may have been presented to a Committee, is also treated as a breach of privilege of the House.

Breach of Privilege: Any act of attack on or in disregard of any privileges, rights or immunities of either the House or its Committees collectively or its members individually by any individual or authority may result in a breach of privilege. It is an offence which is punishable by the House. The fundamental principle is that, anything that hinders, hampers or obstructs the Houses, Committees or members of Parliament from discharging their duties and functions effectively and efficiently and without fear or favour will be treated as a breach of parliamentary privilege. Thus, preventing a member from proceeding to the House to attend a sitting thereof will be a case of breach of privilege. Trying to bribe a member of Parliament will be a breach of privilege. Wilfully misleading the House or deliberately and knowingly giving false information to the House is also a serious offence. Besides breach of specific privileges, actions in the nature of offences against the authority and dignity of the House, such as disobedience to its legitimate orders or libels upon itself, its members or officers, are also punishable as contempt of the House.

Contempt of the House: Contempt of the House may be defined generally as any act or omission which obstructs or impedes either House of Parliament, or its Committees or its members, or its officers in the efficient and effective discharge of their functions and duties or which has a tendency, directly or indirectly, to lower the dignity or prestige of the House, its Committees or its members. The difference between breach of privilege and contempt of the House is very narrow. Normally, a breach of privilege may amount to contempt of the House. Likewise, contempt of the House may include a breach of privilege also. Contempt of the House, however, has wider implications. There may be a contempt of the House without specifically committing a breach of privilege. In fact, the word contempt is not amenable to a strict delimitation or definition. A particular act in one set of circumstances may not constitute a contempt while in another situation, the same act may constitute a contempt. In other words, the sole authority to decide whether a contempt has been committed or not is the concerned House of Parliament itself.

Broadly, contempt includes any attack on the supremacy, authority or dignity of the Houses of Parliament and the Committees thereof. Some of the acts, which could be considered as contempt of the House are:

(i) Speeches and writings reflecting adversely on the Houses, their Committees or their members with a view to bring them into disrepute or lower them in the esteem of the people;

(ii) Questioning the character or the impartiality of the Speaker/Chairman in the discharge of his duties;

(iii) Alleging partiality in the report of a Parliamentary Committee;

(iv) Publication of false or distorted reports of the proceedings;

(v) Publishing portions of proceedings expunged by the Chair or proceedings of secret sessions of the House;

(vi) Moelstation of members on account of their conduct in the House or obstructing members while in the performance of their duties as members or while on their way to or from, attending the House or a Committee thereof;

(vii) Offering bribes to members to influence them in their parliamentary conduct;

(viii) Intimidation of members in connection with their parliamentary conduct;

(ix) Giving false or misleading evidence or information deliberately to the House or a Committee thereof, by a member or witness; and

(x) Obstructing or molesting any witness appearing before the House or a Committee thereof.

Matters not Amounting to Breach of Privilege: There are certain parliamentary practices, usages and conventions which should be followed by the members and others concerned. But the violation of these practices and conventions may not technically constitute a breach of privilege or an instance of impropriety. For instance, propriety requires that when the House is in session, policy statements should not be made outside the House, that due courtesy should be shown to M.P.s at public functions by government officers, etc. and that Parliamentary Committees on tour be extended due facilities and courtesies. Violation of these proprieties, however, does not amount to breach of parliamentary privilege.

Punishment for Breach of Privilege, Contempt, etc.: Each House of Parliament is the guardian of its own privileges. The House may punish a person found guilty of breach of privilege or contempt of the House either by reprimand or admonition or by imprisonment for a specified period. In case of its own members, two other punishments are available to the House, namely suspension from the service of the House and expulsion. A member may be suspended from the service of the House for a specified period or for the rest of the session or in an extreme case, he may be expelled from the House.

Normally, in cases where the offence of breach of privilege or contempt is not serious, the person concerned may be called to the Bar of the House and admonished or reprimanded by the Speaker or the Chairman as the case may be, by order of the House. Admoniton is the mildest form of punishment, whereas reprimand is the more serious form expressing displeasure of the House. The House can punish the offenders with imprisonment for a period normally not exceeding the duration of the session of the House. As soon as the House is prorogued, the prisoner is set at liberty. Both the Houses have, from time to time, committed the offenders to prison till the House rises, for committing a contempt of the House by shouting slogans and/or throwing leaflets from the Visitor's Gallery.

The penal jurisdiction of the House is not confined to its own members nor to the offences committed in its presence, but extends to all contempts of the House, whether committed by members or persons who are not members. It also does not make a difference whether the offence was committed within the House or beyond its precincts. This power of the House to punish the person for breach of its privilege or contempt is the 'keystone' of parliamentary privilege. It is this power which gives reality to the privileges of the Parliament and emphasises its sovereign character so far as the protection of its rights and the maintenance of its dignity and authority are concerned.

The penal powers of the House for breach of privilege or contempt of the House are, however, exercised only in extreme cases where a deliberate attempt is made to bring the institution of Parliament into disrespect and undermine public confidence in and support for the Parliament. It is also a tradition of the House that unqualified and unconditional regrets sincerely expressed by the persons guilty of breach of privilege and contempt of the House are accepted by the House and the House normally decides in such cases to best consult its own dignity by taking no further notice of the matter.

Procedure in Questions of Privilege: The procedure for dealing with questions of privilege is laid down in Rules 222 to 228 and 313 to 316 of the Rules of Procedure and Conduct of Business in Lok Sabha. A member wishing to raise a question of privilege is required to give notice to the Secretary-General of his intention to do so. Notice has to be given before the commencement of the sitting of the day. If the question proposed to be raised is based on a document the notice should be accompanied by that document. After examining the notice, if the Speaker feels that there is no *prima facie* case of breach of privilege or the matter to be raised is not in order, he may refuse his consent to the matter being raised. The member concerned is informed of the Speaker's decision. After the decision of the Speaker that he has withheld his consent to the raising of the matter in the House is conveyed to the member, the member is not permitted to raise the matter in the House. However, if the member is not satisfied, he may see the Speaker in his chamber to explain his case. This has been so laid down so that the time of the House is not taken up by raising a matter which, on the face of it, is not admissible. Where the matter is of an immediate nature and there is no time for a notice being given, the Speaker may permit a member to raise a question of privilege without previous notice in writing.

The question whether a matter complained of, is actually a breach of privilege or contempt of the House is entirely for the House to decide, as the House alone is the master of its privileges. The Speaker, in giving his consent to the raising of a matter in the House as a question of privilege, considers only whether the matter is fit for further inquiry and whether it should be brought before the House. A question of privilege should be raised by a member at the earliest opportunity and should require the interposition of the House. If the Speaker finds that *prima facie* a question of privilege is involved, he may on his own refer the matter to the Privileges Committee or he may give his consent to the matter being raised on the floor of the House. After the Speaker gives his consent, the member when called by the Speaker seeks the leave of the House to raise the question of breach of privilege. While asking for such leave, the member concerned is permitted to make only a short statement relevant to the question of privilege. If objection to leave being granted is taken, the Speaker requests those members who are in favour of leave being granted to rise in their places. If 25 or more members rise accordingly, the House is deemed to have granted leave to raise a matter and the Speaker declares that leave is granted; otherwise the Speaker informs the member that he does not have leave of the House to raise the matter.

Leave to raise a question of privilege in the House can be asked for only by the member who has given notice of the question of privilege. He cannot authorise another member to do so on his behalf. A question of privilege is accorded priority over other items in the List of Business. Accordingly, leave to raise a question of privilege is asked for after the questions and before other items in the List of Business are taken up. Urgent matters requiring immediate intervention of the House may, however, be allowed by the Speaker to be raised at any time during the course of a sitting after the disposal of questions but such occasions are rare.

After leave is granted by the House, the House may consider and decide the issue itself or refer it to the Privileges Committee for examination, investigation and report. The usual practice is, however, to refer the matter of complaint to the Committee and the House defers its judgement until the report of the Committee has been presented. In cases, where the House finds the matter to be too trivial or when the offender has tendered an apology, the House itself disposes of the matter by deciding not to proceed further in the matter.

After the report of the Committee has been presented to the House, the Chairman or any member of the Committee or any other member may move that the report be taken into consideration. After the report is taken into consideration, the Chairman or any member of the Committee or any other member may move that the House agrees or disagrees or agrees with amendments, with the recommendations contained in the report. The motion that the report of the Committee of Privileges be taken into consideration is given under Rule 225 of the Rules of Procedure and Conduct of Business in Lok Sabha. Further action is taken in accordance with the decision of the House on the report of the Committee.

Houses of Parliament, in practice, have always been extremely liberal in matters of breach of privilege. Action has been taken only in a few cases so far. Even in cases where breach of privilege or contempt has been actually committed either by individuals or by the Press, Houses of Parliament have rarely taken a serious view. In majority of cases, they seem to have been guided by the feeling that it is below their dignity to take notice of every petty and insignificant matter. It may, in fact, give undue importance to those who indulge in creating such situations.

Parliament—the Sole Arbiter of its Privileges: A reference is sometimes made to the so-called 'judgement of the Supreme Court' as reported in A.I.R. 1965 SC 745. It may be mentioned that this was not a judgement, but an opinion of the Supreme Court on a special reference made by the President of India under Art. 143 of the Constitution on 26 March 1964. This related to the committal to prison of Keshav Singh by the U.P. Vidhan Sabha for committing a breach of privilege and contempt of the House and his writ petition to the Allahabad High Court for setting him free, which led to a chain of events giving rise to important and complicated questions of law regarding the powers and jurisdiction of the High Court and its judges in relation to the powers and privileges of the State legislature and its members.

The courts of law in India have recognised that a House of Parliament or State Legislature is the sole authority to judge as to whether or not there has been a breach of privilege in a particular case. It has also been held that the power of the House to commit for contempt is identical with that of the House of Commons, and that a court of law would be incompetent to scrutinise the exercise of that power.

In 1959, the Supreme Court held in the *Searchlight case* as follows:

> The provisions of cl. (2) of article 194 indicate that the freedom of speech referred to in cl. (1), is different from the freedom of speech and expression guaranteed under article 19(1)(a) and cannot be cut down in any way by any law contemplated by cl. (2) of article 19.
>
> The provisions of article 105(2) and 194(2) are constitutional laws and not ordinary laws made by Parliament or the State Legislatures and that, therefore, they are as supreme as the provisions of Part III (articles relating to fundamental rights).
>
> The principle of harmonious construction must be adopted and so construed, that the provisions of article 19(1) (a), which are general, must yield to article 194(1) and the latter part of its clause (3) which are special.

In 1965, the Supreme Court in its advisory opinion in the above mentioned Special Reference Case of 1964 (*Keshav Singh case*), observed as follows:

> It would not be correct to read the majority decision in the *Searchlight case* as laying down a general proposition that whenever there is a conflict between the provisions of the latter part of article 194(3) and any of the provisions of the fundamental rights guaranteed by Part III, the latter must yield to the former. The majority decision, therefore, must be taken to have settled that article 19 (1) (a) would not apply, and article 21 would.

> In dealing with the effect of the provisions contained in clause (3) of article 194, whenever it appears that there is a conflict between the said provisions and the provisions pertaining to fundamental rights, an attempt will have to be made to resolve the said conflict by the adoption of the rule of harmonious construction.

It may be stated that the judgement of the Supreme Court in the *Searchlight case* is the definitive one and the guiding principles as set out by the Supreme Court in that case are held to apply in all such matters.

The opinion of the Supreme Court was discussed by the Conference of Presiding Officers of Legislative Bodies in India held at Bombay on 11 and 12 January 1965. The Conference unanimously adopted a resolution expressing its view that suitable amendments to Arts 105 and 194 should be made in order to make the intention of the Constitution makers clear beyond doubt so that the powers, privileges and immunities of Legislatures, their members and Committees could not, in any case, be construed as being subject or subordinate to any other articles of the Constitution.

The Allahabad High Court, in their judgement in *Keshav Singh case* dated 10 March 1965 (i.e. delivered after the advisory opinion of the Supreme Court), observed as follows:

(i) In our opinion, both upon authority and upon a consideration of the relevant provisions of the Constitution, it must be held that the Legislative Assembly has, by virtue of article 194 (3), the same power to commit for its contempts as the House of Commons has.

(ii) In our opinion, the provisions of article 22(2) of the Constitution cannot apply to a detention in pursuance of a conviction and imposition of a sentence of imprisonment by competent authority.

(iii) Since we have already held that the Legislative Assembly has the power to commit the petitioner for its contempt and since the Legislative Assembly has framed rules for the procedure and conduct of its business under article 208 (1), the commitment and deprivation of the personal liberty of the petitioner cannot but be held to be according to the procedure laid down by law within the meaning of article 21 of the Constitution.

(iv) Once we come to the conclusion that the Legislative Assembly has the power and jurisdiction to commit for its contempt and to impose the sentence passed on the petitioner, we cannot go into the question of the correctness, propriety or legality of the commitment. This Court, cannot, in a petition under article 226 of the Constitution, sit in appeal over the decision of the Legislative Assembly committing the petitioner for its contempt. The Legislative Assembly is the master of its own procedure and is the sole judge of the question whether its contempt has been committed or not.

The government, therefore, decided that an amendment of the Constitution was not necessary. It was of the opinion that the Legislatures and the Judiciary would develop their own conventions in the light of the opinion given by the Supreme Court and the judgement pronounced by the Allahabad High Court.

It may, therefore, be seen that the judgement of the Supreme Court in the *Searchlight case* is final till today insofar as matters of privileges are concerned.

Parliamentary Privileges and the Press: The Press is often called an extension of the Parliament. It conveys to the people the substance of parliamentary legislation and discussion and keeps the people informed of what is happening in the Parliament. Freedom of the Press has not been expressly provided for in the Constitution, but is implicit in the fundamental right of the "freedom of speech and expression" guaranteed to the citizens under article 19 (1) (a) of the Constitution. It has been settled by judicial decisions that freedom of speech and expression includes freedom of the Press. It is a breach of privilege and contempt of the House to publish expunged proceedings of the House.

Absolute immunity from proceedings in any court of law has been conferred under the Constitution on all persons connected with the publication of proceedings of either Houses of Parliament, if such publication is made by or under the authority of the House [article 105 (2)]. This immunity does not, however, extend to the publication of reports of parliamentary proceedings in newspapers, whether published by a member of the House or by any other person, unless such publication is expressly authorised by either House. Statutory protection has been given to the publication in newspapers or broadcast by wireless telegraphy of substantially true reports of any proceedings of either House of Parliament, provided the reports are for the public good and are not actuated by malice (Art. 361 A of the Constitution).

The above protection has been accorded within the overall limitation that the House has the power to control and, if necessary, to prohibit the publication of its debates or proceedings and to punish for the violation of its orders. Normally, no restrictions are imposed on reporting the proceedings of the House. If, however, the reports are *mala fide* or there is willful misrepresentation or suppression of speeches of particular members, it is a breach of privilege and contempt of the House and the offender is liable to punishment. Further, the Press is forbidden to publish any part of the proceedings or evidence given before, or any document presented to a Parliamentary Committee before such proceedings or evidence or document has been reported to the House. It is also incumbent on the Press not to disclose the proceedings or decisions of a secret sitting of the House, until the ban on secrecy is lifted by the House. Any such publication or disclosure is treated as a gross breach of privilege of the House. Similarly, publication of such portions of the debates as have been expunged from the proceedings of the House by order of the Speaker is a breach of privilege and contempt of the House and accordingly punishable.

A question that is very often raised is whether the privileges of the legislatures extend to taking action against a writer, speaker or a cartoonist who makes valid criticism of the shortcomings of the legislatures. No doubt, Parliament or any legislature for that matter is entitled to take action for any malicious writing, speech, etc. casting reflection or aspersion on its functioning or on the functioning of its members or its Committees. No action is, however, taken if the criticism is fair and *bona fide*.

The approach that is generally followed in matters of privilege by the Lok Sabha is the same as followed by the House of Commons, U.K.

The Select Committee on Parliamentary Privilege of the House of Commons (U.K.), 1967 made the following recommendation:

> The House should exercise its penal jurisdiction (a) in any event as sparingly as possible, and (b) only when it is satisfied that to do so is essential in order to provide reasonable protection for the House, its Members or its Officers from such improper obstruction or attempt at or threat of obstructions as is causing, or is likely to cause, substantial interference with the performance of their respective functions.

Subsequently, the Committee of Privileges of the House of Commons in their Third Report (1976-77) reiterated this recommendation and the House of Commons, U.K., adopted it on 6 February 1978.

The Committee of Privileges of the Second Lok Sabha in their Thirteenth Report had observed, *inter alia*, as follows:

> Nobody would deny the Press, or as a matter of fact, any citizen, the right of fair comment. But if the comment contain personal attacks on individual members of Parliament on account of their conduct in Parliament or if the language of the comments is vulgar or abusive, they cannot be deemed to come within the bounds of fair comment or justifiable criticism. Even the Press Commission (1954) held the view that 'comment couched in vulgar or abusive language is unfair'. Nor can 'fair comment' be stretched to include irresponsible sensationalism.

The Committee of Privileges of the Sixth Lok Sabha in their Fourth Report had observed:

> The Committee are conscious that the freedom of the Press is an integral part of the fundamental right of freedom of speech and

> expression guaranteed to all citizens under article 19 (1) (a) of the Constitution. The Committee consider it important that in a Parliamentary system, the Press should enjoy complete freedom to report the proceedings of Parliament fairly and faithfully. If, however, freedom of the Press is exercised *mala fide*, it is the duty of Parliament to intervene in such cases. At the same time the Committee are of the view that Parliamentary privileges should in no way fetter or discourage the free expression of opinion or fair comment.

The Committee of Privileges of the Seventh Lok Sabha in their First Report observed, *inter alia* as follows:

> The Committee feel that it adds to the dignity of one and all if power in a democratic system is exercised with restraint; the more powerful a body or institution is, the greater restraint is called for particularly exercising its penal jurisdiction.

Codification of Privileges: Article 105 (3) of the Constitution stipulates that, apart from the privileges mentioned in the Constitution itself, the Parliament may, from time to time, define its privileges by law. No law, however, has so far been enacted by the Parliament in pursuance of this provision to define the powers, privileges and immunities of each House and its members and the Committee thereof. In fact, an important privilege of the Parliament is not to codify the privileges. They must remain as undefined as they are today, as they have always been.

As far as constitutional stipulation 'until defined by Parliament by law' and the question of defining or codifying the parliamentary privileges are concerned, opinions are divided.

The question of undertaking legislation on the subject has also engaged the attention of the Presiding Officers of Parliament and the State Legislatures in India since 1921. The dominant view, however, has all along been that any codification is more likely to harm the prestige and sovereignty of the Parliament/State Legislatures without any benefit being conferred on the Press and that in the present circumstances, codification of parliamentary privileges is neither necessary nor desirable.1 Both the Legislature and the Judiciary are supreme in their own spheres. The Parliament is supreme in its own sphere, and so is the Judiciary. It is the business of the Judiciary to interpret the law in cases which come up before the courts. In this respect the following observation made by Shri M. Hidayatulla, former Chief Justice of India and former Chairman of the Rajya Sabha, is worth recalling:

If there is mutual trust and respect between Parliament and Courts there is hardly any need to codify the law on the subject of privileges. With a codified law more advantage will flow to persons bent on vilifying Parliament, its members and Committees and the Courts will be called upon more and more to intervene. At the moment, given a proper understanding on both sides, parliamentary right to punish for breach of its privileges and contempt would rather receive the support of Courts than otherwise. A written law will make it difficult for Parliament as well as Courts to maintain that dignity which rightly belongs to Parliament and which the Courts will always uphold as zealously as they uphold their own.[2]

(B) Members' Salaries and Perks

Members of both the Houses are entitled to salaries and allowances as may be determined by the parliament by law from time to time (Art. 106).

Pension: There is no mention of pension in the constitutional provision regarding payments to members (art. 106). Parliament has, however, sanctioned to members a pension under the Members of Parliament (Salaries, Allowances and Pension) Act. Every member with four years of service is paid a pension of Rs. 3,000 per month with Rs. 600 additional paid for each year of service beyond five years. In addition to pension, former Members are now provided with facilities like free railway travel for self and a companion in A.C. Second Class for life.

Salaries and Allowances: Every member is entitled to a salary of Rs. 12,000 per month and an allowance of Rs. 500 for each day during residence, on duty, at a place where a session of a House of Parliament or a sitting of a Committee is held. A member is also entitled to daily allowance for three days immediately preceding or succeeding the session of the House and two days preceding or succeeding the sitting of a Committee, or for the purpose of attending to any other business connected with his/her duties as a member of Parliament. Besides, the monthly salary and the daily allowance, every member is entitled to a monthly constituency allowance of Rs. 10,000 and office expenses at the rate of Rs. 14,000 per month.

Travel Facilities: A member is entitled to the following Travelling Allowances: (a) For journey by rail, an amount equal to one first class plus one second class fare; (b) For journey by air, an amount to one and one-fourth of the air fare for each such journey; (c) For journey by road Rs 8 per kilometer; (d) and for journey by steamer, one and three-fifths of the highest class fare.

In addition, every member is allowed 32 single air journeys free each year anywhere within the country with spouse or companion. Also, every member gets a railway pass for self and companion for traveling air-conditioned First class free any number of times anywhere within the country. A separate pass for the spouse is admissible. In rail journey, one other person can also travel free with the Member in A.C. II class.

Telephone: Every member is entitled to free installation of two telephones—one at New Delhi/Delhi and the other at his/her usual place of residence. One MTNL mobile phone is available to every member without payment of any registration or rental charges. Also he/she is allowed 1,50,000 free calls each year.

Accommodation and Conveyance: Every member is provided residential accommodation in New Delhi. For flats there is no charge while for bungalows a nominal licence fee is charged. Electricity (50,000 units) and water (400 kilo litres) are free.

An advance of Rs. 1 lakh during the term is available to each member, free of interest, for the purchase of a vehicle.

Other Perks: Other perks and facilities provided to members include access to the stenographic and typing pools, income tax relief, canteen refreshment and catering, clubs, common room, bank, post office, railway and air booking and reservation, bus transport, LPG service, foreign exchange quota, lockers, super bazar etc. A first-aid post and a well-equipped medical centre also function exclusively for members on the premises of the Parliament Estate.

In addition to all this, every member has at his disposal a sum of Rupees two crores each year under the Local Area Development Scheme.

Furniture of upto Rupees thirty thousand is provided to each member at his/her residence free of cost.

In foreign travel on duty, e.g. as a member of a Parliamentary Committee, Delegation, etc. Members of Parliament are entitled to travel by Air in First Class and receive daily allowance in travel and while abroad.

Expenditure on Parliament: According to the budget figures for the year 2002-2003, the annual expenditure on Parliament exceeds 264 crores. In 1952 this expenditure was less than one crore.

The expenditure on members which was nearly 58 lakhs in 1952-53, has gone beyond 60 crores per year. This does not include nearly 1600 crores per year kept apart under the Local Area Development Scheme.[2]

REFERENCES

1. For another view, see Subhash C. Kashyap, 'Codify Privileges of Parliament', *Time of India*, 5 December 1990.
2. For further study, see Subhash C. Kashyap, *Anti-Defection Law and Parliamentary Privileges*, Universal, New Delhi, 2003 ed. and *Parliamentary Procedure*, op.cit., Vol. 2, Chapter 25.

15

POLITICAL PARTIES AND GROUPS

ANTI-DEFECTION LAW

Parties and Groups

An appropriate party system has not so far developed in India. A large number of parties participate in elections. By and large these are not ideologically oriented or based on any programmatic differences. Many of the parties revolve around personalities, caste, communal, tribal, linguistic and regional identities. All the time these keep getting formed, split, merged, etc. Only for two short periods, with the Janata Party and Congress during 1977-79 and again with the Janata Dal and the Congress during 1989-90, hopes were raised of some semblance of a two-party system taking shape.

Until 1985, political parties did not find any mention in the Constitution. The election law provided for their recognition for the specific purpose of allotting symbols. Presiding Officers under their own discretion and directions recognised parliamentary parties and groups for the purposes of facility of functioning in the respective Houses of Parliament. Thus, in the Lok Sabha, those with a minimum strength enough to keep the quorum, i.e. one-tenth of the total membership were recognised as Parliamentary Parties, and those with a minimum of 30 members were recognised as Parliamentary Groups. Certain functional facilities followed recognition as a Parliamentary Party/ Group. These included allotment of separate seats, accommodation in the Parliament Estate for the party office, supply of parliamentary papers and publications, memberships on committees, allotment of speaking time, consultation in vital matters of the business of the House, etc.

The Constitution (52nd Amendment) Act which added the Tenth Schedule—commonly referred to as the Anti-defection Law—to the Constitution for the first time gave constitutional recognition to political parties and legislature parties. It *inter alia* provides for disqualification from membership of anyone voluntarily leaving or disobeying the party on whose ticket he or she was elected to the House. Only the members doing so following a party split or merger are protected. Following the enforcement of the Anti-defection law, every member of the House who is not elected as an independent or nominated, belongs to his party even if he be the only member of his party. That is, irrespective of the number of its members in the House, every party that is represented in the House automatically comes to get constitutional recognition as a party. But under 'Directions from the Chair' for recognition as a Parliamentary Party, a minimum strength of one-tenth of the total membership of the House is necessary. Thus, there is some contradiction between the constitutional provisions and the 'Directions from the Chair'. It is hoped that early action would be initiated to resolve it.

Majority and Minority Leaders: In a parliamentary polity more or less of the British model, the U.S. Congressional concept of majority and minority leaders does not apply in India. We have instead the Leader of the House and the Leader of the Opposition.

Leader of the House: The leader of the majority party in the Lok Sabha or, in case there is no party with absolute majority, the leader commanding the support of the majority of members in the House, is called upon by the President to be the Prime Minister. As the leader of the majority, he also functions as the Leader of the House. In the rare event of the Prime Minister not being a member of the House, the senior-most minister who is a member of Lok Sabha is designated as the Leader of the House. Similarly, the senior-most minister from among the Rajya Sabha members is appointed by the Prime Minister as the Leader of the House in the Rajya Sabha.

Important parliamentary functions are attached to the office of the Leader of the House. He proposes to the Speaker the dates for summoning and proroguing the House, draws up the programme of the official business and fixes *inter se* priorities.

The leader may propose a secret sitting of the House. He is consulted by the Speaker either directly or through the Minister of Parliamentary Affairs in regard to the arrangement of government business, allocation of time for important discussions, suspension of a member, privilege motions, etc. The Leader of the House is responsible and responsive to the House as a whole. On several important occasions, he speaks for and on behalf of the whole House. He may nominate a Deputy Leader for either House.

Leader of the Opposition: The leader of the largest party in opposition in each House is recognised as the Leader of the Opposition provided that the party has a strength which would enable it to keep the House, i.e. the number should not be less than the quorum fixed to constitute a sitting of the House which is one-tenth of the total membership.

Since a two-party system of the British type has not developed in India so far, the Leader of Opposition may not be the Prime Minister in waiting with a shadow cabinet of his own. In fact, there may be a situation where parties in the Opposition may be more opposed to each other than to the ruling party.

An 'official' Opposition and a Leader of Opposition was recognised for the first time since independence during December 1969–December 1970 when Congress Party split into Congress (R) and Congress (O), the former being the ruling Congress party and the latter the Opposition party with its leader as the Leader of the Opposition. After the sixth general elections in 1977 which brought the Janata Party Government, the Congress Party became the officially recognised Opposition and its leader remained the Leader of the Opposition throughout 1977-79. Again, during December 1989–December 1990 Rajiv Gandhi was the Leader of the Opposition in the Lok Sabha. Thereafter, throughout 1991-94, BJP has been the official Opposition and its leader in either House has been the Leader of the Opposition.

Since 1977 Leaders of Opposition in the Lok Sabha and Rajya Sabha are extended certain official status and facilities like salary equivalent to that of a Cabinet Minister, office facilities in the Parliament House, etc. The salary and allowances are governed by the Salary and Allowances of Leaders of Opposition in Parliament Act, 1977.

The 1977 Act defines the Leader of the Opposition as that member of the Rajya Sabha/Lok Sabha who, for the time being, is the Leader of the Party in Opposition to the government, having the greatest numerical strength and recognised as such by the Chairman/Speaker of the Rajya Sabha/Lok Sabha.

Whips and Party Discipline: In the Indian parliamentary context, the Whip of the Parliamentary Party or Group is the one who has been designated to ensure that members of the party are present in adequate numbers, and vote according to the line taken by the party in important questions. The Chief Whip of the government party in the Lok Sabha/Rajya Sabha is the Minister of Parliamentary Affairs and he is directly responsible to the Leader of the House. It is part of his duties to advise the Government on parliamentary business. The Chief Whip acts as the eyes and ears of the Leader of the Party so far as the members are concerned. During sessions, in his capacity as adviser to the Leader, he has to be in constant touch with the Prime

Minister. The Chief Whip is assisted by two Ministers of State. The responsibility of keeping everybody at his post and keeping his party united, strong and well-knit, falls on him.

The Whips of the ruling party and of the parties in Opposition keep contact with each other to sort out matters of common interest, and to understand and accommodate each other on many crucial occasions. Whips of the ruling party as well as those in Opposition thus play a very significant role in the smooth and efficient functioning of parliamentary democracy.

The ruling party Whip has "to make a House and to keep a House", which means that it is his responsibility to ensure a quorum throughout the sitting of the House by keeping the members within the hearing range of the division bells, particularly when some important business is under consideration. His most important job is ensuring the presence of members and more particularly marshalling his party forces on important issues.

As a floor manager, the Chief Whip of the ruling party has to smoothen differences and plan the business of the House in consultation with the Whips of other parties. He has to act as a liaison between the Houses of Parliament, their Presiding Officers and their Secretariats on the one hand, and the ministers and ministries and departments of the government on the other. In short, the functions of the Whips today encompass those of management, communication and persuasion. They keep their members informed about the business of the House and the party line adopted on various issues and enforce party discipline.

During sessions, Whips of different parties send to their members periodic notices and directives informing them of important debates and divisions, telling them of the probable hour of voting and demanding their presence at that time. Such notices and/or directives are also called 'Whips'.

Whips are said to be of three types—one-line, two-line and three-line Whips. These are so called by the number of lines by which their text is underlined. The number of lines is indicative of the importance and urgency attached to a particular measure before the House. The three-line Whip indicates most important business and a division. A member must obey it and attend the House; it is mandatory and one can disobey it only at one's peril. Disregard of a three-line Whip is almost certainly likely to invite serious disciplinary action.

There are some differences in the language used in the Whips issued by the British Labour and Conservative Parliamentary Party Whips on the one hand, and those issued by the Parliamentary Party Whips in India on the other. The most significant difference is that while the British Whips only 'request' or 'particularly request' attendance or declare attendance 'essential', the Indian Whips go further and not only ask for the presence of members, but direct them to support the government stand or "the vote without fail, in favour of party candidates" in the manner indicated by the Whip. The British Whips never speak of 'support' or 'vote', but are limited to 'attendance'.

The office of the Whip is not mentioned in the Constitution of India or in the Rule of Procedure of the House. In fact, till recently the political parties also found no such mention or recognition. With the passing of the Constitution (52nd Amendment) Act, 1985, popularly known as Anti-defection law, the Whip has assumed very important role in the matter of enforcing party discipline inasmuch a Whip is a party directive and disobedience of the party directive may now entail disqualification from membership.

Anti-defection Law

The Constitution (52nd Amendment) Act, 1985 amended Art. 101, 102, 190, and 191 of the Constitution regarding vacation of seats and disqualification from membership of

Parliament and the State Legislatures, and added a new Schedule (Tenth Schedule) to the Constitution setting out certain provisions as to disqualification on grounds of defection. The Tenth Schedule *inter alia* provides that:

(i) An elected member of Parliament or a State Legislature, who has been elected as a candidate set up by a political party, and a nominated member of Parliament or a State Legislature who is a member of a political party at the time he takes his seat would be disqualified on the ground of defection if he voluntarily relinquishes his membership of such political party or votes or abstains from voting in the House contrary to any direction of such party;

(ii) an independent member of Parliament or a State Legislature will be disqualified if he joins any political party after his election;

(iii) a nominated member of Parliament or a State legislature who is not a member of a political party at the time of his nomination and who has not become a member of any political party before the expiry of six months from the date on which he takes his seat shall be disqualified if he joins any political party after the expiry of the said period of six months;

(iv) no disqualification would be incurred where a member claims that he belongs to a group representing a faction arising from a split in a party or merger of a party in another, provided that in the event of a split the group consists of not less than one-third of a merger or not less than two-thirds of the members of the legislature party concerned;

(v) no disqualification is incurred by a person who has been elected to the office of the Speaker or the Deputy Speaker of the House of the People or of the Legislative Assembly of a State or to the office of the Deputy Chairman of the Council of States or the Chairman or the Deputy Chairman of the Legislative Council of a State, if he severes his connection with his political party;

(vi) the question as to whether a member of a House of

Parliament or State legislature has become subject to disqualification will be determined by the Chairman or the Speaker of the respective House; where the question is with reference to the Chairman or the Speaker himself, it will be decided by a member of the concerned House elected by it on that behalf;

(vii) the Chairman or the Speaker of a House had been empowered to make rules for giving effect to the provisions of the Schedule. The rules are required to be laid before the House and are subject to modifications/ disapproval by the House;

(viii) all proceedings in relation to any question as to disqualification of a member of a House under the Schedule will be deemed to be proceedings in Parliament within the meaning of Art. 122 or, as the case may be, proceedings in the Legislature of a State within the meaning of Art. 212; and

(ix) notwithstanding anything in the Constitution, no court will have any jurisdiction in respect of any matter connected with the disqualification of a member of a House.

Paragraph 7 of the Tenth Schedule which bars the jurisdiction of the courts was held *ultra vires* of the Constitution by the High Court of Punjab and Haryana, and an appeal against this order was preferred by the government in the Supreme Court. The Supreme Court (*Kohoto Holiohan v. Zachillhu & Others*, SC, CWP 17 of 1991) found that there were legal infirmities in the passage of the Anti-defection law inasmuch as the Constitution Amendment Bill had not been ratified by the requisite number of members of State Assemblies before being presented for the President's assent. Also, the Speaker's functions under the Tenth Schedule called for a judicial determination of issues under the law. The process of determining the question of disqualification could not be considered part of the proceedings of the House and, as such, was not amenable to judicial review. The Supreme Court struck down

Paragraph 7 of the Schedule barring the jurisdiction of the Courts and declared that while operating under the Anti-defection law, the Speaker was in the position of a tribunal, and therefore, his decisions like those of all tribunals were subject to judicial review.[1]

Reforms

The National Commission to Review the Working of the Constitution (NCRWC) noted that the last few decades had seen a great deal of political instability. During ten years, there were seven governments and these were unable to provide stable administration and stable policies. The reasons were not far to seek. We adopted the Westminster first-past-the-post (FPTP) model of elections but forgot that it presupposed for its success a two party system.

The Commission felt that the increasing instability of elected governments was attributable to unprincipled, opportunistic political realignments from time to time and defections and re-defections. The administrative and economic costs of political instability and short-lived governments were enormous and unaffordable. The need for political stability became more pronounced because "in administering any economy in the global context, a reasonable degree of stability of government and strong government is important."

The Anti-Defection Law in the Tenth Schedule of the Constitution was supposed to prevent defections but, in effect, it has become an enabling law for larger defections. As the Commission says, "en bloc defections are permitted". Defectors are usually lured with ministerships or other political offices and perquisites "so openly that it really makes a mockery of our democracy". The Commission recommends that all defectors—whether as individuals or in groups—must resign and contest fresh election. They should be debarred from holding any public office of a minister or any other remunerative political post without winning a fresh election. Also, votes cast by them to topple a government should be treated as invalid.

Presumably on considerations of evolving a less divisive and more unifying political party system for the nation, the Commission recommended that the Election Commission should progressively increase the threshold criterion for eligibility for recognition of parties so that the proliferation of smaller political parties is discouraged. It further recommended that only national parties or alliances should be given a common symbol to contest for Lok Sabha.

[Also see under chapter 4, The Electoral System].

REFERENCE

1. For further study, see *Report of the National Commission to Review the Working of the Constitution*, New Delhi, 2002, Chapter 4; Subhash C. Kashyap, *Anti-defection law and Parliamentary Privileges*, op.cit., —, *Blueprint of Political Reforms*, Shipra, Delhi, 2003, Chapters 4 & 5; and —, *Parliamentary Procedure*, op.cit., Vol.2, Chapter 34.

16

INTER-PARLIAMENTARY LINKS

COOPERATION BETWEEN PARLIAMENTS

In the Parliamentary field, as in other fields, exchange of ideas and sharing of experiences by those involved in the working of the legislative institution have their obvious utility and value. Recognising this, the Parliament in India has, through various means, sought to develop and maintain close and continuing links with legislatures within the country and other parts of the would.

Parliament and State Legislatures

Under the Constitution, each House of Parliament and a State Legislature respectively, has the power to make rules for regulating its procedure and the conduct of its business. The Houses of Parliament and State legislatures have adopted similar rules of procedure for the conduct of their business with some variations to suit their local requirements. This uniformity in procedure has been brought about and is maintained by close contacts which Parliament and the State Legislatures keep among themselves through the media of conferences, seminars, symposia, correspondence, discussions, training programmes, orientation courses, etc. Conferences are held periodically by the Presiding Officers, the Secretaries of legislative bodies and the Chairmen of Parliamentary Committees. Similarly, seminars and symposia on select subjects of importance from the point of view of parliamentary practice and procedure and primacy of parliamentary and legislative institutions are held from time to time at the Union level and in the States. These are addressed by Presiding Officers, eminent parliamentarians, members of State Legislatures, distinguished jurists, senior parliamentary officials and experts.

At the Conferences of Presiding Officers and Secretaries of Legislative bodies and the Chairmen of Parliamentary Committees, though only resolutions are usually passed, the discussions serve a very useful purpose in evolving consensus on intricate questions of parliamentary/legislative practice and procedure and on common professional problems.

Conference of Presiding Officers of Legislative Bodies in India

The first Conference of Presiding Officers of Legislative Bodies in India, was held on 14 September 1921, in Delhi, under the Chairmanship of Speaker Whyte. In recent years it has been an annual feature, held for 2-3 days at different State capitals by rotation. It provides a valuable forum where experiences can be exchanged and procedural problems thoroughly discussed. This helps develop healthy parliamentary conventions and traditions and as far as possible establishes uniformity in the practice and procedure in the Parliament and State Legislatures.

The Speaker of Lok Sabha is the *ex officio* Chairman of the Conference of Presiding Officers and the Secretary General, Lok Sabha works as the Secretary to the Conference.

Conference of Secretaries of Legislative Bodies in India

The first Conference of Secretaries of Legislative Bodies in India was held in 1943 and since then it is held almost every year usually on a day preceding or following the Presiding Officers' Conference. The Object of the Conference is to discuss administrative, procedural and other common problems faced in Legislature Secretariats throughout

India; and to consider and report on any matter referred to it by the Conference of Presiding Officers.

Conference of Chairmen of Parliamentary Committees

Periodical Conferences of the Chairmen of Parliamentary Committees, e.g., Committee on Public Accounts, Committee on Estimates, Committee on Public Undertakings, Committee on the Welfare of Scheduled Castes and Scheduled Tribes, Committee on Government Assurance, Committee on Subordinate Legislation, etc. are in the nature of a "get together" for discussing questions of mutual interest relating to these Committees and for exchanging views on important aspects of practice and procedure with a view to evolving a common approach. These Conferences are held in New Delhi (Parliament House or Parliament House Annexe) under the Chairmanship of the Chairman of the concerned Parliamentary Committee, usually once in the life time of the Lok Sabha.

Visits of Parliamentary and State Legislative Committees

The Committee of State Legislatures frequently visit New Delhi and various State capitals and meet their counterpart Committees of Parliament and sister State legislatures to exchange views on matters of common interest. The visiting Committee also witness proceedings of Legislature Committee when the latter take evidence. Parliamentary Committee also meet their counterparts in States during their tours of States for an on-the-spot study of their subjects.

Seminars/Symposia

Seminars and symposia are held in New Delhi under the auspices of the Indian Parliamentary Group and Bureau of Parliamentary Studies and Training on subjects of contemporaneous importance in which members of Parliament and State legislatures Participate. For some years now, a symposium on a subject of topical interest is also held on the last day of the Presiding Officers' Conference.

Indian Parliamentary Group

When India became independent in 1947, there were immediately requests from international bodies such as the Inter-Parliamentary Union and the Commonwealth Parliamentary Association (then known as Empire Parliamentary Association) to become their members and to open Indian branches. In response to these requests an autonomous body called the 'Indian Parliamentary Group" was set up. Its membership is open to members of Parliament. Former members of parliament may become associate members. The Speaker, Lok Sabha is the *ex officio* President and the Deputy Speaker, Lok Sabha and Deputy Chairman, Rajya Sabha are the *ex officio* Vice Presidents. The Secretary-General, Lok Sabha is the *ex officio* Secretary of the Indian Parliamentary Group.

The Group functions as the National Group of the Inter-Parliamentary Union and as the India Branch of the Commonwealth Parliamentary Association.

Inter-Parliamentary Relations

Parliamentarians, as people's representatives, have an important role to play in reducing international tensions and promoting understanding between countries, as they can mould public opinion and influence the Executive of their respective countries and influence the Executive of their respective countries to build brdges of understanding between peoples and countries and promote world peace and cooperation. The Indian Parliament exchanges delegations, goodwill missions, etc. with foreign Parliaments and regularly participates through the Indian Parliamentary Group in the Conferences held under the auspices of the Inter-Parliamentary Union (IPU) and the Commonwealth parliamentary Association (CPA).

The IPU is an association of Parliamentary Groups constituted within the national Parliaments with the object to promote personal contacts between members of all parliaments and to unite them in common action to secure participation of their respective States in the establishment and development of par institutions and supporting the UN objectives. The Union meets in Conference twice a year to be hosted by member countries.

The CPA is an association of Commonwealth Parliamentarians with the aim of encouraging understanding and cooperation between them and to promote the study of and respect for parliamentary institutions. The Association meets in Conference annually and also assists in holding Seminars on Parliamentary Practice and Procedure at regional levels.

From the very beginning of its membership of the IPU and the CPA, India has been taking considerable interest in the working of these institutions. India hosted the 57th Inter-Parliamentary Union Conference in 1969; the Commonwealth Parliamentary Conferences in 1957 and 1975 and the Conference of Commonwealth Speakers and Presiding Officers in 1969 and 1986. Besides, a number of international regional seminars have been organised in India from time of time. Again, in September 1991 the Commonwealth Parliamentary Conference and in 1993, the IPU Conference were hosted by India at New Delhi.

The Sixth Commonwealth Parliamentary Seminar was held at New Delhi in January 1994. In July 1995, India hosted at New Delhi the first Conference of the Speakers of the Parliaments of SAARC countries. A specialised inter-Parliamentary conference on the theme of "Participation Between Men and Women in Politics" was jointly organised by the Indian parliamentary Group (IPG) and the Inter-Parliamentary Union (IPU) at New Delhi in February 1997. At the beginning of 2003 (in January), on the occasion of the Golden Jubilee Celebrations of the Indian Parliament, an International Parliamentary Conference was organised. Presiding officers/representatives of the Parliaments of nearly 80 countries participated.

17

PARLIAMENT BUILDINGS

TOURS FOR VISITORS

The Parliament Buildings Comprise of the Parliament House, Parliament House Annexe, Reception Office and the Parliament Library Complex. Together called the Parliament House Estate, it includes extensive lawns, pools, fountains and roads. The Estate is enclosed by an ornamental red sand-stone wall and iron grills with massive iron gates.

Parliament House (Sansad Bhavan)

The Parliament House which houses the two Chambers of Parliament—the Lok Sabha (House of the People) and the Rajya Sabha (Council of States)—was built during 1921-27. Described as "one of the most magnificient buildings in New Delhi" with "one of the brightest clusters of architectural gems possessed by any country in the world", Parliament House compares very well with the best legislature buildings anywhere. It is a massive circular edifice of about 171 metres in diameter and 0.54 kilometre in circumference. The area covered is nearly 24,282 sq.metres. The building has 12 gates, 5 with porches. The open verandah on the first floor is fringed with an impressive colonnade of 144 creamy sand-stone columns, each 8.2 metres high.

Even though designed by foreign architects, the building was built with indigenous material and by Indian labour and its architecture bears a close imprint of Indian traditions.

The centre and focus of the building is the big circular edifice of the Central Hall. The Central Hall dome, 29.9 metres in diameter and 36 metres in height, is believed to be one of the most magnificent domes in the world. The Constituent Assembly of India met in this Hall (1946-46). The historic transfer of power from British to Indian hands also took place in this Hall in 1947. The Hall is now used for the joint-sittings of the two Houses, Addresses by the President and by visiting dignitaries—the Heads of State or Government. The Hall is adorned with portraits of national leaders. On the three axis, radiating from the Central Hall are placed the three Chambers of the Lok Sabha, Rajya Sabha and the Library Hall and between them lie well laid-out garden courts with lush green lawns and fountains. Surrounding these three Chambers is a four-storeyed circular structure providing accommodation for ministers, Chairmen of Parliamentary Committees, Party Offices, important offices of the Lok Sabha and Rajya Sabha Secretariats and also the Offices of the Ministry of Parliamentary Affairs.

Four Committee rooms on the first floor are used for meetings of Parliamentary Committees. Three other rooms on the same floor are used by the press correspondents who come to the Press Galleries of the Lok Sabha and Rajya Sabha.

The outer wall of the corridor on the ground floor of the building is decorated with a series of panel of mural paintings depicting the history of India from the ancient times, and India's cultural contacts with her neighbours.

Adjoining the Chamber and co-terminous with it are two covered corridors called the Inner and Outer Lobbies. These Lobbies are well furnished to make them a comfortable place for members to sit and have informal discussions among themselves.

In the first floor of the Lok Sabha Chamber are located the various public galleries and the Press Gallery. The Press

Gallery is just above the Chair and to its left are situated the Speaker's Gallery (meant for the guests of the Speaker) and the Rajya Sabha Gallery (meant for Rajya Sabha members). The Public Gallery is in front of the Press Gallery. To the right of the Press Gallery are situated Diplomatic and Distinguished Visitors' Galleries.

The Lok Sabha Chamber with a floor area of about 446 sq.metres and seating capacity for 550 members, is provided with a modern sound amplifying system. The unidirectional low impedance microphones placed in strategic positions on pedestal stands with each seat provided with a loudspeaker concealed in the back of the bench and small loudspeakers provided in the galleries, enable members to speak from their seats without having to move up to the microphones. The Automatic Vote Recording Equipment installed in the Lok Sabha Chamber enables the members to record their votes quickly in cases of division.

The Rajya Sabha Chamber is almost on the same pattern as the Lok Sabha Chamber but is smaller in size. It has a seating capacity of 250.

Pending the completion of its own building, the Parliament Library is located on the ground floor in the Library Hall, in the rooms adjoining it and in a number of rooms on the first floor. A large part of the stacking is outside the Parliament House.

For the convenience of the members of parliament, two main refreshment rooms on the first floor and a few small tea, coffee and milk booths, near the passages leading to the Chambers from the Central Hall, are provided. Other amenities are the railway booking offices, pay office of the State Bank of India, first-aid post, post office, air booking and C.P.W.D. complaint cell.

Several passages of noble words are inscribed on the parliament building, which are expected to inspire the deliberations in the two Houses. At the very entrance, a Sanskrit quotation from the *Upanishads* reminds one of the sovereignty of the nation of which the Parliament is the visible symbol. Turning round and looking at the dome over the passage to the Central Hall one see the Arabic quotation which says that it is the people themselves who can shape and mould their destiny. Another example, of a stanza in Sanskrit from *Panchtantra* greets one's eyes from above the Gate of the Central Hall which means "That one is mine and the other a stranger is the concept of little minds. But to the large-hearted the world itself is their family".

Reception Office

The Reception Office located in a new (1957) circular building of modest proportions, is a friendly waiting place for the large number of visitors who come to meet the members, ministers, etc. or to witness the Proceedings of the Parliament. The building, which is fully air-conditioned, is unique in conception and combines the values of both the old and the new forms of architecture. The central portion of the Reception Office is an inverted cone on a single tapering column like a fountain and the remaining portion is an independent conical shell supported on a ring beam held by twelve columns. The outer portion of the building is finished in red sand-stone and the inner portion is given a wooden lining which radiates the feeling of warmth and comfort. There is a fine cafetaria inside the Reception Office for the Comfort of visitors.

The lounge at the basement level is for the Convenience of members where they can meet and entertain their guests.

Parliament House Annexe (Sansadiya Soudha)

The Annexe building, on plot of 39,660 sq.metres with a total floor area of 35,000 sq.metres, is modern, functional, economical and dignified. It was built during 1970-75. The front and rear blocks are three-storeyed and the central block is six-storeyed with a terrace. The water pool at the basement level with hanging stairs over it and pyramids for diffused natural light adds beauty to the area.

The basement floor at the road level provides an important public area for reception and enquiry. AT the same level, there is a well-equipped medical centre which has almost become a mini-hospital. A spacious lounge has been laid out around the water pool. Telephone exchange, telecom bureau, post office, super bazar are also housed in the basement.

From, the second to the fifth floors, the Secretariats of the Lok Sabha and the Rajya Sabha are located besides the liaison offices of the telephone department, N.D.M.C. and Directorate of Estates for the convenience of the members. The Income Tax Office has been located on the third floor to assist the members in filing their income tax return.

On the terrace floor are situated the Bureau of Parliamentary Studies and Training and the Staff Library. The ground floor is considered to be one of the most functionally viable areas ideally suited for national and international conferences. There is one main committee room and four small committee rooms grouped around a square sunken court with an octagonal water pool in the centre. The Central Court with an overhead mosaic jail screen is landscaped with plants and paved with slate and pebbles. All the five committee rooms are provided with a simultaneous interpretation system as is available in the Lok Sabha and the Rajya Chambers in the Parliament House. Each committee room has an attached room for the office of the Chairman, Parliamentary Committee. The pool is the central feature in this area. A multi-purpose auditorium, a branch of the State Bank of India, a large banquet hall, private dining rooms and refreshment rooms including a milk bar are also located on the ground floor. The ground floor also has a number of lounges.

A modern and efficient PABX telephone exchange has been installed which is exclusively catering to the Parliament House Estate. The same instrument is used as an intercom and for making external calls.

Sansadiya Gyanpeeth

Parliament Library has now moved into its own very large and ultramodern new building within the precincts of Parliament. The foundation stone of the building was laid in 1989 by the then Prime Minister Rajiv Gandhi. It was christened 'Sansadiya Gyanpeeth'. The lay out plans for the building were finally approved on 15 November 1991 and the construction and finishing got completed in 2002. The cost came to around Rupees 200 crores. The total area is 14 thousand square metres. The stacking capacity is 30 lakh volumes. Latest communication mechanisms have been installed inside the building. The communication network is linked with the systems of other Indian legislatures, parliaments of several foreign countries and international organisations and institutions. 'Sanasadiya Gyanpeeth' has an excellent 1100-seat modern auditorium. Other special facilities are an audio-visual unit, micro-film unit, study chambers, computer rooms, etc. i.e. all the state-of-the-art equipment and infotech set up. Parliament of India can be legitimately proud of its new Library building.

Tours for Visitors

Arrangements exist during inter-session periods for taking tourists, students and other interested persons on a guided tour of the Parliament buildings during specified hours. The visitors are accompanied by a staff member who guides and briefs them. Visitors start their tour from the reception office in convenient batches of 40-50 persons roughly every half-an-hour. Special tours are also arranged for groups of students or others particularly interested in knowing about the working of parliamentary institutions. In such cases, the

Bureau of Parliamentary Studies and Training may hold introductory briefing sessions before the tours. The number of all the visitors to the Parliament buildings during non-session periods in ten years has varied from 3,000 to nearly 90,000 a year.

18

HALF-A-CENTURY AND MORE OF OUR PARLIAMENT

ITS CHANGING FACE AND NEED FOR REFORMS

It would be appropriate to review the working of our Parliament during the last half-a-century and more. We need to attempt a balance-sheet of the achievements and failures of Parliament as the supreme representative institution of the people.

The First Parliament

The first Parliament of India came into being on 26 January 1950 with the commencement of the Constitution and birth of the Republic. This was the Provisional Parliament. The first Constitution Amendment was passed during its life. In retrospect, one of the other significant events during the life of the Provisional Parliament was the *Mudgal case*. It was an indication of the high standards that the founding fathers wanted to establish that when H.G. Mudgal, a Congress member was found to have used his position as a member to further the interests of the Bombay Bullion Association for a consideration, Nehru himself moved for setting up a committee to enquire into the matter and Mudgal lost his membership.

The first General Elections under the Constitution were held in 1951-52 and the bicameral Parliament with its two Houses—the Lok Sabha and the Rajya Sabha—was duly constituted.

The Thirteen Lok Sabhas

The first Lok Sabha (1952-57) was constituted on 17 April 1952. Its first sitting was held on 13 May 1952. Though elected by universal adult franchise and as such a truly representative body, the first Lok Sabha, in a sense, was highly elitist. It had a marked dominance, especially on its proceedings, of the people who had their education in prestigious and coveted institutions of learning either in India or abroad. Most of them came from the urban background. The single largest professional group was that of lawyers. Although the House had a preponderance of graduates (37 per cent of the total membership), undermatriculates constituted the next largest group having 23.2 per cent of the total.

The average age of members was 45 years and 8 months. The maximum number of members were in the age-group 50-55 years. 22 members forming only 4.4 per cent were women. It was a treat to hear some of the fighting speeches that came from women members. Renu Chakravarty, a communist member from West Bengal, distinguished herself as a great debator in the House having "strong yet feminine and musical voice". She individually took the maximum time of the House. Other important lady members were Sucheta Kripalani, Rajkumari Amrit Kaur, Tarkeshwari Sinha, Vijayalakshmi Pandit and M. Chandrasekhar.

Although with 364 of the 499 members being from the Congress alone, it was clearly a situation of one-party dominance but it could not be said that opposition was inefficient or was rendered ineffective by the large majority of the Congress. In actual practice, it always asserted itself and made its presence felt on every important occasion. On many matters, the Congress could not afford to ignore the opinion of opposition members. Nehru himself was known to respect the sentiments of the members on the other side sometimes even against the wishes of the members of his own party.

Generally speaking, in terms of quality, the first Lok Sabha consisted of some of the most distinguished men and outstanding parliamentarians, all adept in parliamentary procedure, talented, accomplished and skilled in the art of parliamentary debate. The Congress party included, to mention a few by way of illustration: besides Prime Minister Nehru, other giants like Purushottam Das Tandon, Harekrushna Mehtab, S.K. Patil, N.V. Gadgil, Swaran Singh, R.Venkataraman, N.G. Ranga, Seth Govind Das and Thakurdas Bhargava.

The list of the members from the opposition side was also no less impressive. It consisted of freedom fighters and powerful debators of a high order such as Acharya Kripalani, Ashok Mehta, Dr. S.P. Mukherjee, A.K. Gopalan, H.N. Mukerjee, N.C. Chatterjee, Renu Chakravarty, Meghanad Saha, H.V. Kamath, Sardar Hukam Singh and others. Everyone of these men could be the pride of any Parliament in the world.

The first Lok Sabha functioned at a time when far-reaching and important changes were taking place in the world. And, what happened elsewhere vitally affected India especially because she had just emerged from colonial subjugation and was taking her first steps towards rebuilding and rehabilitating the country's economy on a new basis. Legislation was adopted as the chief instrument of socio-economic engineering. It occupied about 48 per cent of the total time of the sittings of the first Lok Sabha. A large number of legislative measures ushering in great reforms in the social, economic, and political fields were brought on the Statute Book. Seven Private Members' Bills were passed. This remains a record inasmuch as the number has not been surpassed during any other Lok Sabha period.

The first Lok Sabha passed six (second to the seventh) Constitution Amend-ment Acts. The Seventh Amendment was to give constitu-tional effect to the scheme of the reorganisation of States.

During the years 1952-57, the House was in a formative period laying down healthy foundations for building the strong edifice of Parliamentary institutions and procedures. New situations had to be faced, fresh procedures evolved and appropriate rules laid down. And, in all this it fared very well indeed and passed on to the succeeding Houses high standards. Its working earned unanimous acclaim from experienced Indian and foreign observers. *The Manchester Guardian,* for example, wrote on 5 June 1954.

> "Parliamentary institutions have not had good time in Asia... All that is happening in Asia throws a spotlight on Parliament in Delhi as one institution of the kind which is working in an exemplary way... Pericles said that Athens was the school of Hellas. Mr. Nehru without boasting may say that Delhi is the School of Asia."

The second Lok Sabha (1957-62) deserved the credit of having given effect to a large number of legislative measures ushering in significant reforms in social, economic and political fields. Among the bills passed, four amended the Constitution (including the one incorporating Goa into the Indian Union). Two Private Members' Bills were brought on the Statute Book. For the first time, there was a joint sitting of both the Houses to resolve the deadlock on Dowry Prohibition Bill. The importance of the 'Question Hour' as a very potent parliamentary device for ensuring administrative accountability was highlighted by a question which brought to light the Mundhra Scandal and resulted in Minister (T.T. Krishnamachari)'s and I.C.S. Secretary (H.M. Patel)'s resignation.

The opposition, though weak and fragmented, remained active and effective and never missed an opportunity to force a discussion.

On the last day of the second Lok Sabha, Jawaharlal Nehru remarked: "considering everything, we have done rather well and considering the state of the world today when every other day we read about *coup d'etats* in various countries, it is surprising how we have carried on in our normal way". It could be said the tenure of the second Lok Sabha represented the golden period in the history of Indian parliamentary democracy.

In the third Lok Sabha (1962-67), a remarkable change took place in the composition of the House. The lawyers after having formed the largest group in the first and the second Lok Sabha were pushed to the second position, the first position having been taken by the agriculturists. The opposition members generally were even more active now. They included both "the lunged parliamentarians" and the intellectuals who relied less on the volume of their voice and more on the cogency of points and their argumentative skills. Acharya Kripalani, Ram Manohar Lohia, Madhu Limaye and M.R. Masani, were inducted through bye-elections. Madhu Limaye proved very difficult to handle for Speaker Hukam Singh and in a Monsoon session he raised privilege issues almost every day, always in his loud and defiant voice.

Treasury benches consisted of a number of persons of equal oratorical capability, intelligence, sound knowledge and deep interest in parliamentary business. They were never silent spectators to whatever was happening around. On many measures proposed by the government, they fearlessly criticised, expressed genuine doubts, and sometimes even opposed government proposals. On many occasions, they joined opposition members in castigating the government for its fault or in demanding resignation of a corrupt or inefficient Minister.

The third Lok Sabha had 34 women members. Smt. Indira Gandhi became the first woman Prime Minister of India. An interesting development was that the law-making function no more remained the major occupation of the House.

The fourth General Elections marked a watershed in Indian politics. Although the Congress Party retained absolute majority in the House, the losses that it had suffered were the heaviest so far. The most important developments on the political and parliamentary scene in India during the fourth Lok Sabha (1967-70) period were the phenomenon of defections and party splits, of the Congress party losing its undisputed dominant position and of non-congressism emerging as a rallying point and programme for the opposition parties.

The support of Smt. Gandhi to V.V. Giri and his election as President, battle between Smt. Gandhi and the Congress syndicate, the controversy of conscience *v.* discipline, split of the Congress in the Gandhi Centenary Year (1969), the ouster of Morarji from Finance Ministership and the nationalisation of major banks, all had their impact on the functioning of Lok Sabha. The phenomenon of defections characterised the period. The House was dissolved prematurely on 27 December, 1970 and thus had a life of only 3 years, 9 months and 10 days.

The fifth Lok Sabha (1971-77) was significantly eventful. Some of the national and international events gave rise to serious debates, discussions and deliberations on the floor of the House. Simla Agreement in the wake of India's triumphant victory in the Bangladesh War generated a very lively discussion on the floor of the House. A plethora of legislative measures—some 482—were brought on the statute book. As many as 19 Constitution Amendment Bills were passed. These represented by far the largest number of such bills passed by any Lok Sabha. It was through the Constitution 35th and 36th Amendments that Sikkim was integrated with the Union.

Some incidents and developments which were bound to linger on in the memory lane were the introduction of a pension scheme for former members of Parliament, the Nagarwala issue where the Chief Cashier of the State Bank of India made a payment of Rs. 60 lakhs on the basis of alleged oral instructions and the persistent defiance of the Chair by distinguished members like Jyotirmoy Basu leading to suspension from the House. One also remembers the most heated discussion on the MISA and the long debate on the Import Licences case and the alleged role of the Railway Minister, Shri L.N. Mishra and a member, Shri Tulmohan Ram. The latter was said to have accepted a bribe for furthering the cause of applicants for import licences.

While a proclamation of Emergency issued earlier in December 1971 following the Pakistan aggression was already in operation, a fresh Proclamation was issued by the President on 25 June 1975 on grounds of threatened internal disturbance. Opposition leaders linked the declaration of a fresh Emergency with the Allahabad High Court's decision declaring the election of Smt. Indira Gandhi to the Lok Sabha void and disqualifying her "for being chosen as, and for being, a member" of either House of Parliament or of any State Legislature for a period of six years. After a fourteen-hour debate, Lok Sabha adopted the resolution approving the Proclamation of Emergency. The most controversial of the decisions of the Lok Sabha were those extending its own life by two years and passing the far-reaching 42nd Constitutional Amendment. But before completing its extended term, the House was dissolved after being in existence for a period of five years, ten months and six days. The dissatisfaction with the Emergency measures and the movement led by Jayaprakash Narayan had made the position of the Congress Government very uncomfortable.

The fifth Lok Sabha left behind some bitter memories of emergency legislation, administrative excesses and political isolation of Smt. Indira Gandhi. But also, there were many positive achievements and moments of the greatest glory for the nation under the leadership of Smt. Gandhi during the same 5th Lok Sabha period, e.g. return of the Congress with more than two-thirds majority in Lok Sabha, decisive victory over Pakistan, creation of independent Bangladesh, Shimla agreement, Indo-Soviet Treaty of

Friendship, Sikkim becoming an integral part of the Indian Union, successful underground nuclear explosion establishing India's nuclear capabilities, etc.

The 1977 election brought to power a non-Congress government. But, it was a courageous decision on the part of Smt. Gandhi to accept the verdict gracefully, bow out of power and uphold the highest norms of parliamentary democracy. While the ruling party lost, freedom and democracy had won, the system had proved its legitimacy, vibrance, resilience and vitality. It was established that even the most powerful could be defeated at the polls and transfer of power could be effected through constitutional peaceful means. It was hardly surprising, therefore, that the *New York Times* called the results "an inspiration to all democracies" and U.S. President, Jimmy Carter in his congratulatory message said:

> The reaffirmation of the democratic process in India through a free, open and vigorous election had been an inspiration to Americans and to peoples in all parts of the world.

Some of the significant work done by the 6th Lok Sabha (1977-79) included an amendment to the Constitution (43rd) to revert to a five year term for the Lok Sabha and State Assemblies instead of 6 year term. Another comprehensive Constitution (44th) Amendment was passed to omit some of the amendments which were inserted by the 42nd Amendment during the emergency. Almost the entire period was dominated by Janata Government trying to trace out and punish all those guilty of standing with Smt. Gandhi and responsible for the 'atrocities and excesses' of the emergency period. The Shah Commission inquiry, the Maruti affair, the privilege issues against Smt. Gandhi and in one of them her warrant and arrest, jail and expulsion from the membership of the House, all were part of the same exercise.

Before the Janata Government could settle down to positive business, serious fissures between the leaders and diverse groups constituting the Janata Party started coming the surface. Y.B. Chavan moved a vote of no-confidence in the Council of Ministers headed by Morarji Desai. It brought another non-Congress Council of Ministers, this time headed by Ch. Charan Singh who never faced the House and resigned. The 6th Lok Sabha was dissolved after remaining in existence for nearly two years and a half only. The Janata experiment had failed.

The 7th Lok Sabha (1980-84) found Smt. Gandhi back in the saddle. The Congress (I) had avenged its defeat of 1977. Almost all other parties were in bad shape. The single largest group (39.3%) in the seventh Lok Sabha also continued to be that of 'Agriculturists'. In fact, right from the first Lok Sabha onwards, the strength of the agriculturists had been increasing in every successive House. The situation in Punjab dominated the proceedings of the House particularly during the last two years of its term. The Mandal Commission Report which recommended 27 per cent reservations for the backward classes was discussed in a marathon debate till late in the night in the Lok Sabha on 11 August.

On 31 October, 1984 the whole nation was shocked to learn of the dastardly assassination of Prime Minster Smt. Gandhi by her own security guards on duty in her official residence. Shri Rajiv Ghandhi succeeded her as the Prime Minister. Held under the shadow of the assassination of Indira Gandhi, the 1984 elections gave a three-fourth majority to the Congress, which the party did not command even during Nehru's time. In every sense, the 8th Lok Sabha (1985-89) had a new look. In the International Year of the Youth, India had her youngest Prime Minister. Also the House had some top stars from the film world namely Amitabh Bachhan, Smt. Vijayantimala Bali and Sunil Dutt.

The most distinguished characterstic of the 8th Lok Sabha was that an unusually large number of its members were really new. The eighth Lok Sabha had the distinction of having the largest proportion of educated members. More than 71 per cent were graduates or with higher attainments. The number of under-matriculates declined to 7.9 per cent to become the lowest in any Lok Sabha. In terms of professional background, the trend of the last few Lok Sabhas was continued and the agriculturists and lawyers constituted the largest groups in the House. As many as 13 Constitution Amendment Bills were passed. 10 of these were finally enacted during its life time. The two most important were those providing for disqualification of members on grounds of defection and reducing the voting age from 21 years to 18 years.

The Indian Post Office (Amendment) Bill, 1986 caused uproarious scenes in the Lok Sabha when it was taken up for consideration. It was, however passed by both the Houses and sent to the President for his assent. Considerable public debate was generated on the issue. Finally, the Bill was returned by the President to the Government for clarification/reconsideration. It is significant that neither was assent refused nor was the Bill returned to Houses of Parliament. The Muslim Women (Protection of Rights of Divorce), Bill, 1986 generated lively discussions in the wake of the *Shah Bano case* and the Bill was passed at a marathon sitting on 5-6 May 1986 at 2.45 a.m.

The eighth Lok Sabha will be remembered in India's Parliamentary history for many important debates under various procedural devices. Some discussions were marked by pandemonia and procedural wrangles which also saw the suspension of 63 members of the Opposition on a single day—15 March 1989—for the remaining days of the week. The same was the case with discussions on matter relating to the purchase of the 155 mm. Howitzer guns from the Bofors company of Sweden.

Closely linked to the Bofors debate was the debate on the Report of the Comptroller and Auditor General of India on the purchase of these guns from Sweden. A record of sorts was created when the House was adjourned eight times on a single day—20 July, 1989. These developments ultimately culminated in *en masse* resignations by Opposition members from the Lok Sabha. 124 members resigned their seats in the House. Of these, 107 resigned during the Fourteenth Session (Part I) alone; 73 tendered their resignation on a single day—24 July, 1989. The eighth Lok Sabha verily was a historic House in many respects. It will be remembered for beginning the system of Departmental Standing Committees.

In the ninth Lok Sabha (1989-91) though Congress was still the largest single party, the number of parties represented was an all time record. There were as many as 24 parties. Also, it was for the first time that no party had secured a clear majority. A minority government of the Janata Dal was formed by V.P. Singh with the support of the BJP and the Left Parties from outside. The ninth Lok Sabha had the unique distinction of having the single largest party—the Indian National Congrees (I) with 197 members—as the officially recognised opposition and the former Prime Minister, Rajiv Gandhi as the Leader of the Opposition with the rank of a Cabinet Minister to sit as the Leader of the Opposition in the Lok Sabha. The new members in Lok Sabha included Mayawathi of BSP from U.P., Uma Bharti of BJP from M.P., Uma Gajapati Raju of Congress from Andhra, Subhashini Ali of CPI from U.P., M.J. Akbar of the Congress from Bihar and Atinderpal Singh, Simranjit Singh Mann and Bimal Khalsa (widow of Beant Singh, assassin of Mrs. Gandhi) from Punjab. Simranjit Singh never took his seat in Lok Sabha as he was not allowed to enter and take oath with a sword on.

The situation in Jammu & Kashmir, Punjab and Assam dominated the proceedings. On 7 August, quite suddenly it seemed, V.P. Singh announced in the two houses his government's "momentous decision of social justice" on the report of the Mandal Commission. V.P. Singh's announcement, it was alleged, was politically motivated. Intense and massive agitation launched by the students, teachers, lawyers and others accompanied by self-immolation of young boys and girls on open streets virtually rocked the Lok Sabha.

V.P. Singh Government could not complete even a year in office. Following the withdrawal of support by BJP and its allies in retaliation against the arrest of L.K Advani and stoppage of his Rath Yathra to Ayodhya for construction of the Ram temple, it was obvious that V.P. Singh had lost majority support in Lok Sabha. However, he refused to resign and instead offered to prove his majority on the floor of the house. On 7 November, the motion of confidence was defeated by 356 to 151 votes with six members abstaining. This established another record in as much as it was for the first time that the government was defeated on a vote of confidence. The President invited Chandra Shekhar to form the new Government. But, his minority government also was short-lived.

On 6 March, Chandra Shekhar referred to the crisis created by the boycott by the Congress (I) Party and said "I am unable to lead the Government and propose to meet the President and offer the resignation of the Council of Ministers of my government". The same day, the President in a letter to the Prime Minister conveyed his acceptance of the resignation. The week-long political uncertainty was ended on 13 March, with the President dissolving the ninth Lok Sabha.

The biggest casualty during the ninth Lok Sabha period was institutional; the rules, conventions and time-honoured traditions in many respects were given a go-bye. There were more than the usual instances of pandemonia, noisy and uproarious scenes, walk-outs, crowding in the well of the House and raising of slogans, frequent adjournments and the like. When the ninth Lok Sabha was dissolved on 13 March no less a person than the distinguished parliamentarian and socialist leader, Madhu Limaye wrote that it had "at last made its inglorious exit." Limaye added, the entire tenure of the ninth Lok Sabha was disappointing and the last day was a day of national shame. At a time when the nation was passing through a grave economic crisis, Members were allowed to vote for themselves increased pension, allowances and facilities by relaxing rules. The most outrageous and indefensible of these was proportionate pension for life on completing only one year as a member. By this one act, the members of all parties proved that they were more concerned with petty self-interests than with the larger national issues and could not care less for public opinion or susceptibilities. A wave of nation-wide indignation followed the hasty adoption of the Bill by the two Houses. And, finally the President did not give his assent to the Bill. Secondly, financial business including voting on demands for billions of rupees for the Union, Vote on Account for 1991-92, Supplementary Grants for 1990-91 and the budgets of four States and one Union Territory under President's rule were passed within minutes without any scrutiny or discussion, making a farce of the role of Parliament. Also, as many as 18 Bills were passed again without discussion within less then two hours, setting a record of sorts but a rather dismal one.

Fortunately, the ninth Lok Sabha's tenure was brief. Experiment of minority governments run with outside support having flopped, the country was back at square one facing another general election within less than two years.

The tenth Lok Sabha (1991-96) was constituted under the shadow of the grim tragedy of the most gruesome and ghastly assassination of Rajiv Gandhi who was not only a candidate for Lok Sabha membership but also the most likely person to take over as Prime Minister after the elections. The tenth General Election was the most brutal and violent election in Indian history. Congress (I) emerged as by far the largest party in the House but a little short of absolute majority to form a stable government on its own. The sympathy generated as a result of the assassination of Rajiv Gandhi did add a few seats to the Congress (I) tally but it was not enough. The party was almost completely routed from two of the most populous States—U.P. and Bihar. The unanimous election of P.V. Narasirnha Rao first as the president of the Congress and then as the leader of the Congress Parliamentary Party and his appointment as the first Prime Minister of India from the Southern States strengthened the integration sentiment.

During the period 1991-1994, the Congress Government headed by Narasimha Rao strengthened its numerical position in Lok Sabha and acquired simple majority largely through managing splits in Opposition parties and allowing Opposition members to defect to its ranks allegedly through outright cash prizes and promises of ministership and the like. The defectors were not disqualified from membership as they were held rightly or wrongly to be covered by the provisions pertaining to splits in parties.

In an unusual move to placate members of Parliament and create greater vested interests in somehow continuing to be members for the full term, each member was allotted a crore of rupees each year to be spent under his directions in his constituency. From the procedural angle, the most noteworthy development during the tenth Lok Sabha was that of setting up a full-fledged system of 17 Departmental Standing Parliamentary Committees *inter alia* entrusted with the task of making an in-depth scrutiny of budget proposals and demands for grants.

The eleventh Lok Sabha (1996-97) had the distinction of more than half of its members being entirely new to Parliamentary life. They had never been members of a Parliament. Also, persons with criminal records had the largest ever representation in this House. Again, it would be remembered for the shortest ever life-span and the inability of political parties to form a stable government with support of majority of the members. As many as 28 political parties were represented in the House. It saw three governments and Prime Ministers come and go: Atal Bihari Vajpayee for 13 days followed by Deve Gowda and Gujral. It was a strange phenomenon that the two largest parties in the house—the BJP and the Congress—were outside the government while some 13-14 tiny parties of diverse and opposite persuasions cobbled majorities in the lust for sharing the spoils of power. Both Gowda and Gujral were members of Rajya Sabha. During the short life of the 11th Lok Sabha there were as many as four confidence motions from the Prime Ministers themselves.

The average age of the 11th Lok Sabha members was 52.82 years. Women members numbered 40 or 7.36 per cent. In terms of educational background, 77.36 per cent members were graduates or above. The largest single professional group continued to be that of agriculturists.

Indiscipline, disorder and pandemonia resulting in house not being allowed to function and getting repeatedly adjourned became routinised but the show lasted only 18 months. Be it as it may, the 11th Lok Sabha will be remembered for electing to the office of the Speaker for the first time a member of the opposition, P.A. Sangma who was also the first tribal, the first Christian and the youngest ever Speaker. At his initiative, a special 6-day session of the two houses was held to commemorate the Golden Jubilee of Independence. For the first time in the history of Parliament, the Speaker delivered a speech in the House. He gave a clarion call from the Chair for a second freedom struggle.

It was an interesting coincidence that on his 50th birthday on 1 September 1997, both Lok Sabha and Rajya Sabha, as part of the celebrations of the 50th Anniversary of India's Independence, unanimously passed a historic resolution setting a national agenda of electoral reforms, transparency, probity and accountability in public life, preserving the authority and dignity of Parliament and all the political parties starting a powerful national campaign for eradicating criminalisation from politics and controlling population.

In the 12th Lok Sabha also, no party could secure a clear majority. A BJP led coalition government headed by Atal Bihari Vajpayee was formed but it could last only 13 months. Since no alternative government could be formed, fresh elections had to be called. The 12th Lok Sabha thus became the shortest lived Lok Sabha. Obstructions in the proceedings of the house, not allowing it to function and forcing frequent adjournments continued to be parts of the strategy of the opposition. About 10 per cent of the time was taken only by these. A first during the 12th Lok Sabha was presentation of the budget at 11 a.m. instead of the traditional time 5 p.m.

In the matter of the background of members: 77 per cent of the members were university graduates or above. The number of women members had gone up to 44 or 8 per cent plus. Professionwise the agriculturists now constituted a majority. For the first time, a member of the Scheduled Castes, GMC Balayogi of the Telugu Desam Party was elected Speaker.

At the beginning of the present 13th Lok Sabha, Balayogi was again elected Speaker but due to a tragic accident he died prematurely and could not complete the term. Atal Bihari Vajpayee formed a coalition government of some 23 parties which despite many stresses and strains and a succession of crises is continuing and proving considerably stable with no alternative in sight. Fierce trials of strength were made on the floor of the house first on the Prevention of Terrorism Bill and then on the motion on Gujarat. For the third time in the history of Parliament, the President had to call a joint sitting of the two houses to pass the anti-terrorism Bill. By March 2003, Vajpayee had become the first non-Congress Prime Minister to have completed five years in office.

An Overview

An overview of developments in Parliamentary institutions since the first Lok Sabha reveals some very interesting and some disturbing facts. The number of days on which the Houses of Parliament sit each year and the time that is devoted to transacting business has come down considerably in recent years. Even when they do meet, often little gets done. In the face of disturbances and shouting, the Houses have to be adjourned frequently. Even in Parliamentary circles now it is widely recognised that the ugly scenes of indecorous behaviour, indiscipline, pandemonia, etc. lead to waste of precious Parliamentary time and loss of respect for the supreme representative institution of the people. The special sittings of Parliament held to mark the 50 years of independence, unanimously adopted a resolution on 1 September 1997 pledging adherence to rules of decorum and discipline. But, in practice, nothing has changed.

Parliament was conceived as the Legislature or the law making body but of late law making has ceased to be even the most important of its functions either qualitatively or quantitatively. From about 48 per cent, it has come down to occupy less than 14 per cent of its time.

The character of Parliament has also changed as a result of changes in membership composition. In the early years, our Parliament could legitimately boast of having some very outstanding and accomplished parliamentarians who could do honour to any Parliament of the world. Once when a member drew the attention of Acharya Kripalani to the fact that he was criticising the Congress Party which had attracted his own wife, the quickwitted Acharya retorted: "All these years I thought Congressmen were stupid fools. I never knew they were gangsters too who ran away with other's wives". The whole house roared with laughter. When Dr. Ram Manohar Lohia was pleading for Stalin's daughter Svetlana being given asylum in India on the ground of her marriage with an Indian, the charming lady member, Tarkeshwari Sinha interjected to say that when Dr. Lohia was not married how could he talk of conjugal sentiments? Dr. Lohia hit back: "Tarkeshwari, when did you give me any chance". Later, on one occasion, the heavy-weight member Piloo Mody was accused of showing disrespect to the chair by speaking with his back towards the Speaker Mody defended himself by saying "Sir, I have neither front, nor back, I am round." Such wit and humour, of late, have largely disappeared from the houses of Parliament.

The average age of a member of Lok Sabha which was 46.5 years in the First Lok Sabha came to be 55.5 years in the Thirteenth Lok Sabha. The percentage of women members which was 4.4 in the First Lok Sabha rose to over 9 per cent in the Thirteenth Lok Sabha. In recent years, even though the number of graduates rose from 37 to 48 per cent and the number of non-matriculates was reduced from about 25% to less than 5% we had more representatives coming from mofussil towns and villages. The largest professional groups came to be those of agriculturists and whole-time 'political and social workers' with the agriculturists now constituting a majority.

Until 1977 i.e. for the first 30 years of Independence, Congress remained the dominant party with an undisputed majority. Interestingly however, the opposition while small in number was more effective and had greater impact in the earlier years. Perhaps, it was so because of the high quality and character of membership on both sides and largely because a stable government and secure leadership could show greater magnanimity and accommodate opposition viewpoints without losing face. Once while rejecting an amendment moved by Rajaji, Nehru said: "you see Rajaji, the majority is with me". Rajaji retorted: "Yes, Jawaharlal, the majority is with you but the logic is with me". Nehru laughed with the House and accepted Rajaji's amendment. Such gestures are hardly conceivable now.

Attention needs to be drawn towards a distinct change in the content, canvas and culture of debates right from the first Lok Sabha days. In the earlier Lok Sabhas, there was much greater emphasis on discussion of national and international issues. Regional issues and local problems were left to be taken up in the State Legislatures. People would flock to hear Nehru initiate debates on international situation, on foreign affairs, etc. which were followed by high level discussions from a national angle. It seems that gradually but increasingly more regional and even local problems are coming to acquire greater relevance and importance for our members. What perhaps may cause the greatest concern is not only the sift in emphasis but the fundamental change in approach and outlook. Sometimes it appears as if we are more and more looking at national problems from regional, communal, linguistic or otherwise parochial angles rather than the other way round.

The representative democracy and parliamentary institutions have endured in India for five decades is a great tribute to their strength and resilience. There has, however, been in recent years quite some thinking and debate about decline of Parliament, devaluation of Parliamentary authority, deterioration in the quality of Members, poor levels of participation and the like. Today, one notices a certain cynicism towards parliamentary institutions and an erosion in the respect for normal parliamentary processes and the parliamentarians. We have an unending debate in regard to the falling standards in the conduct of legislators as evidenced by poor quality of debates, niggardly attendance in the houses of legislatures, unruly behaviour of members, scenes of pandemonia and the like. Once a Lok Sabha Speaker said that he had to take aspirin tablets before taking the Chair. Legislatures having members with criminal records, sale and purchase of legislators to obtain majority and stay in power or somehow come to power, mortgaging the interests of the nation and of future generations for self-interests in the business of power politics are the most common topics of popular discussion today. The people are aghast and, and what is worse, they feel helpless.

Bashing Parliament and parliamentarians has become a fashion with self-proclaimed intellectuals. This has to be deprecated because other institutions have perhaps declined more. But, it is true that in parliamentary polity, there can be nothing sadder or more dangerous than the representative credentials of the representatives, with some honourable exceptions, becoming suspect and an increasing alienation taking place between the people and their representatives with the representatives losing the respect of the people. Today, we are in a situation where sanctity of means has lost all value, meaning and relevance. If dacoits, smugglers, gangsters and foreign agents can help put us or sustain us in power, we are prepared to compromise with them. We do not hesitate to buy stability of our chairs by bribing fellow legislators. The people feel that the new breed of politicians in all parties are selfish, power hungry, greedy, dishonest hypocrites and power merchants for whom the nation comes last and the welfare of the people is at the bottom of priorities. Their only concern is to amass wealth and somehow get to and stay in power. They are so busy in the struggle for power that they have no time or energy left for serving the people. In the words of the former President R. Venkatarman, they are "no longer competitors in endeavour to serve the nation but are bitter enemies drawn in battle array".

Need for Reforms

Very little effort, seems to have been made to examine and analyse what really plagues Parliament or to find out the reasons for the erosion of the traditional authority, high esteem and pristine glory of the institution of Parliament. We must deliberate on the highest priority basis why things have come to such a pass? Perhaps, something can still be done to restore the legislatures and legislators to their old glory and bring about a renaissance of democratic faith and parliamentary culture.

One of the most cardinal and fundamental functions of Parliament in a parliamentary system is to provide a responsible and responsive representative Government. In the words of the National Commission (NCRWC):

> One way to judge whether the system is working well or not is to see whether it has brought into being governments that last their terms and succeed in providing good governance to the community. The overriding objective has to be to make both government and Parliament relevant to meet today's challenges which bear little comparison to those faced by our society in the middle decades of the twentieth century. The fundamental challenges are economic and technological. Parliament has a decisive role in refashioning the national economy, keeping in the forefront the ideals of a self-reliant economy that serve the real needs an aspirations of our vast masses. Parliament can play this historic role only if it consciously reforms its procedures and prioritises its work.

A constitutional way would have to be found to meet the situation when no party or leader is able to form a government. Parliament has to be made to discharge its responsibility. It cannot be left only to the whims and machinations of professional politicians or parties. Also, frequent elections can provide no solution. One simple constitutional remedy may be found in article 86 of the Constitution whereunder the President can send a Message to Lok Sabha asking it to elect its leader. The person so elected may be asked to form the Government and the Government so formed may be made removable only by a constructive vote of no-confidence i.e. it goes only when someone else can be simultaneously elected. If Parliament has to retain its relevance and legitimacy some such steps would have to be taken. It would require only a small amendment in the Rules of Procedure.

The information explosion, the technological revolution, the growing magnitude and complexities of modern administration cast upon Parliament other vastly extended responsibilities. Inadequacy of time, information and expertise with Parliament results in poor quality legislation and unsatisfactory parliamentary surveillance over administration. Inadequacy of education and training in the sophisticated mechanics of parliamentary polity and the working procedures of modern parliamentary institutions have adversely affected the performance of both the legislators and the bureaucracy. Little effort has been made thus far to develop the essential prerequisites for the success of parliamentary polity—discipline, character, high sense of public morality, ideology-oriented two-party system and willingness to hear and accommodate minority views. Several of the archaic practices and time-consuming procedures most unsuitable for present day needs are being continued unnecessarily.

Members irrespective of their party affiliations have themselves become a new caste and parts of the establishment and co-sharers in the spoils. Again, some honourable exceptions apart, politics and membership of Parliament have emerged as a whole-time, highly lucrative hereditary profession for majority of those involved. Following the changed composition of the Houses, there has been faster devaluation of all the old values and increasing disorders and pandemonia on the floor during the "Zero Hour" and at other times. There is general apathy among members, Ministers and public at large in the work of Parliament. Absenteeism among members has assumed alarming proportions and defections for money and office have been a common phenomenon.

Legitimacy of government and of representative institutions under the system are inextricably linked to free and fair elections and to the system being able to bring to power persons who truly represent the people's will and have the necessary abilities to govern. Therefore, as a first step, it would be necessary to reform the electoral system and the political party system. What is needed is a holistic approach to electoral reforms and a comprehensive legislation for the purpose.

Reforms and urgent remedial action seem imperative for making parliamentary institutions and processes effective and potent instruments of ensuring sustainable economic growth so vital for the success of the new economic policy also. Role expectation of Parliament is linked with the role perception of the State. NEP should lead to cutting back on government involvement and drastic reduction in the role of the State in national economy. This should naturally get reflected in the reduced role for Parliament and its Committees. Also their processes, control mechanisms, debating and decision making procedures would have to be revamped and made faster. Floor management techniques would have to be professionalised at the level of whips, parliamentary officials and the Presiding Officers.

For Parliament, it is of the utmost importance constantly to review and refurbish its structural-functional requirements and from time to time to consider renewing and reforming the entire gamut of its operational procedures to guard against putrefaction and decay. The case for reforming Parliament is unexceptionable and, in a sense, has always been so. The real question is of how much and what to change to strengthen and improve the system. We have to be clear about the precise need, the direction and the extent of the reforms that would be desirable at present. It is obvious that mere tinkering first-aid repairs and trifling cosmetic adjustments would not anymore be enough. What is needed is a full-scale review. We have to be prepared for fundamental institutional—structural, functional, procedural and organisational—changes.

Parliamentary Reforms would have to include (a) building a better image of Parliament, (b) improving the quality and conduct of members, (c) reducing expenditure on Parliament, (d) making membership financially less attractive and more motivated by the spirit of sacrifice and service, (e) improving information supply to Parliament and efficacy of committee scrutiny, (f) legislative planning and improving the quality of laws, (g) setting up standing committees on the Constitution and on Economy, (h) codifying parliamentary privileges, (i) improving working of parliamentary parties, floor management, parliamentary time table and (j) rationalising and modernising rules of procedure to meet today's needs. Finally, parliamentary reforms would have to be a part of an integrated approach to reforms in all sectors — in education, judiciary, administration and the rest.

REFERENCE

1. Subhash C. Kashyap, *History of Parliament*, op.cit., Vol.6, Chapters 3 and 4, pp. 498-559; ——, *Parliamentary Wit and Humour*, Shipra, Delhi, 1992; ——, *Blueprint of Political Reforms*, op.cit., Chapter 5, pp. 147-177.

Select Bibliography

Books

Altekar, A.S.: *State and Government in Ancient India*, Delhi, 1949.

Belavadi, S.H.: *Theory and Practice of Parliamentary Procedure in India*, Bombay, 1988.

Bhargava, P.L.: *India in the Vedic Age*, Lucknow, 1971.

Hardas, B.: *Glimpses of the Vedic Nation*, Madras, 1967.

Institute of Constitutional and Parliamentary Studies, *Journal of Constitutional and Parliamentary Studies* (Quarterly).

Ilbert, C.: *The Government of India*, Oxford, 1922.

IPU, *Who Legislates in the Modern World? 4th Inter-Parliamentary Symposium*, Geneva, Inter-Parliamentary Union, 1976.

——: *Parliaments of the World*, 2nd ed., 1986.

Jakhar, Bal Ram: *The People, the Parliament and the Administration*, New Delhi, 1982.

Jain, R.B.: *Indian Parliament: Innovations, Reforms and Developments*, Calcutta, 1976.

Jayaswal, K.P.: *Hindu Polity*, Bangalore, 1955.

Kashyap, Subhash C.: *Human Rights and Parliament*, New Delhi, 1978.

——: *Our Constitution—An Introduction to India's Constitution and Constitutional Law*, New Delhi, 3rd ed. 2001.

——: *Blue-print of Political Reforms*, Delhi, 2003.

——: *Parliamentary Procedure, Law, Privileges, Practice and Procedures*, 2 Vols, New Delhi, 2000.

——: *Parliamentary Wit and Humour*, Delhi, 1992.

——: *The Ministers and Legislators*, New Delhi, 1982.

——: *The Parliament of India: Myths and Realities*, New Delhi, 1988.

——: *The Speaker's Office*, New Delhi, 2001 ed.

——: *Anti-defection Law and Parliamentary Privileges*, New Delhi, 2003 ed.

——: *History of Parliamentary Democracy*, Delhi, 1991.

——: (ed.) *Practice and Procedure of Parliament* (4th edn), New Delhi, 1991.

——: *The Ten Lok Sabhas*, New Delhi, 1992.

——: *History of Parliament of India*, Delhi, 6 Vols, 1994-2000.

——: *Legislative Management Studies*, New Delhi, 1995.

——: *Jawaharlal Nehru, the Constitution and the Parliament*, New Delhi, 1982.

——: *Govind Ballabh Pant—Parliamentarian, Statesman and Administrator*, New Delhi, 1989.

——: (ed.) *National Resurgence through Electoral Reforms*, Delhi 2002.

——: *Eradication of Corruption and Restoration of Values*, New Delhi, 2001.

——: *100 Best Parliamentary Speeches, 1947-1997*, New Delhi, 1998.

——: *Parliaments of the Commonwealth*, Delhi, 1989.

——: *Dadasaheb Mavalankar-Father of Lok Sabha*, Delhi, 1989.

Kaul, M.N.: *Parliamentary Institutions and Procedure*, New Delhi, 1979.

Lok Sabha Secretariat, *Parliament of India: The Seventh Lok Sabha 1980-1984*, New Delhi, 1985.

——: *Constitution Amendment in India*, New Delhi, 1986.

——: *Parliamentary Privileges—Digest of Cases 1950-1985*, New Delhi, 1987.

——: *Parliamentary Committees*, New Delhi, 1988.

——: *Directions by the Speaker*, Lok Sabha, New Delhi, 1989.

——: *Government and Parliament*, New Delhi, 1989.

——: *Handbook for Member of Lok Sabha*, New Delhi, 1989.

——: *President's Rule in the States and Union Territories*, New Delhi, 1989.

——: *Rules of Procedure and Conduct of Business in Lok Sabha* (10 edn), New Delhi, 2002.

——: *Presidential Ordinances, 1950-1989*, New Delhi, 1990.

——: *Parliament of India: The Eighth Lok Sabha 1985-1989*, New Delhi, 1991.

——: *Parliament of India: The Ninth Lok Sabha 1989-91*, New Delhi, 1992.

——: *Parliament of India: The Tenth Lok Sabha 1991-96*, New Delhi, 1997.

——: *The Tenth Lok Sabha: A Statistical Profile*, New Delhi, 1996.

——: *Parliament of India: The Eleventh Lok Sabha*, New Delhi, 1999.

——: *Parliament of India: The Twelfth Lok Sabha*, New Delhi, 2000.

——: *Fifty Years of Indian Parliament*, ed. G.C. Malhotra, New Delhi, 2002.

——: *Fifty Years of Indian Parliamentary Democracy 1947-97*, New Delhi, 1997.

Mishra, S.N.: *Ancient Indian Republic*, Lucknow, 1971.

Mookerjee, R.K: *Local Government in Ancient India*, Oxford, 1920.

——: *Glimpses of Ancient India*, Bombay, 1970.

More, S.S.: *Practise and Procedure of Indian Parliament*, Bombay, 1960.

Mukherjee, A.R.: *Parliamentary Procedure in India* (3rd edn), Calcutta, 1983

Nehru, Jawaharlal: *The Discovery of India*, New Delhi, (1981 edition).

——: *Glimpses of World History*, New Delhi, 1982 edition.

Pachauri, P.S.: *Law of parliamentary privileges in U.K. and in India*, Bombay, 1971.

Rajya Sabha Secretariat: *Handbook for Members of Rajya Sabha*, New Delhi, 1982.

——: *Rules of Procedure and Conduct of Business in the Council of States (Rajya Sabha)*, New Delhi, 1982.

Roy, S.K.: *Democracy in India*, Calcutta, 1960.

Shakdher, S.L. (ed): *Constitution and Parliament of India: The 25 Years of the Republic*, Delhi, 1976.

——: *Glimpses of the Working of Parliament*, New Delhi, 1977.

——: *The Budget and the Parliament*, New Delhi, 1997.

Sharma, J.P.: *Republics in Ancient India*, Leiden, 1968.

Thompson, E. and G.T. Garrat: *Rise and Fulfilment of British Rule in India*, London, 1935.

Verma, S.P.: *Indian parliamentarians: A Study of the Socio-political Background*, New Delhi, 1986.

Journal of Parliamentary Information

Journal of Constitutional and Parliamentary Studies

The Journal of Legislative Studies

The Parliamentarian

The Table

Monographs

Joshi, Manohar, *Fifty Years of Lok Sabha*, L.S.S., New Delhi, 2003.

Kashyap, Subhash C.: *Orientation for Legislators*, New Delhi, 1971.

——: *Parliaments and Information Dissemination*, New Delhi, 1986.

——: *Parliamentary Museum and Archives*, New Delhi, 1986.

——: *The Parliament of India*, New Delhi, 1986.

——: *The Parliament and the Executive in India*, New Delhi, 1987.

——: *Parliament as a Multi-functional Institution*, New Delhi, 1987.

——: *Parliament in the Indian Polity*, New Delhi, 1987.

——: *Servicing Parliament—Staffing the Legislatures and Training in Parliamentary Institutions and Procedures*, New Delhi, 1987.

——: *Socio-economic Background of Lok Sabha Members*, New Delhi, 1987.

——: *The Legislative Manager*, New Delhi, 1988.

——: *Party Whips, Parliamentary Privileges and Anti-defection Law*, New Delhi, 1988.

——: *The Office of the Secretary-General*, New Delhi, 1989.

——: *Information Service in the Parliament of India*, New Delhi, 1989.

——: *Sixty Years of Servicing the Central Legislature*, New Delhi, 1989.

——: *Dissolution of the Lok Sabha*, New Delhi, 1990.

——: *The Ninth Lok Sabha: Socio-economic Analysis of Membership*, New Delhi, 1990.

Lok Sabha Secretariat: *Question Hour in Lok Sabha*, New Delhi, 1985.

——: *Voting and Division in Lok Sabha*, New Delhi, 1985.

——: *Central Legislatures Since 1921—Sessions and Presiding Officers*, New Delhi, 1986.

——: *Legislators in India, Salaries and other Facilities*, New Delhi, 1990.

——: *The Salary, Allowances and Pension of Members of Parliament Act, 1954 and Rules Made Thereunder*, New Delhi, 1994.

——: *Parliament in the Era of Globalisation*, New Delhi, 2003.

——: *Parliament As a Vehicle of Social Change*, New Delhi, 2003.

——: *Application of Information Technology in Lok Sabha*, New Delhi, 2003.

——: *The Changing Profile of Lok Sabha: A Socio-economic Study of Members (1952-2002)*, New Delhi, 2003.

——: *Parliamentary Practices and Procedures: Need for Reforms to Secure Greater Executive Accountability*, New Delhi, 2002.

Shakdher, S.L.: *The Codification of Legislative Privileges*, New Delhi, 1973.

——: *Working of Indian Parliament: A Review*, New Delhi, 1974.

——: *System of Parliamentary Committees*, New Delhi, 1976.

——: *The Process of Legislation*, New Delhi, 1976.

Articles

Dandavate, Madhu: Role of Parliament in Indian Political System, *The Journal of Parliamentary Information*, Vol. XXXIV, NO.1, 1988, pp.3-12.

LARRDIS: Members of Tenth Lok Sabha—A Socio-economic Study, *Journal of Parliamentary Information*, Vol.XXXVII, No.3.

Kashyap, Subhash C.: Role of the Speaker, *Indian Political Science Review*, Vol. III, No. 1-2, 1968-69, pp. 62-70.

——: Information Management for Members of Parliament, *Monthly Public Opinion Surveys*, Vol.XVIII, No.6, 1973.

——: Means of Information at the Disposal of the MP: Services, Experts and Other Facilities, *The Member of Parliament: His Requirements for Information in the Modern World*, 3rd International Symposium, CIDP IPU, Vol.I, Geneva, 1973.

——: Parliamentary Orientation and Training Needs, *The Parliamentarian*, Vol.LVII, 3 July 1976.

——: Dissolution of the Lok Sabha, *The Parliamentarian*, Vol.LVII, 3 July 1976.

——: Lees, John D & Malcolm Shaw (Eds.): Committees in the Indian Lok Sabha in *Committees in Legislatures: A comparative Analysis*, Durham, 1979.

——: The Parliament and the Executive in India, *The Table*, Vol.XLIX, 1981, pp. 68-78.

——: Setting up Parliamentary Museum and Archives, *The Parliamentarian*, Vol.XLV. April 1985.

——: Practice and Procedure: Recruitment and Training of Parliamentary Staff, *The Parliamentarian*, Vol.XXVII, No.3, 1986, pp. 134-136.

——: Decline of Legislatures—Some Questions, *Freedom and Legislature: 75 Years of Old Secretariat*, Delhi, 1988.

——: Rule of the House: What MPs May Not Say, *The Statesman*, 23 April 1988.

——: The Office of the Speaker, *Speaker and Democracy*, New Delhi, 1989.

——: Parliamentary Institutions in the Country, *National Herald*, Golden Jubilee Supplement, September 1989.

——: Ninth Lok Sabha: Socio-Economic Analysis of Membership, *The Journal of Parliamentary Information*, Vol. XXXVI, No.1, March 1990.

——: It Takes All Types to Constitute a Lok Sabha, *The Times of India*, 15 March 1990.

——: Analysis of the New Lok Sabha, *Free Press Journal*, 17-18 May 1990.

——: Legislative Behaviour in India, *Journal of Parliamentary Information*, Vol.XXXVI, 2 June 1990.

——: A New Parliamentary Initiative—Subject-based Standing Committees of Parliament, *Economic and Political Weekly*, 6 October 1990.

——: No-Trust Motion First, *The Hindustan Times*, 6 November 1990.

——: A Case for Budget Committees, *National Herald*, 16 November 1990.

——: The Speaker Par Excellence, *National Herald*, 27 Novermber 1990.

——: Codify Privileges of Parliament, *The Times of India*, 5 December 1990.

——: Leader of the Opposition, *The Hindu*, 6 December 1990.

——: Anti-defection Law—Raising Fundamental Questions, *Financial Express*, 10 January 1991.

——: Defections—Flaws in the Tenth Schedule, *The Hindustan Times*, 10 January 1991.

——: Budget and Parliament: Need for Innovations, *Economic Times*, 3 March 1991.

——: Dissolution Can Wait..., *Business and Political Observer*, 8 March 1991.

——: Vote on Account by Ordinance, *Financial Express*, 10 March 1991.

——: Hung Parliament Could Entail New Constitution, *Business and Political Observer*, 3 April 1991.

——: M.P.s and Their Pensions, *The Hindustan Times*, 5 April 1991.

——: Anti-defection Law Does Not Apply, *The Times of India*, 7 April 1991.

——: Return the Salary Bill, *Financial Express*, 7 April 1991.

——: Rajya Sabha Can Hold Session Despite a Dissolved Lok Sabha, *Financial Express*, 2 June 1991.

——: A Hung Parliament, *The Hindustan Times*, 10 June 1991.

——: Towards Politics of Consent, *Business and Political Observer*, 29 June 1991.

——: Return of the MPs Pension Bill, *The Hindustan Times*, 2 April 1992.

——: Constitutionality of Dissolution Politics, *Financial Express*, 8 April 1992.

——: Committees Must Vet Demands for Grants, *The Times of India*, 8 May 1992.

——: Law and Farce of Parliamentary Privileges, *Financial Express*, 18 May 1992.

——: Urgent Need for Electoral Reforms, *The Times of India*, 6 July 1992.

——: Is Parliament Becoming Dysfunctional?, *Financial Express*, 29 July 1992.

——: Anti-defection Law: Plug the Loopholes, *The Hindustan Times*, 18 August 1992.

——: In the Speaker's Court, *The Hindu*, 4 September 1992.

——: Subject-based Parliamentary Panels I & II, *Financial Express*, 2 & 3 October 1992.

——: Parliamentary Committee—Doing Without Secrecy, *The Hindustan Times*, 16 November 1992.

——: Speaker's Role in Crisis..., *The Times of India*, 9 December 1992.

——: The Speaker Speaks..., *Financial Express*, 5 June 1993.

——: Speaker's Judgement..., *Observer of Business and Politics*, 8 June 1993.

——: He (Speaker) Should Steer Clear, *Indian Express*, 16 August 1993.

——: The Seven Saviours, *Indian Express*, 27 September 1993.

——: Coalitions: Stability Factor, *The Hindustan Times*, 8 October 1993.

——: Personal Honesty—Ministerial Responsibility, *Indian Express*, 29 December 1993.

——: JPC's Indictment, *The Times of India*, 30 December 1993.

——: JPC Report and the Debate, *The Hindu*, 31 December 1993.

——: MPs—A Pampered Lot, *The Hindustan Times*, 7 January 1994.

——: Electoral Reforms: The Seshan Suggestions, *Observer of business and Politics*, 31 May 1994.

——: Electoral Reforms: Large Scale Reforms Needed..., *Observer of Business and Politics*, 1 June 1994.

——: Legislators are Not a Privileged Class, *The Times of India*, 20 May 1994.

——: Protecting Privileges, *The Hindustan Times*, 25 May 1994.

——: Ministers and Bureaucrats, *The Hindu*, 14 June 1994.

——: No Back-door Entry to Rajya Sabha, *The Times of India*, 24 June 1994.

——: The JPC and the Action Taken, *The Hindu*, 30 July 1994.

——: Electoral Reforms—Challenge and Response, *The Hindustan Times*, 5 August 1994.

——: A Revised ATR..., *The Times of India*, 8 August 1994.

——: Democracy in the Party, *The Hindu*, 25 October 1994.

——: Reforming the Anti-Defection Law in Alladi Kuppuswamy (ed.), *Pearls of Justice and Progress*, Warangal, 1994.

——: Parliamentary Privileges: Use and Misuse, *Indian Express*, 20 January 1995.

——: Parliamentary Culture under Threat, *Indian Express*, 1 May 1995.

——: Standing Committees Must Learn to Run, *Times of India*, 20 May 1995.

——: Ensuring Stability (Election of the leader of the House, Constructive vote of no-confidence), *The Hindustan Times*, 6 October 1995.

——: Lok Sabha under Shadow of Death, *Indian Express*, 7 December 1995.

——: A Decade of Anti-Defection Law, *Rashtriya Sahara* (English Monthly), III, 9, January 1996.

——: The Timing of Lok Sabha Dissolution, *Indian Express*, 6 February 1996.

——: If vote on Account is not passed, *The Observer of Business and Politics*, 1 March 1996.

——: Judiciary, Legislature must show Restraint, *The Hindu*, 4 March 1996.

——: Portraying an Ideal Parliamentarian, *The Hindu*, 6 May 1996.

——: Power struggle and Procedural constraints, *Observer of Business and Politics*, 20 May 1996.

——: An Article of Confidence (Legitinacy of confidence motion over no-confidence motion), *Observer of Business and Politics*, 27 May 1996.

——: Role of Ministry of Parliamentary Affairs, *The Hindu*, 10 July 1996.

——: Parliamentary Whipcraft, *The Hindustan Times*, 15 July 1996.

——: Parliament—Changing Flavour, *The Gulf Indian Weekly*, 16-22 August 1996.

——: Renewing Parliamentary Polity in Ajit Banerjee & K.S. Chandrasekaran (ed.) *Renewing Governance*, Tata Mcgraw, New Delhi, 1996, pp, 227-304.

——: Are MPs, MLAs Public servants?, *The Pioneer*, 16 January 1997.

——: Making M.P.s 'crorepatis' *Outlook* III, 11, 12 March 1997.

——: Judiciary-Legislature Interface, *Politics India*, I, 10, April 1997

——: Hung Parliament could entail new Constitution, *Observer of Business & Politics*, 3 April 1997.

——: The Constitutional options (The Budget), *The Hindu*, 8 April 1997.

——: Issues in a Crisis (Financial control of Parliament), *The Hindustan Times*, 9 April 197.

——: Should House Proceedings be Televised, *The Sunday Times*, 20 April 1997.

——: 50 Years of Opposition, *The Hindu*, 22 & 23 July 1997.

——: Members of Lok Sabha (1962-1996) Socio-economic Background Analysis, *Parliamentary Affairs*, July-August 1997, Vol.15, Nos 15-16.

——: The Opposition—An ineffectual force, *Times of India*, 12 August 1997.

——: Half-a-century of opposition in Parliament, *Politics India*, October 1997.

——: Parliament: Changing Face and Functions in U.N. Narayanan and another (ed.), *India At 50: Bliss of Hope and Burden of Reality*, New Delhi, 1997.

——: Parliament of India—Case for Reforms, S. Subramanian (ed.), *50 Years of India's Independence*, New Delhi 1997.

——: Changing Lok Sabha Profile Tells it All, *The Tribune*, 30 January 1998.

——: Lok Sabha can Elect its Leader, *Deccan Herald*, 3 July 1998.

——: MPs – The Most Despised Lot, *The Indian Express*, 15 August 1998.

——: Are Defectors Beyond Legality, *The Pioneer*, 24 September 1998.

——: 50 years of Indian Parliament–its Changing Face, Function and flavour *Career Scan*, October 1998.

——: Five Decades of Parliament, *India: 50 Years*, ICCR, Oxford, 1998.

——: Parliament–a Mixed balance Sheet in Hiranmay Karlekar (ed.), *Independent India-The First Fifty Years*, Oxford, New Delhi, 1998.

——: Government Formation and Passage of Budget, *Economic Times*, 21 April 1999.

——: Fixed term for Legislatures–the Bait of Security, *Deccan Herald*, 3 September 1999.

——: Fixed Term Legislators and Coalitions, *The Hindustan Times*, 13 September 1999.

——: Power Perks, *Eminence*, September 1999.

——: Fixed Term Legislatures–It's Citizens who Need Security, *Tribune*, 13 November 1999.

——: Parliamentary System in India, *Panchnad Research Journal*, X, 1, 1999.

——: Elections to Rajya Sabha, *Observer of Business and Politics*, 16 May 2000.

——: Empowerment of Women Through Reservation, *Vidhanmala*, Jan-Dec. 2001.

——: Public Funds for MPs, *Tribune*, 27 May 2001.

——: Amending Defects–Loopholes Plugged (in Anti-Defection Law), *The Pioneer*, 7 April 2002.

——: Overdue Reforms–Recipe for Stability, *The Tribune*, 19 June 2002.

——: Keeping the Criminals Out, *South Asia Politics*, 1 August 2002.

Kushwaha, Shivnath Singh: Role of Presiding Officers in the Evolution of Parliamentary Democracy in India–Their Status and Mutual Relationship, in S.S. Bhalerao (ed.), *Second Chamber: Its Role in Modern Legislature: The 25 Years of Rajya Sabha*, Delhi, pp. 177-83.

Mavalankar, G.V.: Office of the Speaker, *The Journal of Parliamentary Information*, Vol.III, No.1, 1956.

Mukherjee, Pranab: Role and Position of the Leader of the House and Whips in Parliamentary Business, *The Journal of Parliamentary Information*, Vol.XXVII, No.3, 1981.

Mukherjee, Hirendranath: Parliament in Decline, in Amal Kumar Mukhopadhyay (ed.), *Society and Politics in Contemporary India*, Calcutta, 1974.

Pachauri, P.S.: General Principles of Parliamentary Procedure, *Journal of Constitutional and Parliamentary Studies*, Vol.XV, Nos. 1-4, 1981.

Rastogi, K.C.: Parliament at Work: An Appraisal, *Journal of Parliamentary Information*, Vol.XXXVII, No.3.

Sinha, Veena: Some Recent Studies in Ordinance Making in India, *Journal of Administrative Science*, Vol.XXXIV-XXV, 1979-80.

Supakar, Sharddhakar: Question Hour, *The Journal Of Parliamentary Information*, Vol.XX, No.3, 1974.

Tripathi, M.: Committee System in Indian Parliament, *Journal of Constitutional and Parliamentary Studies*, Vol.XIV, 1980, pp.442-64.

Venkataraman, R.: Parliament in the Indian Polity, *The Journal of Parliamentary Information*, Vol.XXX, No.2., June 1984.

Yadav, Shyam Lal: Question Hour—How to Make it More Effective?, *The Journal of Parliamentary Information*, Vol.XXVIII, NO.1, 1982.

Index

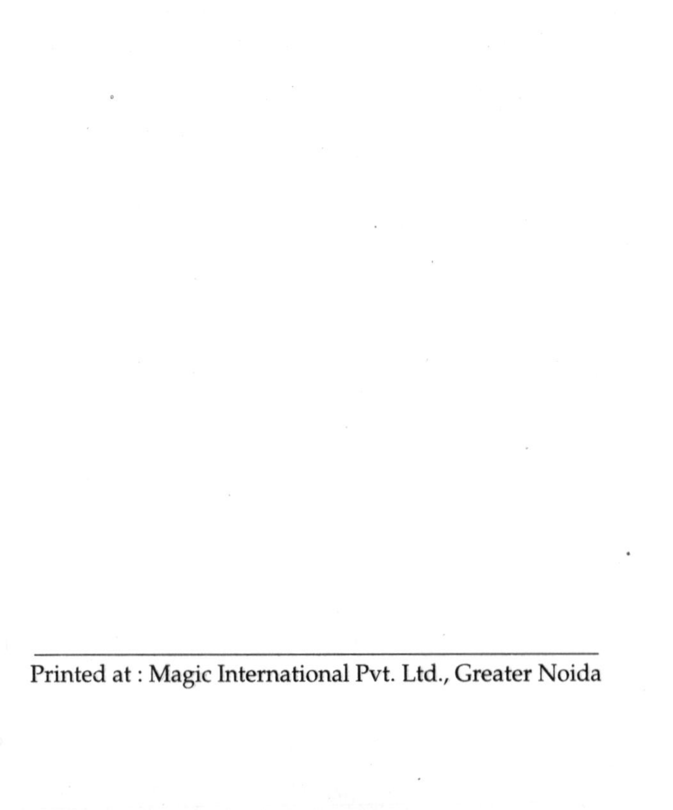

Printed at : Magic International Pvt. Ltd., Greater Noida

PART IVA

Article 51A

Fundamental duties

It shall be the duty of every citizen of India -

(a) to abide by the Constitution and respect its ideals and institutions, the National Flag and the National Anthem;

(b) to cherish and follow the noble ideals which inspired our national struggle for freedom;

(c) to uphold and protect the sovereignty, unity and integrity of India;

(d) to defend the country and render national service when called upon to do so;

(e) to promote harmony and the spirit of common brotherhood amongst all the people of India transcending religious, linguistic and regional or sectional diversities; to renounce practices derogatory to the dignity of women;

(f) to value and preserve the rich heritage of our composite culture;

(g) to protect and improve the natural environment including forests, lakes, rivers and wild life, and to have compassion for living creatures;

(h) to develop the scientific temper, humanism and the spirit of inquiry and reform;

(i) to safeguard public property and to abjure violence;

(j) to strive towards excellence in all spheres of individual and collective activity so that the nation constantly rises to higher levels of endeavour and achievement;

(k) who is a parent or guardian to provide opportunities for education to his child or, as the case may be, ward between the age of six and fourteen years.